Slugs, Snails
&
Casino Tales

True Stories of Casino Life

by

Rowntree Travis

Slugs, Snails & Casino Tales

Copyright © Rowntree Travis 2015

All rights reserved. Printed in the United Kingdom. No part of this book may be used or reproduced in any manner whatsoever without written permission except in the case of brief quotations or embodiment in critical articles or reviews.

Names, characters, businesses, places, events and incidents are either products of the author's imagination or used in a fictitious manner. Any resemblance to actual persons, living or dead, or actual events is purely coincidental.

Book and Cover design by JAG Art and Graphics

First Edition: December 2015

10 9 8 7 6 5 4 3 2

While this book is based on fact, some of the characters have been composited or invented and a number of incidents fictionalised.

Dedicated to

Davina.

May she live on

in these crazy words.

CONTENTS

CHAPTER ONE 1

CHAPTER TWO 36

CHAPTER THREE 68

CHAPTER FOUR 110

CHAPTER FIVE 143

CHAPTER SIX 205

CHAPTER SEVEN 228

CHAPTER EIGHT 311

CHAPTER NINE 331

CHAPTER TEN 377

Chapter One

Business as Usual

"Get his money!"

The job was simple; to relieve him of as much of his wealth as possible.

There were methods that had been learned over the years, skills diligently honed and ruthless tricks that were continually devised and revised.

"A fool and his money are easily parted," was Jenny's soliloquy.

"Go on girl, go for the jugular," snarled Dixie to himself, pressing his lips tight together with a modicum of venom, "Stick him with a 36!"

Jenny thrust the ivory weapon into a furious trajectory that rattled the air with gravity defying momentum. Ancient wood held the sphere of ivory firm on its centrifugal course, an uneven dance that was innately fickle, one that could make or break with impunity.

Ivory was still the popular tool of choice, chosen for its natural properties; it was forgiving of sweaty fingers which prevented slippage at those crucial times when stress, anxiety and fear might cause an unwelcome or embarrassing halt to the proceedings; it resisted fluctuations in temperature as well as preventing any illegal alterations. Then there was the wood, the finest of which was always used, sourced and fashioned into what was no less than a work of art that reflected true craftsmanship along with marquetry skills of the highest order. Radica, Eucalyptus, Oak, Walnut and beautiful Mahogany all heavily protected and sealed in a crystal clear coating of polyurethane; a wheel of fate to determine the fortunes of those who dared an encounter.

Jenny flicked her eyes across the green expanse that filled her vision, right-angled lines of yellow stretching this way and that, regular shapes, perfectly perpendicular forms to define the various gateways of destiny. More often than not they delivered despair and loathing. Another quick look as the ivory piece begins to slow, teasing like an enticing stripper who never quite bares all, then the pace starts to wane and an uneasy anticipation descends upon the moment, like a preacher's loathed sermon.

The rattle of skipping ivory caused the fat man's heart to change rhythm as it beat in time, adrenalin straining overworked and exhausted pulsating muscle. A common prelude to a heart attack. As internal organs prepared for expiration, the fat man held his left shoulder and panted heavily as he awaited the dealer's final blow. Sweat glistened in oversized beads upon his ruddy face and large swathes of sodden cotton were clearly visible under his fat enveloped armpits. In the small of his back and around his perfectly laundered collar, under flabby breasts that no man should ever be proud of, stains began to appear and this would necessitate an immediate change of clothing with wanton disposal of a very expensive shirt. His thick neck hung loosely, layers corralled within a crumpled neck-tie that looked as if it had already been complicit in the murder of his body and the disposal of his soul.

Jenny's hands waved in front of the fat man's face, a controlled motion of thin, outspread arms and spindly fingers, a visible indication that no more bets would be accepted or tolerated. Her milky-white rakes with dapplings of minute freckles, tan-less barriers with little strength other than authority, expertly defined the area that no one dared to penetrate now. There was a bone rattling series of clunks as silver diamonds made their impassioned attempt to thwart the ivory's final fall from grace; chrome studs momentarily sending it on a new course, then another and then just one more before the deed was done. A restless sphere in the perfect, captive harmony of a spinning prison.

"Thirty-six... Red... Even!" announced Jenny with a wry smile that she could barely contain. She dipped her hands and dived onto the green baize, elegantly collapsing tall towers of plastic table chips and stacked French plaques, to finally clear the layout. Number thirty-six, down at the end of the roulette table, lay profitably empty.

Dixie squeezed the fingers of his left hand, his right hand exerting a force that clearly expressed deep satisfaction but it would only be visible to the most observant of bystanders. All eyes watched the brightly coloured casino chips and high value plaques being swept from the roulette layout into the chipping area to be chipped up and stacked around the roulette wheel or placed back into the Perspex covered float. £750,000 had been wagered and lost on a single spin of the ball, in a matter of seconds, on a European roulette table, in one of the most prestigious casino clubs in the world, by one of the wealthiest gamblers obscene enough to squander it. A large droplet of sweat fell onto the table, the expanding stain heralding the inevitable outburst.

Jenny could not understand most of what was said. Lebanese she thought, maybe Egyptian, possibly an Arabic dialect of some sort? The punter was Greek but known to be multi-lingual. The small offerings of English that Jenny did catch pleased her enormously, for they were the sweet sounds of an irate loser.

"An yu see kay. An yu see kay. You fuck whore bitch. You nothing, this is you, An yu see kay."

The fat man held out an oversized, but reassuringly expensive, glass ashtray full of cigarette butts, some chewing gum and the remnants of an extinguished Cuban cigar along with a ball of tissue that was sodden with saliva.

"Thank you, place your bets please," announced Jenny, with that matter of fact tone that all croupiers adopted in order to belittle their punters without being too obvious.

There were no payouts to make. Number thirty-six, the splits, corners, streets, six line and all the outside bets stood empty – another one for the house. Dixie turned to whisper to the Number One Pit Boss as they stood shoulder to shoulder,

"I don't care how rich you are, that sort of money's gotta hurt?"

The Pit Boss raised his eyebrows to concur but his gaze was firmly fixed upon the fat man as he constantly gauged his reaction and any adverse response from Jenny. It was the fat man's sixth straight loss in a row and if he was going to explode, it would probably be right about now.

Dixie could not move fast enough to prevent Zayer from

lifting the table up by its edge, a sideways tilt that caused all twelve hundred of the satin smooth, table chips to slide from their stacks around the roulette wheel. Zayer was furious with another empty number and a daily loss of somewhere in the region of eleven million pounds. Silently, he now demanded satisfaction with his destructive exhibition of childish behaviour. The float cash chips: yellow coloured 25 pence, green 50 pence, blue and white £1, red £5, brown £10, black £25, pink £100, white £500, blue £1000 and the French plaques of marbled yellow £5000, marbled green £10,000, marbled gold £50,000, marbled blue £100,000, marbled pink £500,000 and the marbled white £1,000,000, all lay in a muddled heap. The table Inspector, sitting on a chair at the head of the table, in a position not unlike that of a tennis umpire, had had the foresight to quickly slide the float cover into place to secure the float chips before they could all spill out on to the table layout or even worse, onto the casino floor. Such a catastrophe did not bear thinking about but had indeed happened once before, some years ago, causing chaos and even a death.

***

A less than popular pop singer had wandered into one of the more down-market casinos that were plentiful in London's West End during the eighties, in search of a late night drink, a little entertainment and some company. Fancying himself to play Craps, he ordered that the dice table be opened as soon as possible. Dice was never a popular game due to its unfathomable odds, not to mention the loud manner in which it was usually operated. As such, many a dice table in many a British casino stood empty and they were rarely, if ever, opened for gaming. If they were, it was only on request and very reluctantly at that; notwithstanding the best American punters who knew how to play and could afford the minimum bet, not many punters were worthy of the service. Dice dealers were legends, a law unto themselves, or so they thought - revered but also ridiculed at the same time. Working such difficult odds meant only the most cognitively agile staff were trained to deal the game and this led to some outlandish and arrogant behaviour which, unfortunately, was both commonplace and encouraged. Dickey was a mediocre croupier who had modelled himself on some of the glitzy pop stars of the day; the ones with the bouffant hairdos, a dab of rouge to the cheeks and a little eyeliner for good measure. He carried a Denman hairbrush in his back pocket at all times whilst out and about, using it frequently to sweep his blond hair back from his cherub face. A career in show business, professional magic to be precise, had not materialised so Dickey had done the next best thing by securing himself a croupier position believing it was the closest he would ever come to being in front of an appreciative audience.

"Open the dice table!" ordered Jael, the lead singer of the boy band Kalazoo; the one hit wonders who had a mediocre following and occasionally released a new single to teeter on the fringes of respectable music.

The Pit Boss, neither a fan of Jael nor particularly attentive to his casino duties, casually phoned for the dice crew who were sat at their 'reserved' table in the staff canteen upstairs. It was there they talked their nonsense and chatted about exaggerated libidos, girls they had liberated and fast, unaffordable cars. The all-male crew eventually appeared on the gaming floor then waited to receive due authorisation before proceeding to the dice table at the far end of the casino. Females were rarely given the job of dealing dice due to the unsavoury language that was often used, the banter being crude, racist, misogynistic and homophobic. Overtly discriminating, the dice dealer positions were considered too much of an unacceptable risk for the fragile female, one who might shed a tear at the mere mention of schoolboy expletives.

Dickey made for the cash desk, running his fingers through his hair as he did so. He knew both staff and punters were watching him and like those astronauts we see walking in slow-motion towards their waiting space-shuttle heading for the stars, Dickey lapped up his own adulation and adoring looks. Lacking the necessary skill and finesse to conjure a white rabbit from a black top hat, this was the closest Dickey would ever come to being famous for a trip he would never forget and one that would go down in the annals of casino legend.

The 'cash chip' float was an oblong, wooden box with a clear Perspex lid that was secured by two hinges and a metal flap. A small, brass padlock was supposed to prevent unauthorised access although this was more for show than to prevent idle pilfering. The whole affair was neither strong, secure nor discreet. Every punter knew what was in the box and as Dickey walked across the casino floor towards the dice table, none of them could help but steal a look into the £1,000,000 float and imagine, what if...?

Dickey, with his misconceived wisdom, decided that he wouldn't walk around the outskirts of the Roulette Pit, as he should have done, but decided to go straight through the middle of it and by so doing, he hoped to demonstrate some ridiculous air of authority. Holding the float tray at both ends and keeping it close to his chest, Dickey peered over the top to spy the red velvet rope - the one that keeps the punters from edging behind the roulette tables - before gingerly stepping over it. First, one leg and with a sideways flick of his trailing limb, he was miraculously in the clear and over the obstacle. On the other side of the Roulette Pit Dickey attempted the same manoeuvre however this time, he was less fortunate and fate took full advantage of his over-confidence and lack of coordination. His leading foot was not raised high enough and the second rope was shorter than the first so it hung higher between the two brass poles to which it was attached at either end. By no more than a few centimetres, the merest fraction of a margin, the toe of Dickey's shoe, specifically the welt edge of his handmade Loakes, clipped the red velvet roll and flicked it higher up his shin. As his body momentum carried him forward, the rope pressed hard into his lower leg and with no way to release the strained restraint, Dickey was propelled heel over arse. Head between outstretched arms, boyish good looks contorted in fear, face heading straight for the inevitable collision with a hard surface, there was no way Dickey could maintain his grip on the float box. Survival instinct kicked in and the float tray was released as Dickey tried protect his facial features with both hands. A large sum of money in cash redeemable gaming chips were violently propelled into an unstable orbit.

An almighty crash announced full contact with the floor and the float box instantly broke apart like a schoolboy's hastily constructed woodwork project. Splinters and cracked Perspex glass lay scattered about the carpet, much of it disappearing from view amongst the intricate patterned weave of Chinese red dragons and blue Koi Carp interlaced with yellow bamboo stems. The float padlock, now separated from the metal clasp as well as the box itself, remained firmly secure but pathetically redundant. The sound startled almost every punter in the house and when Dickey actually made contact with the floor himself, it left a nasty but highly amusing carpet-burn across his entire forehead; even the loud thud of his fleshy torso striking the ground caused everyone to smile with guilty amusement.

There was a deathly silence, just momentarily, before pandemonium erupted. Cash chips of every denomination were sent flying through the air and across the vast expanse of casino floor to flip, skip and roll their way into waiting, straining, thieving little hands. For most punters it was a dream come true as money, literally, fell from above. Then, just as one might view a scene from the old Wild West, a hoard of normally sedate customers engaged in shameful fighting and indecent squabbling as they scrambled and crawled over each other to stake their claim and grab as much of the casino's money as they could. Nearby staff joined in the foray too, although their motives were more in keeping with honesty and integrity, as they tried to wrestle back that which belonged to the house. For some of the staff this was seen as an open invitation to vent their frustrations upon the most annoying of their loyal customers. A whole lot more than the occasional jab was inflicted as staff tried to recover that which did not belong to the light-fingered felons. Respect for order and basic human rights went careering out of the door as sheer determination was focused solely on grabbing cash chips. Of course, it was no more than natural instinct which produced such abysmal behaviour and Dickey was no exception to these forces of nature. However, his particular instincts were a deep rooted desire not to be seen as the fool that he clearly was so, he quickly sprung to his feet and waded into the recovery process with the hope that no one had noticed. For those not involved in the furore, there was no resisting a good laugh at the expense of poor Dickey, his incompetence and the pandemonium he left in his wake.

Most of the cash chips were eventually recovered; none of the high value plaques were missing and as anything over a £25 denomination chip was tracked and logged, it was little more than minor annoyance at having to confront those who presented their finds for redemption at the cash-desk. After a short time the majority of the float was recovered, with the exception of a very small number of low value chips which, it could only be assumed, had disappeared into kleptomaniacal pockets or slipped between pieces of furniture – maybe where the small people live who hide the things we drop? Unfortunately, during the mêlée, an older gentleman of dubious fitness, it can only be assumed, began the process of expiration. Maybe it was all the excitement, maybe it was the crushing weight of body upon body or possibly the concealed punches that were inflicted by overzealous employees that contributed to his demise; it was impossible to determine with any degree of accuracy. Actions that did form the basis of many a complaint however were of an alleged, sexual nature. Females of all ages, some of whom should really have been much more grateful of the attention, complained of being groped about the breasts and some went so far to claim that wandering hands had entered those forbidden and confined areas. One complainant even demanded that her assailant be identified as she was determined to marry him, based on some foreign premise that goods which had been handled determined ownership. Suffice to say, she was neither young nor attractive.

The cadaver was quickly removed in order to allow gaming to continue; manhandled into a side room that was dark and full of discarded casino furniture, the deceased was pronounced life extinct at exactly 21:17 on Friday 1st August 1980. One, Harold Arthur Swann had spent his last moments on this earth scratching around in the filth, dust and dirt of a badly soiled, flea infested, Chinese styled carpet, trying to grab at something he would never use or appreciate - a few cash chips that might have bought him the satisfaction of a salmonella laced chicken sandwich from the casino snack bar at best. Such was the expectations, needs, wants and desires of the average punter.

***

Dixie was now inside the dealer's area pulling Jenny back from the table as Zayer lifted it with all his might. Huge, thick, table legs of ornately carved hardwood added to the considerable weight of the table. Huge, thick, flabby legs strained at the knees in support of the arms that held the table aloft. Ordinarily, the wheel alone would take two men to lift whereas a full size roulette table, this would normally need at least six, able-bodied men to manhandle it.

"Whoa!" whispered Dixie, mindful not to cause a scene or excite the few remaining players that were, as yet, unaware of what was happening on table number four. Dave, the roulette Inspector, heard a whirring in his right ear as the miniature CCTV camera that was secreted amongst the glass crystals of a wall light adjusted its position to catch all the action. Somewhere deep in the bowels of the casino building was a small, rotund man of dubious integrity who was sat in an over-sized chair, switching his view between pornography and a bank of video screens. Zooming in and out on the mayhem with his CCTV control joystick, he recorded every moment for later review, should it be required by management. Although preserved solely for such purposes, extra copies were always made for private screenings amongst industry personnel, for amusement purposes only you understand, and never for the eyes of the general public or, more importantly, the clutches of the Gaming Board.

"Mr Zayer, please put the table down," urged Dixie.

This was a small part of the Pit Boss and Management communication arsenal, coercing punters to comply with orders that were cleverly disguised as polite requests.

"C'mon now, don't be silly, let's go and talk about it."

As it was, Zayer was struggling to maintain his grip on the table, the weight being too much for him to lift any further and his sweaty hands making for a slippery grip. But, were he able, he would undoubtedly have tipped the whole thing over if he could have managed it. As a last show of defiance, Zayer lifted the table just a little higher by standing on his tip-toes, then released his grip to send the table crashing back to its horizontal rest, a thunderous thud announcing its rightful return to position. Almost in unison, the other players in the room shot a look, discovered that there was nothing more than an unhappy player in their midst, then returned to their private preoccupations of being entertained with winning and losing plastic discs.

Not a moment could ever be spared from gambling, no loss of play could ever be justified. It was this mind-set that brought about far too many unhygienic, covert episodes that were perpetrated by those who would not even take a break in order to relieve themselves. Any form of rest break would mean missing a spin of the ball or a hand of cards where there lay the slim possibility of a winning bet materialising. And, just like the Law of Sod, it would all happen right at the very moment one was elsewhere attending the call of nature. For most it was a scenario that did not bear contemplation so continuous play took unquestionable precedence over the emptying of bladders and the discharging of irritable bowels. At the end of the gaming day, there was always a wet seat where some punter had been unable, or most likely unwilling, to drag their pathetic bodies away from the gaming table to go to the toilet; they simply relieved themselves where they sat. On other occasions the stains were a lot more troublesome to comprehend and women were the worst offenders, especially those who sat on their knickers or knickerless arses. Where skirts had been draped over the stools so as not to crease the material - fully acceptable and understandable - it was menstrual blood that was often the unwanted calling card left behind. Some men were no less guilty by allowing their weeping haemorrhoids to stain not only the expensive casino furnishings on which they sat, but also their ow attire.

Jenny took umbrage at Zayer's behaviour and the barrage of abuse.
"Fatch-e-yer gats, doubray-peachka," he spat.
Maybe it was Italian? Yugoslav perhaps? No matter, it

sounded offensive and Jenny was now in the mood for confrontation. Dixie quickly placed himself between the two fuming parties and facing Jenny, almost nose to nose, he whispered to her face.

"Leave it Jen, he isn't worth it. Get yourself on a break."

"Fat bastard!" Jenny scolded, knowing full well that were Zayer to hear the remark or the mini microphone, installed into a small recess in the dealers working area of the roulette table, to catch her voice, she would be instantly dismissed for gross misconduct.

"Fat, stinking, sweaty bastard!" she protested one last time before Dixie, in the manner of an impromptu dance routine, side-stepped Jenny to the door that led to the back stairs and up to the staff room.

Not once diverting his look from Jenny's eyes, Dixie ensured that no matter what happened next, Jenny would not do anything that both of them would later regret. The embrace, although purely professional, hinted at something much more sexual and sadistic with its veiled intentions of pleasurable abuse. For now, Dixie had done his job admirably, with Jenny at least, but he needed to direct his attention towards Zayer, who was now berating Dave.

Dixie interlinked arms with Zayer in a manner of friendship but it was anything but, nothing more than a well-rehearsed and professional ploy with which to placate an irate punter.

"Bring me... One," demanded Zayer, an indication that he wanted a further million pounds from his line of 'credit'.

Although it was called credit it was not quite what it appeared. Punters, instead of carrying large amounts of cash on them, could deposit cheques or cash into the casino's own bank account and draw on that amount later by using a casino cheque or 'kite', as it was affectionately known. Cheques, in casino terms, were often referred to as kites but this was for reasons that no one could explain. Something to do with flying away or being high up? No one knew for sure.

An alternative to cash was to seek a reference from a punter's personal bank to twice the value of what they proposed to draw per day, per week or per month. The bank would confirm that they were good for this amount and essentially agree to honour any cheque that was drawn on that account to the sum specified. It was these, and other similar methods, that allowed players to receive 'credit' for gaming purposes.

"We'll have a drink first," comforted Dixie, "We'll set up the roulette table for you while we have a drink in the restaurant". The two men swayed their way up onto the mezzanine floor, Zayer reluctant to leave the gaming floor and Dixie persuasively leading him by the elbow.

On route, Dixie ushered Zayer into the restroom where a very attentive attendant named Alsop offered a top quality service with pretty much everything one could possibly desire, dependent on a decent tip, of course. Hidden amongst the array of designer colognes, hair brushes, clothes brushes and all things cosmetic, precisely arranged on the marble shelf, lay hidden a few grams of pure cocaine – an absolute rarity and reserved for the most discerning of the casino's clientèle. Dixie, on this occasion, declined the shrouded wink of Alsop and motioned for a new shirt for Zayer to squeeze into. Alsop, being a career toilet attendant, had made sure he was able to offer the most valued clients anything that he thought they might need. Sweaty shirts were often an item for attention so Alsop bought some good quality, but relatively inexpensive, shirts during the sales and being of a neutral colour and design, he offered them as replacements for the saturated garments that were often presented to him. With affirmations overheard and acknowledged by Dixie, Alsop was instructed by Zayer to dispose of the damp shirt as he saw fit. It was well known that the following week, having been professionally dry cleaned, the discarded shirt would appear 'for sale' at only £50, a snip from the £375 it cost new. It helped towards the financing of Alsop's collection of toileteria products and all those little extras, those illegal extras, which were always in great demand by Alsop's valued clients. More often than not the tips alone paid for everything Alsop needed but he had a reputation to uphold and was always looking to increase customer satisfaction.

A replacement cotton shirt was taken from its wrapper and handed, still folded, to Zayer who inspected the collar size before putting it on and throwing his used one into the used towel bin under the sink. It would remain nestled amongst the discarded cotton hand towels until Zayer had left, then immediately retrieved for 'recycling,' as Alsop always put it. Zayer stood in front of the urinal, searched under some folds of flab for his inadequate appendage and shook it at the pristine, white porcelain. At the same moment, Alsop employed his expertise and took one of the hand-towels and twirled it in his hand whilst pinching the end with his fingers. Held taut, he then directed it with great precision between Zayer's legs and with an artistic flick of the wrist (in the manner of a schoolboy during P.E. changing time), caused the automatic flush to start where water would be silently drawn into the urinal from a hidden tank behind a mirrored wall. Aim had to be perfect - there was no margin for error lest a man be injured, insulted or simply confused. The motion detector demanded a perfect aim and this usually resulted in a good tip along with some very surprised looks, not to mention the odd gasp. As it was, there was barely anything to flush away from Zayer's effort and as the final drip was shaken free from its temporary mooring, it missed its target and fell onto his trouser front. Zayer farted loudly before coercing himself back to respectability. After washing his hands and having them dried by Alsop, Zayer dug deep into his trouser pocket and fumbled amongst a collection of odds and sods to find the familiar round shape of a casino chip. No more than loose change to Zayer, he tossed a pink into a bowl that was labelled, *'THANK YOU'* in large, black letters and held in place by three, one pound coins and a five pound note. By displaying anything smaller in terms of cash might be seen as an indication of what should be left and showing anything bigger, well that risked it being stolen by a thieving punter in dire need or desperate times.

"Thank you, Sir," Alsop said with a nod of his head, showing subservience more than respect.

Dixie raised his eyebrows. A pink was almost an insult for such service as it was not unusual for Zayer to toss a grand to the prettiest waitress. Then again, the prettiest waitress deserved everything she got.

Dixie led Zayer through a glass panelled swing door to the restaurant and was instantly greeted by the Croatian Maitre D'. who was a tall, thin man, impeccably manicured and with manners to suit. He welcomed both men in with a swing of his arm and an open palm to guide them through,

"This way gentleman, please," ushered Victor, a big tip always forefront in his mind.

He led Dixie and Zayer to the best table, which was partially hidden at the far end of the restaurant, in front of the display cabinet that housed an enviable collection of vintage decanters. Possibly the most dangerous place for entertaining volatile players but dining location could not be compromised for such high ranking, high rollers, no matter what their temperament. A stunning, perfectly proportioned curved ceiling arched angelically over the heads of the two men as they sat down to drink and dine; delicate Wedgewood reliefs of brightly painted exotic fruit appearing to float upon the pristine, white plaster background, beautiful and exquisite... and totally ignored by most. Once seated, the finest food and wine available was presented as words between the folds of a sumptuous, leather bound, dining menu.

"Might I recommend the Beef Wellington," said Victor. "Finished to your liking," he quickly added.

Dixie looked up from his menu, satisfied that some of the finest chefs in the city were ready and waiting to cater for every customer's diverse, dining requirements. There was the Executive Chef, an award winner with Michelin Stars to his credit, an Indian Chef specialising in Southern Indian cuisine, a Chinese chef from Hong Kong who was famous for his divine fish lip and sea-slug soup, a Japanese Tappanyaki Chef and a general Chef who could knock up just about anything ordered, including a full English breakfast, if requested.

"I have Big Mac and fries," stated Zayer with impudence.

"I beg your pardon, Sir," responded Victor, who knew all too well that an awkward customer such as Zayer might mean a difficult time ahead where jobs could be on the line.

"You hear me," retorted Zayer. "Bird's Eye frozen peas also!"

There was always a chance that that was exactly what Zayer desired however, it was more likely that he was just being bloody awkward and testing the patience of the restaurant staff as well as the resolve of Dixie, who would be in the thick of another commotion if Zayer didn't get his own way. The Sommelier presented himself and appeared to be a little flummoxed.

"A bottle of Chateauneuf-du-Pape, perhaps," he suggested, dreading the response but wondering what fine wine might actually go with a Big Mac and fries.

"Don't give me that filthy," barked Zayer. "I want good stuff. Bring Richebourg."

At £1800 a bottle it would go down very well with burger and fries, Victor mused. The dinner order went to the kitchen and a faint voice was heard to express total dissatisfaction and contempt.

"What the fuck is this!?"

Immediately, a club driver was dispatched to satisfy the whim of a man who could not win in life other than to demean those around him. Stranger orders had been met so this would be no problem, as long as there was a McDonalds open somewhere in central London. The Chef de la Cuisine put a small, copper pan onto the hob, all rings fired up in readiness, to boil some water for the frozen peas. The chefs stood watching, resplendent in their crisp, white tunics with their names embroidered in blue cotton on their left breast, just above the name *Chantilly's Casino Club;* each and every one of them capable and adept in the preparation of the finest cuisine, now left standing impotent as the water began to bubble in the pan.

"You need to calm down," said Dixie, encouraging the conversation back to a more sedate level. "You have to think of your heart Mr Zayer. All this excitement, it will make you ill."

"The whore laugh at me," responded Zayer, looking for any excuse to justify a continuation of the abuse. "I could see her laughing at me, whore. I don't mind lose, I lose always, I don't like laughing and she the laughing whore," he continued.

"I can assure you that she wasn't laughing Mr Zayer, but I'll check the CCTV and audio and if I find she was, she will be in big, big trouble. Okay?"

"Thank you, is good," Zayer said, nodding in agreement as the flesh of his thick neck washed over the collar of his fresh, shirt like a wave lapping at the seashore.

Dixie had no intention of checking the CCTV because he knew the matter did not warrant it, it merely gave Zayer the way out that he needed in order to 'save face'. Dixie had no intention of reprimanding the secret love of his life either.

"Do you really want a Big Mac?" questioned Dixie, with an incredulous tone to his voice.

"It's what I order," Zayer confirmed.

It was a few minutes to midnight and the restaurant was starting to empty. The Number One Pit Boss stood at the swing door in order to catch Dixie's eye and he waited for the invitation to approach their table. The Cashier had refused to issue Zayer with another cheque, his line of credit having already been exceeded by taking three, excess amounts – the absolute limit that could be given in any one, gaming day - he could have no more. The Pit Boss was an aggressive career climber who would relish the commotion that would no doubt ensue. He hoped that Zayer would go crazy on being refused any further opportunity to continue playing and any chance of winning his money back. Dixie could mess it all up and this would leave a nice little promotion opening to step right into, or so the Pit Boss thought.

Dixie beckoned for the Pit Boss to approach and it was into Dixie's ear that he whispered the words, "He's had his lot."

Oh fuck! Were the words that Dixie heard inside his head but as he opened his mouth, thankfully, he heard himself say, "Thanks for that, tell the cashier I'll be down later."

The Pit Boss turned on his heels knowing full well what was about to follow.

"What is it?" asked Zayer. "Why whispering?"

Dixie needed to pre-empt a volatile situation that may well occur right there and then, or possibly even later on the casino floor.

"You're up to your credit limit Mr Zayer," said Dixie. "But don't worry," he quickly added, "I'll go and speak to the cashier after dinner."

Zayer knew damned well how much he had played and exactly what his line of credit was; he was an astute businessman who hadn't joined the elite group of billionaires by being slow with figures. Nevertheless, this was an excuse to vent a little rage and partake in some argumentative rhetoric.

"I get more at the Moritz Casino. Blue Elephant Club give me anything I want… you don't want me to customer here anymore… I go then," said Zayer gesticulating wildly, none of which matched the words that came out of his mouth. It was like a movie that was out of sync, the action and the sound being a second or two apart.

"I spend millions and you must be best to me. I look after you. I pay your salary."

"Not a problem," Dixie offered by way of consolation. "We'll get it sorted. I'll speak to the cashier after dinner. Relax Mr Zayer, enjoy your meal."

Emerging from the heavy, wooden swing doors to the kitchen appeared Victor with two plates perfectly balanced on one arm, enormous dinner plates sitting atop a white cotton cloth draped over Victor's left forearm. Dixie's usual order appeared before him - he always had the same and rarely needed to remind the waiter of his dinner choice - a salad Nicoise and it was beautifully proportioned with a sprinkling of tuna and decorated with glistening, brown strips of anchovy. On the top was a quartered boiled egg which looked as if it had been dropped from a great height and landed on its end and split into four, perfect quarters atop the middle of piled high, oil drenched, lettuce leaves. Dixie preferred a salad as it did not offend vegetarians that he might dine with, it looked healthy and light and as it was a working meal so it would not make him feel sleepy before his shift was complete. On Zayer's plate of white, bone china sat a sad looking, decidedly unhealthy, Big Mac and fries with a generous serving of peas to one side. Zayer looked at it with amusement. Manipulation of the staff was his true fare that evening but even having gorged on it already, he remained unsatisfied.

"These not 'Bird's Eye' peas," said Zayer, disbelief resonating in his voice.

"I can assure you they are," stated Victor with authority.

"They not," corrected Zayer, now verbally squaring up for the fight. "Bring me bag!"

As luck would have it, Chef had indeed taken a packet of Bird's Eye frozen peas from the staff canteen freezer and the multitude of green balls that sat staring Zayer in the face were, in fact, of the 'Bird's Eye' brand. Victor excused himself and immediately returned with a smoothed out, empty bag with *'Bird's Eye Frozen Garden Peas'* clearly printed on the front with a small picture of a ploughed field and a pea popping out of its homely pod. The bag was wet with condensation, which somehow gave verisimilitude to Victor's argument.

Zayer did not turn to look at the bag, he just nodded in agreement. He dismissed Victor by resting his left elbow on the arm of the sumptuously covered dining chair then, leaning sideways, he raised his right buttock to let rip an obnoxious conflagration that quickly filled the air.

"I not eat this Mac," surrendered Zayer. "Is very bad and not good to me."

Dixie motioned with his fingers for Victor to approach, all three well aware that the game was not yet over.

"I like eight ounce steak, please - very rare," ordered Zayer with a contrived tone of humbleness to his voice.

"And anything to go with that, sir," enquired Victor, with a contrived tone of servitude to his.

"That all for now," said Zayer, raising his palm to reiterate his position in this most contrived affair.

The plate containing the Big Mac, with some congealed juice having formed an unsightly puddle under the peas, was whisked away at an angle that was far too dangerous under the circumstances; the risk of food slipping from the plate was an unnecessary taunt of fate. Fortune did indeed favour the brave, on this occasion, as the soggy bun and thin meat(ish) burger managed to stay put, possibly glued in place by the solidified fat which prevented what could, possibly, have been the start of World War Three and man's final demise. A clever ploy by Victor perhaps?

"That put the shit up him," sniggered Victor as he entered the kitchen to be met by a group of disdainful chefs.

Before it could escalate any further, Dixie played his trump card.

"Did you see Chelsea play yesterday?"

"Yes, I like Manchester United."

"We have a box at Stamford Bridge if you would like to see Chelsea play?"

"Yes, I like to see Manchester United."

"I'll arrange some tickets for you to see Man. U. then. Where do they play?"

"Manchester!"

Do you know which ground?"

"Manchester!"

"I'll see if I can get you there."

"Good!"

And so went the dialogue between Dixie and Zayer until the steak arrived, courtesy of Victor's adept, right hand, delivered in front of Zayer with a gliding motion not unlike an airplane touching down smoothly on a very short runway with full flap.

"What this?" enquired Zayer, as though something extraordinary had appeared before him.

"An eight ounce steak, sir," replied Victor, a sense of despair forming in his voice.

"Eight ounce? No!"

"It is an eight ounce steak, sir. As you ordered," Victor said, with all due conviction, although a little unsure yet optimistically hopeful of having got all the facts right.

"No eight ounce," insisted Zayer, "Bring weigh scales."

Dixie felt he had to interject before the matter escalated.

"Mr Zayer, come on, please. Enjoy your steak. The wine is here now. Let's have a drink and enjoy ourselves."

"Bring scales, not eight ounces here today, please."

"It would have been pre-cooked weight, sir," Victor explained then quickly added, "The cooking will cause some loss in weight."

"Bully shit. It rare. Little cooking. Weighs machine, please!"

"Some scales," surrendered Dixie, somehow resigned to whatever fate this episode would unveil.

Electronic scales were delivered to the table by the Sous Chef, eager to see what the fuss was all about.

The pitch of Zayer's voice now rose as he attempted to deride both Victor and the Sous Chef jointly,

"Weigh steak, no eight ounces, I telling you!"

Gingerly, the Sous Chef speared the steak with a table fork provided by Victor and placed it centrally in the plastic dish on top of the scales. Everyone watched the green lines dance on the LED screen which quickly formed recognisable numbers that read... '8.2 oz.'

Now there's a stroke of luck, thought Dixie, what are the odds on that one?

Zayer could not be humiliated, even if it was of his own making.

"Scales are not good, not trust electrics. Bring weigh and tray," he demanded.

The Sous Chef was now up for the fight and spoke before Victor could offer the necessary polite, submissive response.

"We haven't any scales with weights!" he declared.

A chef did not have the training, experience or verbal dexterity to avoid such pitfalls when trying to conciliate an irate punter – he was now asking for trouble and both Dixie and Victor already knew what it would be.

"GET SOME!" bellowed Zayer. "NOW!"

Finding a set of traditional scales, at one -thirty in morning, was not going to be easy. Fortunately, being centrally placed in London, it meant there were some 24 hour stores in the area, especially in those parts which catered for tourists, immigrants and insomniacs that might have a kitchen equipment fetish. In fact, almost anything could be bought in such places, day or night, for a price.

The club driver was dispatched, once again, to go in search of a set of traditional scales so that the weight of an eight ounce steak could be verified. Zayer, taking a huge swig of the *Henri Japer Richebourg Grand Cru*, almost downed the entire contents of the bulbous wine glass in one go.

"Good!" was his offering of satisfaction.

His meal lay untouched, the steak slowly getting cold, as Victor's temper slowly heated up. There were other, well behaved and civilized customers, good tippers still to be attended to in the restaurant and Zayer was making it very difficult to get the serving concluded. Dixie could see Victor in his peripheral vision becoming agitated, fidgeting and muttering to himself. He motioned for him to move away and attend to some of the other diners that were looking to pay and leave.

"How's your swing?" Dixie asked, trying once again to find a neutral topic of conversation with which to pacify Zayer.

"Good," responded Zayer, giving no leeway for Dixie to do his job.

"What's your handicap now?"

"Scratch!"

"We must play a round soon. I can book us in at my golf club if you like?"

"Good!" answered Zayer.

Dixie had been an aspiring golfer before deciding that the casino business would be far more lucrative as a career. Golf had held him in good stead for many years since as he taught the casino directors and entertained those V.I.P. players who loved to win and knew they would. It meant paid days out for Dixie and promotion came quickly by way of appreciation for the corporate attitude he eagerly adopted. He was an excellent player and could have made it in the big league, but laziness was his nemesis.

The last of the wine slipped down Zayer's thick throat, sliding effortlessly into his oversized, ulcerated gut. He had calmed down now, the bright red complexion of fury, caused by surges of Adenosine Triphosphate, Cortisone and Adrenalin, had now dissipated to be replaced by the warm glow of mild intoxication. Zayer farted loudly and thought little of it.

Dixie sat motionless, trying not to laugh but, more importantly, trying not to inhale through his nose. The stench was nauseating and Dixie was glad he had not touched any of his salad as it would surely have made an unwelcome reappearance back on the plate.

"Here come the scales," Dixie gagged.

Victor delivered the scales to the table in a heavy cardboard box which he placed to the left of Zayer. Slicing through the securing tape with a small penknife, Victor opened the cardboard flaps to reveal a set of cast iron scales painted bright green. A domed, shiny brass dish and a set of black weights of various size were tucked down the side, separated by corrugated card and opaque plastic sheeting. Each item was separately wrapped in its own plastic bag with a small strip of sticky-tape securing the flaps. The assembled apparatus was inspected by Zayer and the Executive Chef, who had now come out to do the honours.

"If you'll excuse me," said Chef, taking the steak by each end with two, spotless, table forks. Victor quickly wiped the convex dish in a thoughtful display of hygiene as the cold, blood red, fibrous flesh neared its target.

The steak was placed into the brass tray and a heavy clonk of iron against iron was heard as the see-saw hit home upon the solid base. One of the weights was carefully lowered onto the flat, iron plate at the other end of the rocker - the weight was round and matt black with dimples across its surface, '8oz' had been stamped on its top and filled in with white enamel. Chef did not let the see-saw hit home this time but held the weight just long enough for the balance to start gently rocking up and down, then he released it to let the scales search for equilibrium and to determine who it was that would be having humble pie for desert. Zayer, Dixie, Victor, Chef, the other chefs looking out of the swing doors to the kitchen, the security officer monitoring the whole episode on

CCTV, the remaining diners and the Pit Boss, who had returned to catch the finale, all watched in silence, craning their necks as the arguing weights rose and fell to reveal which side would be declared the heavier. There was no great climax; a small arrow set against a pointer on the front of the scales indicated that the circular, cast-iron weight was marginally lighter than the steak, but not so much that it could be argued about. The see-saw appeared to rest horizontally, as far as the eye could tell.

"Good!" stated Zayer, who cocked and lowered his globular head sideways so he could take a closer look at the scales. Once more, he was looking to save face because, yet again, he had proven himself to be an argumentative menace but he could not, and would not, be seen to lose in this or any other conflict.

"These are good scales," he surmised. "Buy for everyone here." He motioned with a sweeping right arm that all the other remaining diners should receive a set of scales at the casino's expense, in order to appease this most valuable player. Twelve grateful diners awaited their unexpected gifts.

Once again, the club driver was dispatched.

Chapter Two

A Croupier's Life

LIFE WAS NOT so bad for Jess. When he thought it through, there was not too much in his life he was worried or concerned about. For now, there was a lull in gainful employment but something would turn up – it always did. A cloudy sky of thick, foamy suds formed an intermittent, chilly shade upon the ground and this caused Jess to momentarily tense as he tried to relax against a mound of daisy freckled grass. Summer was drifting along sedately and in light of recent events, things were considerably better than they had been for a long time. The public park was busy but not overly so; most people were at work but dotted about the vast expanse of lush greenery were society's unemployed and unemployable: a few mums, some pre-school kids, pensioners with partners, pensioners without partners, pensioners with small dogs to replace deceased partners and one suspicious chap with a highly questionable interest in young children playing. There were the work-shy, some down-and-outs, an alcoholic, an obvious drug addict and, of course, Jess. Unfortunately, Jess did not know what his talents were or whether he was actually capable of doing anything productive - he considered himself to be 'inbetween jobs' because he had no work and no immediate prospects of getting any. He had walked out of his last job as a tailor in an outfitters after an unfortunate incident involving a greasy finger and a V.I.P. customer. Lunch had always been a rush and an urgent, personal call to serve had resulted in a greasy fried chicken stain being left on the lapel of a very expensive three-piece suit. The customer in the suit had complained bitterly and Jess had responded inappropriately with some frothy spit. With no more than a hastily scribbled letter, Jess had removed himself from the debacle without working any of his resignation notice. What the hell, he had thought. He had just been paid, had a little by way of savings and didn't give a toss for the consequences. Some things, he considered, just didn't make sense until you looked back on them. With this thought foremost in his mind, he forged ahead with an air of confidence.

Solid arms outstretched above his face, he lay on the ground holding a newspaper where a half page advertisement slowly drew him in like a kid to candy. He read it slowly, out loud and with admiral enunciation:

'BECOME A CROUPIER. WORK IN ONE OF LONDON'S PREMIER CASINOS. TRAVEL THE WORLD WORKING ON LUXURY CRUISE LINERS. FULL TRAINING GIVEN. FREE MEALS ON DUTY. UNIFROM PROVIDED. OPEN INTERVIEWS...'

Jess sat bolt upright, poorly toned stomach muscles contracting to pull up the weight of his body from the lazy, prone position he had adopted for most of the afternoon, if not his entire life. He read it again and again searching for any small print that might exclude him from applying. It read like a personal request so he would do himself no favours to ignore the invite. He was familiar with the odd Bond film, knew very little of casinos but then, full training was offered so there would be no worries in that department. It meant there would be few expectations and nothing to live up to, unlike the past experience and qualifications he had often lied about for previous jobs. Jess mentally checked off his personal wish list: travelling the world was definitely up there in the top three, along with sky-diving and a date with Felicity Kendall or Debbie Harry. This was it – opportunity was hammering on his door and it wouldn't hang around forever, so Jess decided to act upon it right away. He walked home with delirious enthusiasm for this unknown, yet to unfold, chapter in his life. Reading again and again the advertisement, like a winning lottery ticket, it seemed too good to be true. Once back home however, a disgruntled middle aged woman with one leg would quickly dismantle his enthusiasm.

As he excitedly described his plans to the seemingly disinterested, caustic old crone that was his mother, he felt elation slowly ebb away. This sad, blood relative that bore him scoffed at his ideas and eagerness as she plotted an act of pure malice, a deed borne of jealousy and loathing that would manifest itself in the ugliest of acts.

***

The police arrived shortly after 5pm. Jess was sat on his bed, his mind meandering, floating freely with all things casino and how his life was to be immeasurably enhanced. Imagined, exciting thoughts and ideas drifted in and out of his mind with visions of travelling the world, meeting the rich and famous and maybe even finding a girlfriend who might lift him out of the social quagmire of a life he now found himself in – it was all edging just within reach and he was ready to embrace it.

The knocking on his bedroom door woke him from the beauty of his new, illusory life.

"Jess?"

"Err...yes," replied Jess, with a curious tone.

"Can I come in?" enquired a woman's voice, authoritative yet somehow calming.

Jess jumped up and cautiously began to open the door, preparing for the unknown. This was definitely not a voice he recognised.

"Hurry it up lad!" commanded a male voice, with no authority whatsoever.

With few female friends and a father who was working in Africa, there should not have been anyone else in the house other than his mother. Jess considered his options as he cautiously opened the door; wisely thinking better of the baseball bat lying next to his bed, he decided to opt for the element of surprise. He quickly pulled open the door and pushed his body into the empty frame to fill the space, puffed up and ready, he threatened,

"What d'ya want?"

Stood slightly back from the door, in a position of professional anticipation, was a well-built, slightly masculine woman in her mid-thirties. Dressed in a white, short-sleeved shirt, she spoke quietly with an officious tone that was very difficult to ignore or interrupt.

"Jess, I want you to listen to me very carefully," she said.

A reflection of light flashed from a silver badge that was pinned to her left breast. Jess looked at it, initially attracted by the light, then read it twice, moving his lips as he did so but making no sound. He spelt out the reflective, silver letters in his head, M.E.T.R.O.P.O.L.I.T.A.N-P.O.L.I.C.E. Jess' eyes darted around the police issue leather belt that carried an officer's armoury: a pair of handcuffs - chrome arcs of steel poking from the top of a pouch, a cylinder - completely concealed but for a rubber handle that offered pain were it to be extended, a baton of steel with a solid metal ball at the end. A small canister with a red plastic safety catch held Jess' gaze and he knew from pub stories of bravado what it meant to be on the receiving end of this particular weapon - CS gas in the eyes, an uncontrollable stinging that would burn long and deep, red hot grit grinding under eyelids for several minutes. CS spray was a badge of honour that was reserved only for yobs and the foolhardy, a club which Jess did not want, need or wish to join the ranks of.

"Yeah sure," Jess replied, "What's this all about then? If it has anything to do with that bloke down the pub then I'm.."

A slightly older male colleague joined the female officer at her right shoulder and interrupted.

"Don't say anything lad, just listen. An accusation has been made against you and we're obliged to take you in."

"Bloody what?" quizzed Jess. "It's that bloke from the pub isn't it?"

"Jess, listen to what I have to say," began the female officer. "Calm yourself and just listen."

There was a momentary pause while the officer formulated the well-rehearsed words in her head. "Jess Vere-White, I am arresting you on suspicion assault. You do not have to say anything but anything you do say may be taken down and used in evidence against you. Do you understand?"

Jess' face distorted, screwing itself up in a useless show of utter astonishment.

"I don't understand," he replied, inflicting as much denial into the statement as he felt appropriate. "Who the hell am I supposed to have assaulted?"

"Mary," came the male officer's curt reply.

"I don't know any Mary. She's a lying bitch whoever she is. I don't know anyone called Mary. Mary who?"

The female officer quickly wrote down as much of Jess' reply, contemporaneously, as she could then showed it to Jess with the offer of a black, ballpoint pen with which to sign the page. "Sign this," she ordered.

"What is it?" asked Jess, eyes trying to focus on the hastily scribbled notes.

"It says, reply after caution, I don't understand, I don't know any Mary. She's a lying bitch. Who is she?"

"I'm not signing anything until I talk to my brief!" said Jess. But Jess did not have a brief, counsellor, solicitor or anybody else remotely connected with the legal services. Nonetheless, he thought it was the right thing to say under the circumstances.

The officer added to what she had written in her plastic covered notebook, 'Declined to sign,' then signed it herself with the initials AGW and then PC 9231.

***

In his mother's eyes, Jess was a lazy, untidy bugger and she blamed his father for this, as well as everything else that had gone wrong in her life. Just as Alfie Vere-White had gone off to some far flung place in Africa to help some starving kids, Jess' mother felt that Jess was about to perform a similar disappearing act by working in a casino or on a cruise ship. She always believed Alfie should have been at home to lend a helping hand and not half way around the world in some god-forsaken patch of wasteland caring for kids he didn't even know or really care about. Alfie didn't even like black people, everyone knew that.

Jess had left his washing on the floor at the end of his bed for no good reason. Concealed amongst the jeans, T-shirts and a pair of tartan boxer shorts lay his leather belt that he'd stripped from his denims the previous night. Dark leather held a tarnished buckle that had worn to a faint orange glow, a sign of quality with a patina that could not be manufactured. Rounded and smooth it carried a badge of wings with the name Harley Davidson but at some point, one of the wing tips had broken off.

Firmly held between long fingernails painted bright red and liberally applied, the belt dangled limply with the weight of the buckle causing it to gentle swing back and forth.

"Untidy little shit," muttered Jess' mother. "He's had a dolly-bird in here, I bet."

Like a bag of radioactive plutonium that might contaminate the entire world at any moment, Jess' dirty laundry was walked at arm's length into the bathroom and dunmped unceremoniously in the wash basket.

Jess could be seen coming in from the park and through the kitchen window his mother watched him like a cat ready to pounce on a mouse to torment it to death. She resented the joyous spring in his stride, she resented his youth, she resented his father and she resented life in general. She truly believed that if she was miserable then Jess should be too.

Jess burst through the kitchen door that led inside from the driveway. Holding up the newspaper in front of his face he shone with excitement.

"You won't believe this, look at this. It's an ad for croupiers and look, it says you can travel the world on cruise ships. I'm gonna apply for it, it's what I've always wanted and who knows, I could meet up with Dad on the Ivory Coast someday. There's an interview on Friday so I'm going into town. It'll be brilliant, casinos are full of gorgeous girls and there'll be loads of famous people I expect. Place your bets please, Mr Bond," sang Jess with such enthusiasm that he barely took a breath.

The one-legged, disgruntled, middle-aged hag spoke to snatch the moment of elation from him.

"Spag Bol for dinner... y'want cheese?"

Jess bounded off to the toilet, barely able to control his enthusiasm or his bladder. He flushed the toilet, the rinsing water sounding as though life itself was being flushed down the pan with the crashing, splashing, gurgling of an old cistern that was being forced back into life for yet another, squeaky clean performance. Jess dropped heavily into an armchair in front of the television in the lounge and was soon transfixed by a loud news flash: *'Local company lays off workforce'*. Somewhere in a place you would not choose to live, someone was having bigger problems than Jess was about to face.

"You finished in there?" squealed Jess' mum as she pushed open the toilet door to walk straight in without waiting for an answer. "Dinner's in five!" she hollered.

The door was firmly shut behind her and a feeble lock could be heard wedging into the door frame to shut out the world and conceal the wickedness within. Atop a stained, porcelain bowl, on a plastic toilet seat, was perched a flesh coloured false leg that was stretched out straight and alongside it, a real leg limply hung sideways from the poorly crafted prosthetic piece. Reaching into the nearby wash basket from her seated position, she reached in and held in front of her the thick leather strap and jangling buckle. Bracing herself with a deep breath, leaning forward, she whipped the length of the belt over her shopulder in order that the buckle made full contact with her back. There was a momentary pause while she bit her lip and then, as if awakening from a trance, she shook her head slowly from side to side before wiping a tear from the corner of her eye. She leant back to ease the initial pain then leant forward once more to receive two more lashes. Bright, red welts began to show on lily white skin where the image of wings, one with its tip missing, was clearly visible. Quietly, she stood up, lifted her blouse, then admired her handywork in the mirror that hung above the bath. An uncomfortable aching caused her to make some stretching adjustments before she filled the hand basin to wash her face of any visible pain that might show. Flushing the toilet, the cistern springing back into life, another unsavoury secret was flushed away. A quick tug at her poorly fitted false leg and it was out into the hallway, a mobile phone close to her ear with a victorious tone in its dialled purr. The only sign of her visit to the toilet was a wet towel and a casually discarded leather belt where wings could not be attributed to anything angelic.

The Bolognaise began to boil dry.

'Emergency, which service do you require?"
"Police!"
"One moment caller, connecting you now..."
'Police, emergency, how may I help you?'
"Hello... I've just been attacked by my son. My name is Mary... Mary Vere-White."

***

Jess sat in the back of the police car, a neighbour peered out from behind lace curtains two doors down.
"These cuffs really hurt, can you loosen them?" pleaded Jess, "It wasn't necessary to cuff me you know."
The voice without authority spoke,
"It's for your own protection as well as ours. We'll take them off when we get to the station. Anyway, they're not designed for comfort."
Jess could offer no more resistance. The accusation was

spinning around in his head. His own mother was accusing him of the most heinous of crimes. The thought alone disgusted Jess but the motive was the blow that he just could not fathom. Jess began to weep uncontrollably.

Fortunately, Mary had a history of lying, false accusations, petty theft, harassment and anti-social behaviour. She was well known to the Police and Social Services so the false accusation would soon be cleared up but the motive; it was the motive that felt as though it was wringing the life out of Jess. It didn't make any sense. Why would his own mother want to destroy him?

Down at the station, Jess was booked into custody with the reason for his arrest noted as – 'to investigate the offence and secure evidence.' The Custody Sergeant had approved the detention on the grounds as stated and the process of evidence collecting began. In a clear plastic 'evidence' bag sat Jess' leather belt, duly handed over by Jess' mum who knew exactly what she was doing.

Mary was sitting in the cold confines of an interview room, a warm cup of tea with five sugars sitting in her right hand. Mary was enjoying the moment, her mind relishing the havoc she was causing in Jess' life, not to mention the long forgotten feelings of having this amount of attention afforded her. The anticipation of what would happen to Jess was a simple pleasure and a just reward, she reasoned.

In cell number fourteen sat Jess staring at the wall trying to read the scribbles of previous detainees. A suicide blanket sat folded at his side and he wondered what, in fact, it would actually be like to attack your own mother.

***

Jess looked around him as he stood in the queue that snaked its way down the street and around the corner. God only knew how long it stretched back for. Jess had been waiting for almost four hours and it looked like it would be another four until he was through the street door of the Top Clubs Training Centre. There was a short man in front of Jess, dressed in a manner that suggested a desperate playboy of times past. An enormous, black velvet bowtie was in the process of garrotting the little fella. Affixed like a giant bat to his throat, it sucked from him all sense of style and fashion and Jess could not take his eyes of it.

"Won't be long now," said Jess, trying to strike up a conversation with the bow-tie.

"You should really come dressed for the position you are applying for. Slacks and shirt won't get you past the first round," informed the bow-tie's owner.

"Cripes!" mocked Jess, "It was all a bit of a rush. I've only just got out of nick for beating me mum."

"Bloody Nora!" You've got no chance then. You need to be squeaky clean to work in a casino," explained the short-arse with the bat-like accessory.

"Shouldn't be a problem," concluded Jess, with all due confidence. "My uncle Jeff plays golf with the Chief Constable, he'll sort it all out."

Maybe Jess had inherited his penchant for concocting stories from his mother. No matter, it was no more than a harmless dig at a nuisance of a man who was of no consequence. Another two and a half hours passed by before Jess was finally seated in front of a clean shaven, nicely turned out, possibly gay, interviewer.

"Says here that you've recently been arrested?"

"That's right," replied Jess, enthusiastically, "for attacking my mum."

"Fuck me. That's a first! You're joking, right?"

"Nope!" said Jess, his tone changing to a more serious and meaningful level, just in case it was important to his job prospects. "My mother has a mental problem and she accused me of whipping her with a belt. It's all been sorted out now but the arrest cannot be removed from my police records apparently. Here's a copy of the police notice that states no further action will be taken. She's quite ill, my Mum, in the head like and she's in a mental hospital now undergoing some sort of electro-convulsive treatment or other."

"I'm so sorry," offered the overweight, over-effeminate interviewer, a small curl of blonde hair cutting loose to swing across his silky smooth forehead as he sat back into his chair with a thud.

"Not a problem," said Jess, "I'm coping with it as best I can." It was at this point Jess secured his position in the school for casino croupier training. Selection by sympathy Jess supposed, but he was not ashamed to admit or accept it.

"I'll see you at the training school then. My name's Derrick but people call me Daisy," said Derrick, or Daisy. "Well done! Keep this card with you."

Jess looked briefly at the piece of card handed to him. A signature in blue ink was flamboyantly etched across the whole face of the card whilst underneath were some instructions about joining the training school the following week. Jess got up and unconsciously acted out a small routine he'd seen in a film once. Palms facing forwards and held firm at his hips, he spun around one and a half times on the carpet to leave him pointing directly in front of the exit door. As he walked away he heard the faint sounds of a dainty clap and a high-pitched, 'Ooooh!' in appreciation.

Down at the underground train station, Jess rode the long escalator down to the southbound platform and was ecstatic but showed little more than a cool, calm exterior. What comes around goes around he thought as he dropped a five pound note into the guitar case of a busker who was playing an unrecognisable tune. Jess hoped for eye contact, some form of appreciation from the musician, but no acknowledgement came so Jess continued on towards platform two. Displeased at the lack of gratitude, Jess wished he had kept his fiver.

The training induction meeting was held in the casino training room and Jess made sure he removed his sleeper earring, as advised by Daisy during the initial interview, before class commenced. Jess had worn an earring for such a long time that he was barely aware of it. Back in the day, when lads were considered to be a gypsy, a fairground worker or even a pirate, Jess had had his left earlobe pierced, not so much as a mark of rebellion but more of an embellishment to his boyish good looks. Decidedly straight, in terms of sexuality, Jess had no leanings towards other men but for this moment in his life, Jess would happily use any admirers to his advantage, should it become necessary to do so. Daisy put down his knitting and stood to welcome Jess.
"Come over here and sit next to me poppet," instructed Daisy, patting the seat to his left. Daisy then left his hand upon the seat, just a moment too long for Jess' liking. Jess recognised the ploy and was determined not to let Daisy ruin any chance he had of making it through the training school.

Unfortunately, it appeared that Daisy was one of the trainers so Jess would have to keep him sweet, maybe flirt if he had to, but no more than was absolutely necessary to ensure he qualified as a casino croupier.

"Your attention, please!" called a tall, well groomed Indian man dressed in a light grey suit. He delivered a well-rehearsed speech which outlined the role of a croupier, the training, company expectations, the things that could go wrong and the necessity to declare any convictions, cautions or arrests that would affect the granting of a Home Office licence to work in a casino. Jess had already sought advice from Daisy who had told him that all would be well as long as he declared his arrest and stated that there was nothing pending. The evening was spent filling in forms with a question and answer session at the end and Jess desperately tried to think of something clever to say, to ask something that might get him noticed, something relevant, something intellectual, something that would set him apart from the rest. Jess wondered why the meeting was being held so late. It had started at 9pm and it was already 11.50pm – he would ask why this was and whether it was really necessary. Jess put up his hand along with those who had questions of their own.

"Yes, you," invited the tall Indian, pointing to a slightly built, dark haired lad just in front of Jess.

"Can you tell me why we have to be here so late? Is it really necessary?" the lad asked.

"Shit," muttered Jess, "I was going to ask that."

"If you have a problem with the time of day and your attendance here, then this is not the job for you. What's your name?" responded the Indian.

"Ian."

"Well, Ian..." There was a disturbingly long pause. "I suggest this is *not* the job for you and I thank you for your interest, but you need not report for training."

An audible gasp could be heard from the back of the room as Jess' hand slowly melted out of sight. The meeting was obviously part of the selection process.

"Casino business is conducted during the afternoons, evenings and until two in the morning," explained the tall Indian. "You will be required to work shifts, so if you are concerned with working during the night or unsociable hours then this is not the career for you. If you feel this might be you, as Ian over there clearly does, then please make yourself known."

There was a deathly silence in case the slightest sound got the tall Indian's unwanted attention. Nobody dared breathe lest they drew his gaze and dismissing words. The tall Indian then further explained the training process, what could be expected, how croupiers should conduct themselves, the pros and the cons, the whys, the wherefores and some surprising whatnots. Jess thanked his lucky stars that he had not asked his question. Maybe that fiver to the busker was money well spent after all, he thought. It was way past one o'clock in the morning as Jess made his way out of the training room and as he left, he momentarily caught sight of Ian remonstrating with the unconcerned, nonchalant, tall Indian. Daisy squeezed Jess' arm.

"Catch you later, hun," he squeaked.

"Yeah, cheers," replied Jess, not wishing to encourage or offend. "See you on Sunday for training, bright and late, 6pm sharp."

There was little humour in Jess' voice but then again, this relationship would clearly need none.

Training was, at first, an exciting affair with all manner of casino things to learn. Facts came thick and fast, for example: there were no windows on the gaming floor, no clocks would ever been seen either as casinos didn't want to advertise the time of day as this might encourage players to stop playing or leave, croupiers were not allowed to wear watches for this reason as well as security issues, all gaming floors were situated on upper floors so as to avoid robberies with a quick getaway. Far too many stairs to contend with for your average robber, or so it was believed! As for training, all croupiers would learn to deal European Roulette with a single zero. The tall Indian began his tutoring:

"This is called zero," he said, placing his right forefinger on the hole of the zero printed in yellow on green baize. "It is not naught, nor is it Oh – it is zero and NOTHING else! If I hear you say anything other than zero, you need not attend the next training session."

Word had already spread that sixty candidates had been accepted for training but only twenty were actually required. There was to be some fierce competition to ensure that hopefuls, including Jess, would remain training and not be one of the unfortunate souls that would seemingly disappear overnight. Jess would have to curtail his usual, jovial behaviour, bin the jokes and flippant remarks and keep his head firmly down – in Daisy's lap if necessary. Daisy assisted the well-manicured tall Indian and as the trainees began to recite the first of their times tables, Daisy made eye contact with Jess and gave a promiscuous wink. Jess smiled and winked back, only to see the tall Indian scowling at him.

"Are you paying attention, Jess!" called the tall Indian in such a condescending manner that it tore through Jess' confidence.

"Yeah! Yes, of course," Jess replied.

"Good. Seventeen times seventeen?" snapped the tall Indian.

"289!" shrieked Jess, amazed with himself.

"Come and see me after," said the Indian.

Jess' heart sank. Surely not the end? Not now, he despaired. Surely it would be nothing? Just a slap on the wrist? He consoled himself by refusing to allow any negativity to erode the enthusiasm that stil remained. Jess held on to what little determination he could muster. It would be good, he thought, all good and it was going to be good, forever!

The ride home with Daisy was quiet. The trains had stopped running and Jess had no option but to accept the offer of a lift home. Jess toyed with his left earlobe where a raised mound of flesh with a hole in the centre had once held a small, gold, sleeper earring. How stupid he had been to forget to remove it before going to the training school. The tall Indian had been right; having noticed it, it really wasn't the sort of look casinos wanted to encourage and Jess had been thankful for just a final warning. He scratched at the back of the earlobe and catching a small piece of dried skin under his fingernail, he brought it to his face in order to inspect the sliver of dermis.

Daisy broke the silence.

"I can swallow a banana, whole!" he chirped.

"Really?" replied Jess, a little too enthusiastically.

"I managed to train my gag reflex, for the obvious benefits," explained Daisy. "Then, one night down at Homéres - you have to go to Homéres Night Club, it's brilliant - someone gave me a banana and I took it down in one go."

"Blimey!" said Jess, genuinely impressed.

Jess was starting to become a little uneasy but somehow

enjoyed the titillation along with the taboo subject and the anticipation of the question that he knew would follow.

"What about you?" asked Daisy, with an inflective tone of hope leeching into the question. "Gay, straight, bi, bi-curious, all of the above or still undecided?" he asked.

"Straight I think," he answered, with a depth of sentiment that suggested a good degree of shame.

"Pity. If you ever change your mind, remember... Daisy does!" said Dasiy.

Jess felt safe all of a sudden, like the obligatory gay at a girl's sleepover. The threat melted away and Jess felt like he could flirt a little, tease maybe and get a kick out of the sexual connotations that would pass back and forth. However, caution was required as it would be far too easy to overstep the boundaries and with Jess being Jess, everything was highly likely.

"Daisy knows best if you're ever up for it," said Daisy, as he pulled the car over and waited for Jess to alight.

"I'm not gay," asserted Jess, slight panic somehow getting the better of him.

"Of course you're not sweetie," concurred Daisy. "None of us are!"

For the six months of training, learning the times-table for roulette: thirty-fives, seventeens, elevens, eights and fives, it was none too taxing for Jess as rote learning was usually done on the train. Classes had been re-scheduled which meant Jess could now get the night train home, mostly avoiding Daisy's advances... but not always.

* * *

Friendships were formed from the very early days of training, friendships that would develop into flat-sharing relationships later on and some of those friendships were more emotional than others.

"How's your luck?"

An obvious, 'somewhere up north,' accent pierced Jess' concentration as he read the London evening paper.

"Dickey's the name, and you are?"

An almost pure white hand, fingers straight and knife sharp, invited Jess to take a hold and shake.

"Yeah, how you doing? Jess, Jess Vere-White," said Jess.

Dickey sat down and offered a blue and white flip-top cigarette packet for Jess to take.

"No, cheers," said Jess, raising the palm of his hand to reinforce the refusal of a cigarette.

"No mate. You'll be needing this," said Dickey and he handed Jess the packet.

A waft of fresh tobacco filled Jess' nostrils as he popped open the top to see that there was nothing inside but a few flecks of golden tobacco. Jess studied it for a while and Dickey stood up to repeat himself to the next person sat nearby.

"Gather round you lot!" called the tall Indian in a voice that was neither appreciative nor accommodating.

The cigarette packet was an aid in the development of the manual dexterity that was required of all croupiers. Handling casino chips, discs of plastic about thirty five millimetres in diameter, was an essential element of the dealer's craft. The forefinger should be placed on the flip-top edge of the cigarette packet while the little finger is held opposite, then thumb to the left side and the remaining two fingers opposing the thumb. With slight pressure, the packet was held firm. The art was to draw back the forefinger, over the top edge of the packet and across the opening. As the forefinger pressed down and ran across the join, the top would 'pop' slightly and this would mean the procedure had been carried out successfully. Should the fingernail snag against the join, then this was a disaster for it demonstrated a 'hooked' finger which was considered a failure and would warrant a serious black mark against your progress if detected. If the error wasn't corrected, then a bad habit would be established and that would never, ever, do. The performing of this action was to be repeated over and over and over again. Many flip-top cigarette packets were worn out before the art was perfected and this could not be achieved with just an hour's practice. Oh no! This action required endless hours of practising, constant adjustment and refinement, before it could be performed as a seamless act of manual dexterity. Then, when one was deemed proficient at it, the handling of real casino chips was allowed but only after several weeks of exhaustive practise. This is where the craft, the skill, the mastery would be refined and honed to perfection. Constant, incessant repetition was vigorously undertaken with strict, almost religious fervour where any established Obsessive Compulsive Disorder would be relegated to mere insignificance and regarded as little more than a minor affliction by comparison; practise would take precedence over everyone and everything else, consuming one's life, one's being, one's every waking moment. On the train, in the pub, sat watching television, at the breakfast table, sitting on the toilet and even next to the bed, a stack of twenty casino chips would be handled, caressed and coerced into graceful movements by manual manipulation. Such skills would eventually become part of a croupier's persona, his life-blood, his true worth. A fully trained croupier can comfortably hold, juggle, flip, spin and cut casino chips with such dexterity, finesse and style, that any professional magician would seethe with jealousy were they to witness it for themselves. Casino chips are always stacked in twenties, twenty chips to every stack and any croupier worth their salt can feel this exact amount in their hand without looking. A casino croupier can hold a stack, "wiping off" from the bottom any excess, every time, every single time, to leave exactly twenty chips cradled in the fingers of their hand, either hand, left or right, or both simultaneously. A croupier will hold a stack of chips in one hand and with seamless elegance be able to manoeuvre that hand into any position, sideways, upside down or at any other angle and all the chips would be firmly held in the embracing grip – all this wondrous skill having evolved from those early days flicking empty, flip-top cigarette packets. As time progressed, the same dedication was given to learning new tricks, spreading chips between all five fingers, separating chips, spinning chips and all manner of other impressive showpiece tricks which were often employed by the most skilled and extrovert of croupiers during their dealing routines. Skills were demonstrated at every opportunity but only the very proficient could get away with such overt displays. Ridicule was swift and prolonged for those who failed in their attempts. Competition was fierce and rivalry was never, ever modest.

Throughout the remaining six months of late afternoons and evenings, Jess and twenty four other hopefuls continued their initial training. Candidates were swiftly rejected, never to be seen or heard from again and tears were shed as enthusiastic bodies turned up for training only to be turned away with unsympathetic words of rejection. This was paid training so the few places available, sought by so many hopefuls, meant the selection process was ruthless. Jess considered the sadistic manner in which the dispatching of trainees was gleefully executed. The trainers were employees with a lot of experience and it was more than likely that Jess would be working under, or even alongside, some of them in the very near future. Acceptance into the fold would mean becoming the very thing that Jess despised about them the most. He needed to be one of them. He need to be ruthless.

For training purposes, only one casino game was being taught and that was European Roulette, which is different from American Roulette by way of the double zero (which increases the 'house edge' or profitability of the game for the house). The premise for learning just one game was that a croupier would become proficient, if not a master, of that particular game before going on to learn any others. The minimum exposure to dealing European Roulette was eighteen months. The next game to learn would be Blackjack, the second most popular game played in British casinos after roulette, but that would be a little way off for Jess who, as luck would have it, would have to embark on emergency training before joining the Queen Boadicea II cruise ship as she set sail to cross the Atlantic Ocean on her regular trips to New York.

With all the necessary times-tables firmly fixed in his head and with fingers that could graciously manipulate cash and wheel chips, Jess picked up his pre-ordered dinner suit and held it up in the flickering, fluorescent strip light of the seamstress' workshop where he admired it and felt rightly proud of his achievement. Satin lapels, sewn up pockets and a brand new, black bow-tie that dangled limply from the hook of the coat-hanger, were all his; finally, he had earned the free uniform and meals whilst on duty. This was the start of something special – a glorious adventure, dreams to fulfil, goals to realise and experiences to enjoy. For the forthcoming years there would be ups and downs, a rollercoaster of a ride, an experience like no other where tears of laughter would be quickly followed by tears of despair, a journey to look back on and recite with wonderment. Jess had finally made good and was on his way in a new life, a colourful life where immense highs and extremely dark lows would become the norm. But for now, Jess could barely contain his excitement as he made one, final visit to his mother in Vallington Psychiatric Nursing Home.

"Hello Mum," spoke Jess quietly, still afraid of the withered hag that sat in the chair beside the picture window.

Jess looked out onto the manicured lawns as he spoke and watched intently as sparrows frantically fed from an ornamental bird table that leaned precariously to the left. Hopping on and off, darting back and forth, the flurry of feathered wings were finally chased away by a gang of bullying starlings. Every bird sought its fill from the fat cakes, nuts, seeds and bread crumbs on offer before moving on... to somewhere else, somewhere new, somewhere different.

"Fuck off," spat the poor excuse for a human being that was, unfortunately, still Jess' mother. "Fuck off you, little bastard."

Jess took from his pocket a broad band of bright red ribbon. "I won't ever come again Mum," he said. "This is the last time."

"Fuck off," came the parental response. "Fuck off, you bastard."

In better times, Jess and his Mum had talked about a lady they had once seen in an old people's home whilst visiting a relative. Back then, the elderly woman who they saw was sat on her bed waiting for death to come and claim her. She was totally unrelated but Jess and Mum could not take their eyes off her, or the broad length of bright red ribbon that had been tied in her hair. Like an oversized, garish doll she sat there, no longer a part of the outside world and clearly suffering, she could do no more than pray for the embarrassment to end.

'Don't ever let me get like that. Don't ever let them tie a ribbon in my hair!' Mum had made Jess promise back then. She had repeated it occasionally in the following years and seemed to have a very real hatred, maybe even a phobia, about looking like a rag doll, or just looking like an elderly woman waiting to die. She hated the idea of being an object of ridicule and not being aware of it. She hated ribbons that were bright red.

Jess looped the red ribbon he had brought around the back of his Mum's head and pulled the ends up onto the hairline of her sallow forehead. He tied the biggest bow that the ribbon's length would allow, then let it stand proud as a beacon to all who would pass by.

"There Mum," said Jess, "Don't you look lovely now?"

Jess turned and walked away, the snarling sound of his mother's voice disappearing into his past.

"Fuck off... fuck off.... fuck off... fu..."

Chapter Three

Dealing with the Big Boys

SO THE INTERVIEW, encouraged and lubricated by a couple of pints of the finest Hook Norton Best Bitter, went something like this:

I used to work in London's West End, 'Up West' as we 'Sarf Londoners' call it. Where the lights are all twinkly and you can get hold of anything for a price. I started in a Chinese casino, off Piddington Square, after leaving the training school. I had a bad time during training, it was all faggots and sucking up; sometimes sucking off if you know what I mean and pardon my French! People were chucked out for no good reason and there were one or two characters that deserved a bloody good slap. I can think of one in particular, a right ponce he was and I'll tell you more about him later, if we have time. Yeah, so, I started at The Golden Cat Casino in Mavebury Avenue, just across the road from here.

What was it like?

In the beginning, it was all awe and wonder. Bright lights, things happening at a million miles an hour, just like any new job I suppose. Things to learn, adapting to routines and different ways, living up to expectations and generally trying to fit in really. It's known as an entertainment industry so there's a lot of glamour and excitement to go with it. I have good memories of the time, I think. Of course, there were some bad points, things that went wrong and on a couple of occasions I was close to jacking it all in. But I didn't, and I'm glad I didn't, because it has given me some great stories to tell and a somewhat 'colourful' history to remember in my old age.

Tell me about the punters. What were they like? Did you meet anyone famous?

Ah! The obvious question. You know, you always get asked

the same questions: 'Have you met anyone famous? Do the casinos cheat? What's the most someone has ever won? What's the most someone has ever lost?' Well, I started out at The Golden Cat which is right on the edge of China Town so all the Chinese would pile in at every opportunity. They love the gambling they do, can't get enough of it. Morning, noon and night they would come in, even on their tea-breaks from the restaurant kitchens around the back there. Mad for roulette most of them.

Go on then, what's the most you've ever seen someone lose?

There was this one guy called Zayer. Nasty piece of work he was, although there were times he could be quite polite and charming but that was always to the girls and never to the blokes. They say he got his fortune from arms dealing – dealing in death I call it. Apparently, one per cent commission from trading in guns and ammo worth hundreds of millions. Well, I wouldn't mind some of that action if it was handed to me on a plate. I think he was a Turkish-Cypriot or something, a fat bastard and a real pain in the arse to deal with. This one time, he really goes for it. The wheel is against him and the angrier he gets the more he seems to lose. It's like a negative force, when you're on a losing streak you start to think negatively and you almost will yourself to lose – it's like you know you're going to lose because you keep losing so you continue to lose. It's like an avalanche, a snowball effect and it's difficult to stop once you get caught up in it. 'It's bound to happen and so it does,' if you get my drift? He has a few hits but the many losses are stacking up. He takes hit after hit and presses all the way – doubles up and then doubles again and again chasing his losses. You could see the pressure building up, head like a powder keg he was ready to detonate and he was sweating like a Catholic Priest in a primary school. His neck was throbbing and bright red like it was about to burst. No word of a lie, he smothers the layout with chips and plaques, there must have been nearly a million on the layout and he forgets to play one number, just one – thirty-six I think. He literally overlooks to put anything on it and it's an obvious oversight, a mistake, a very costly mistake and one he would regret. Well, bugger me and Bosh! Straight in thirty six the ball goes and he loses his marbles. Ranting and raving, he lifts up the roulette table and practically shoves it at the dealer. The dealer's crapping it – nice girl, Jenny's her name - and Zayer sees the fear in her eyes and lets the table drop, out of compassion or maybe he just bottled it. The chips go everywhere and the management intervenes to sort it all out. They bundle Jenny off the floor and Zayer gets led into the restaurant to calm down. Everyone was watching, all the other punters preparing themselves for the ruckus. It was bonkers.

Well, at the end of the day, he was about eleven minus eleven. I could almost feel the Christmas bonus wedging itself into my back pocket.

What do you mean, eleven minus eleven?

He bought in for eleven million pounds and lost eleven million pounds. I think he lost some on Blackjack too but I can't be sure. I did see the score card and it definitely said eleven doing eleven.

And what about winners?

It wasn't so much the size of the win that struck us the most. It was this particular bloke and the manner in which he won that we all remember. There was this regular Larry of a punter, nothing special to speak of, a regular who came in, did a few hundred quid and left. He was a cabbie, private hire he was, and he popped in most afternoons before his late shift. He played a few numbers on roulette, some neighbours and a French bet or two.

Neighbours?

If you look in the roulette wheel you see lots of numbers. Pick a number and either side of it you will see two more numbers. Well, those two numbers, either side of your chosen number, are the neighbours of your chosen number. Example, zero has the numbers three, fifteen, twenty-six and thirty-two either side of it so, if you played zero and the neighbours, you would be playing the numbers, zero, three, fifteen, twenty-six and thirty-two. That's a five piece bet. We learnt the wheel, all of the numbers and their positions in relation to all the other numbers, while at the training school. We had to recite the exact location of all the numbers and all of their respective neighbours. It was simple rote learning and anybody with half a brain can do it but some trainees struggled and subsequently found themselves heading home for an early shower.

And French bets?

Same thing really. A series of numbers that cover complete sections of the wheel. It's like playing half or a quarter of the wheel and all those numbers in that section. You have Voissons, Tier and Orphans in that department. Where was I?

Regular Larry?

Yeah, so this cabbie plays his normal game. His name's not Larry by the way! Anyway, he has a bit of luck from the off and he's in for a hundred quid but still SP after an hour.

SP?

Starting Price – the situation you would be in at the point you started, neither winning nor losing. Okay? Then, out of nowhere, Bish, Bash, Bosh! We turn over the staff for a new shift and he's suddenly five grand ahead. Alarm bells start ringing and a small crowd starts to gather. The alarm bells aren't actually ringing, it's just a manner of speaking so don't take everything I say literally otherwise you'll think I'm barking. Now, suspicion is immediately aroused because the games are designed for punters to lose, not win. The Pit Boss is at the head of the table and croupiers are changed so an experienced dealer can take over and try to claw the money back. The Inspector is replaced for a more experienced one as well, the cameras are looking on and the manager is hovering in the wings ready to give someone a bollocking. Then, before we know it, it's game on.

It doesn't sound like much money though, not compared to eleven million?

In another casino, more upmarket, that would be true but this casino was more of a grind action sort of place. The action was provided by those players who had a few quid to spare on their special night out or the regulars who would do a few hundred a day.

Small time then?

Not really. A couple of hundred a day, every day of the week! It doesn't sound much but you would need to be earning quite a decent living to be spending that sort of money on a regular basis, especially back in the day. Two hundred a day, seven days a week, fifty two weeks of the years, it all adds up you know. Seventy-two thousand eight hundred, to be exact.

That's quick. Your maths training coming in useful then?

Not really. I've told this story before. So, grind action is more to do with the pace of play than the financial limits of the clientèle, although the two do really go hand in hand I suppose. The games are fast and sometimes furious, speeded up as the percentages are based on the number of plays completed. Example: When we calculate the house edge, that's the winning percentage in favour of the casino, that is our mark-up and on roulette this is based on ten thousand spins of the ball. Now, you might think that a game which pays thirty-five to one and has thirty-seven numbers is crooked but, in reality, that difference is the profit margin or what we term the house edge. You see, the more spins of the ball, or cards that are dealt, the more, theoretically, the house will win, right?

Got it!

Right then, so it all kicks off and it is definitely game on. This cabbie guy cannot lose, every spin he picks up and where some of us ordinary folk would count our winnings and quit while we're ahead well, he just keeps piling it on until he reaches the table maximum.

Maximum?

Every casino will have a maximum amount that can be wagered, otherwise you could keep doubling up after your losing stake and eventually win, as long as you had the money to do it. Maximums are imposed to prevent this happening. Otherwise a casino wouldn't make any money, would it? The maximum on roulette is proportionate so if you have a thousand pound maximum on a single number, a two number split will have a two thousand maximum and four numbers, four thousand, etc., etc. Outside bets are different but still proportionate. A casino's bankroll, the amount it must prove to the gaming authority to get its operating licence, is based on these maximums. As I was saying...

This cabbie geyser ensnares lady luck and a fair few scroungers to boot. You know the sort of poncing beggars, the ones who pray for you or mumble some stupid incantation so that when you win they try to make out it was their prayers that caused it. Handouts given for such services usually take the form of a couple of table chips or a few quid in cash but it is rarely accepted without an initial display of some well-rehearsed, sham, polite refusal. Most punters are highly superstitious and a lot of them dare not take any chances with their gambling, just in case, just in case it *was* an incantation, a wish or muttered charm that brought up the winning number. Tarts, prostitutes and all manner of scumbags are attracted to a winner; like moths to a flame they are. Anyway, the winning goes on and on and we all start to wonder if there's something up. The CCTV footage will no doubt be reviewed by security later but for the moment something's got to be done. Casinos are just as superstitious as the punters, moreso sometimes. To combat this run of casino bad luck, the dealer and inspector are replaced every ten minutes to try and get this bloke to lose. The top dealer and inspector desperately try to work their magic but the winning streak just goes on and on. Into the night he plays and the casino decides to further reward this punter with complimentary food and drink, which they hope will keep him playing. All we can do is hope against hope that luck will soon swing into the casino's favour. If he does decide to get up and leave, we can only guess about his return as he might well favour one of our competitors in which to gamble his winnings, 'our' money. For that night though, there was one less taxi on the streets. He stayed right up until closing time, the last spin being at 2 am in those days. Finally, he wobbles out of the casino with a cashier's cheque for fifty odd grand. All from a hundred quid! As I said, the CCTV was later checked but everything seemed to be in order. Just luck, sheer luck and it happens that way sometimes. We even changed the roulette wheel, the entire thing, because they are handmade and some are known to have a bias towards certain numbers or sections of the wheel.

What, like crooked?

No, not crooked as in cheating crooked but a natural bias due to the nature of the assembly or the materials used. I'll tell you an amazing true story about wheel bias one day.

Now then, normal people like you and me, would sit at home and count our money, roll naked in the filthy notes and never set foot in a casino again. Even if you did gamble again you would limit yourself to only a few quid so as not to lose it all back like a proper mug. As you can imagine, we really didn't expect to see the punter in again, at least not so soon. However, Customer Relations had done their job admirably and in he came, the same time as usual the following day and he had a couple of girls with him. A girl on each arm, like literally, one on each arm. That's two birds!

I see the Maths is kicking in again?

Cheeky mare! Honestly, it was so corny, like an old black and white movie. All he needed was a top hat and cane. I'll tell you, he was Fred Astaire reincarnated. They came down the staircase onto the casino floor and it was laughable really. Talk about rags to riches. Talk about gold-diggers!

He was ushered to an empty, waiting table, roped off from the ogling dregs of casino society, where he sat down and straight away the waitresses were all over him like a rash. A hundred quid tip for a cup of coffee was worth fighting for but it would have to be returned if it was seen by the management. Tips have to be commensurate with the service given and anything excessive, which might be considered as a direct result of gaming, is forbidden and against the law as well. This necessitated that the waitresses become very friendly with management, for financial reasons if nothing else. Well, Larry-no-mates, or now Larry-everyone's-mate, sits right down and we thought he would ask for a few free spins, to get him in the mood but...

Free spins?

When the dealer spins the ball for you and you don't actually bet anything, that's a 'free' spin. It's so you can get a taste of how the wheel is behaving and how the dealer is spinning the ball, if you believe in that sort of hocus-pocus stuff. You know, some punters sit for hours and hours and hours writing down winning roulette numbers, looking for a pattern, a sign, anything that will give them a clue or the slightest edge over the casino. Nothing ever works of course, but it's not just the crazies that do it. Eminent professors, mathematicians, statisticians, they've all had a go, all of them, searching for the alchemist's dream, a pattern or a system that will turn their bets into riches.

Our Larry doesn't waste any time. BOSH! A grand on number seventeen, max on red and max on the third dozen. 'Bloody hell!' says the Pit Boss, 'Here we go again.'

Straight in my son! His number is like a magnet and the ball is pure iron. You see, everyone is staring at the number with a grand on it. Everyone's eyes boring into it and willing it to happen. The dealer's eyes were looking in the wheel at the number as it spun round and round, trying to calculate whether it would hit or miss, the Inspector was watching the layout number to make sure the bet was all in order. The chipper was also staring at the number, as was the CCTV operator and the Manager and the Pit Boss and numerous lookers-on. All those eyes, all those greedy, beady staring eyes looking at number seventeen, burning right into it, subconsciously willing it to happen then... BOSH! Straight in, thank you very much! Thirty-five grand payout, plus ten grand for the dozen and another ten for the outside bets. Fifty-five thooooousand pounds, on the first spin of the ball, plus the stake. None too shabby! Larry-boy's in no mood for quitting so, on he trundles as before with some minor losses but all in all the winning streak holds out. Questions will soon be winging their way around the Director's board room, we surmise. Day number two and the guy is holding just short of four hundred grand. Eventually, he quits but this is only because it's chucking out time so he leaves with an additional two girls on each arm; all off back to his place for a right old jolly with Mr Big Time Charlie Potatoes. He takes ten grand for holding-folding and puts the rest on deposit for safe keeping. Quite frankly, we don't expect him back – ever, but like the twat he is, he rattles in the next day good as gold. He seems to be soaking up the attention from management and the other punters, the focus is all on him and he loves it. The classic fifteen minutes of fame I suppose. No hoper cabbie, no friends, no admirers then suddenly, Mister Popular, basking in wealth and adoration. Now you would think, at this point, if that was you or me, we'd go out and buy a house or something, then at least you wouldn't lose it all back to the casino, at least you'd have something to show for it all, but not this guy. Oh no! Same M.O. as before...

M.O.?

Modus Operandi – Latin I think, for doing something the same way? Bish, Bash, and Bloody Bosh! Stacking it up like a good 'un and the manager is sweating buckets. No doubt the Directors have asked some searching questions and the Head of Gaming can be seen desperately holding onto his clackers as well as his sanity. Fuck me! The bloke just cannot lose. On the whole, every spin is a winner but his stakes are beginning to taper off now. Slowly he reduces his stake and that, I can assure you, is worse than him winning. Management must now consider how they will get their money back if he isn't even laying it out in the first place. Winning is acceptable because at the end of the day, every casino knows that as long as you keep them playing they will, eventually, lose. As a player, if you reduce your stake then your losses are obviously minimized. This was a superb tactic if it was planned and it certainly got some management hearts missing a beat or two I can tell you. Worse was to come. Even before the night crowd started to drag their sorry arses in he had decided that enough was enough and away he did trot.

The next day – NOTHING! ZILCH! ZIPPO! Or that night shift, nor the next day or the next. I went off for my weekend and on my return I was told that he had not been seen, not even by his wife, who had been in looking for him as he really hadn't been seen, by anyone, anywhere. In fact, he wasn't seen for a whole week and the winner's cheque he'd taken, on his last visit, some seven hundred and twenty thousand smakeroonies, had not, as yet, been cashed. Then the shit seriously hit the fan and just as we're about to issue a profit warning and expect some serious bollockings from the owners, in he strolls all tanned and with a gorgeous bird in tow - Russian I do believe. She's dressed in an expensive looking, clingy, white frock with a serious plunging neckline, earrings all a drip with sparklers and leading her by the arm, the former cabbie who was enjoying his new, playboy lifestyle, pretty much as anyone would in such circumstances. It transpired that he had buggered of somewhere on holiday and who were we to criticise? Seven hundred and twenty grand, a holiday in the sun and a dejected missus back at home. Who wouldn't be out having the time of his life? I know I would. Funny thing was, this 'couple' didn't look so out of place dressed as they were, all formal like, as you might expect for an evening at the opera. Somehow we weren't shocked by him, or her as it happens, it was sort of predictable.

First, he larges it up in the restaurant with a bottle of Chateau Petrous at a thousand quid a throw, brought over special from one of our sister casinos in Mayfair. Eventually, in a lovely little V.I.P. section we had sectioned off for him, he sat down to play. Now, whether he was trying to impress the Russian bird or maybe the sun had gone to his head, we couldn't tell but he started gunning it. Eight, twenty, twenty nine, complete to the maximum. You're talking a hundred and twenty grand a bet, let alone the stuff the Russian bird was chucking on the layout like money was going out of fashion. From that point on, it didn't take too long. It seemed Lady Luck had been left lying on a sun-lounger somewhere in the Asiatic as she no longer gave a toss for the cabbie or his consort. At one point, when things were looking particularly grim, the Russian had excused herself and failed to find her way back - accidently on purpose I should imagine! By the time chummy realised that she was not coming back, he is about to wave goodbye to the last of his stash with a thousand quid sat on good old number seventeen. Yep, we all stared at that number and the ball rattled around, ivory clattering on ancient wood where, finally and decisively, it dropped... into number twenty-eight. This, ladies and gentleman, concluded the demonstration of luck and stupidity. It was gone, all of it, not a bean left.

The whole lot?

Well, apart from ten grand or so, which we assumed he'd blown on holiday somewhere whilst picking up the Russian trollop. Yep! he did it all back. How mad is that, I ask you?

Wow!

When you consider it, he wasn't the biggest winner I've ever seen but the difference in his initial stake to the amount he won sets him apart. Wealthier punters have won a lot bigger, like thirty-five million over the course of five days I can recall, but that particular episode raised one or two questions as to whether external influences or devices were being used to assist in the winning process? Nevertheless, to a billionaire it was nothing but for a cabbie, the win was monumental. It must have seemed like billions but, when you think about it, how much did he actually lose?

Seven hundred and…

Nope! A hundred quid. That's all his initial stake was. That's all he bought in for. All he actually lost, out of his own pocket, was a hundred pounds. The rest was never his, it was the casino's money. That's why he was so brave gambling it the way he did. He said he never considered the winnings to be his so he was only playing with the casino's money and I know this to be true, because he told me so himself.

I would have felt awful if it had been me!

He was quite philosophical about it all really. He stated it was never his money and that he only lost a hundred quid of his own, drank some great wine and had a bloody good time on the ten grand. As for his missus? Well, she disappeared with the kids and hasn't been seen since. As he said, that was bit of a bonus too.

Does he still play?

He does, just as before, a few hundred quid but to date, Lady Luck has not seen fit to pay him any more courtesy calls. Once again he is just a regular Larry, no friends, no family and a no hoper. He still drives a taxi. As I say, it was the amount that he won from such a small, initial stake and the speed with which he won it, the risks he took and just how quickly it was squandered that makes this story so memorable. I'm sure he won't forget it either.

Talking in terms of millions, do these amounts of money become normal?

They do. Once you've seen millions won and lost, after it has been a part of your everyday, working vocabulary, it becomes very normal. Like an accountant who writes figures with loads of zeros after them. It's not real money and it definitely isn't yours, so it doesn't mean anything, other than numbers on a page.

So the money isn't real?

Don't get me wrong. The money is very real indeed. Packets and packets of cash, carrier bags full to the brim sometimes. It's just that the more times you see and hear about it, the less impact it has on you. As for hard cash… I've been on the back stairs, on my own, bringing cash up to the top cash desk, metres away from the fire exit, with over a million pounds cradled in my meaty, well defined arms.

Yeah, nice biceps! Ever been tempted?

Too right, but where would you go? A million doesn't last long these days.

So what's the story there then?

Nothing exciting really. I was just bringing up a bundle of money from our downstairs V.I.P. rooms to the cash desk on the main gaming floor. It seemed like a good idea to use the fire stairs rather than the punter's stairs. I thought there'd be less chance of being hit over the head and robbed but then, that left the temptation of me legging it out onto the street. Most of us think this way; the 'what if' syndrome but when you actually think about it, it's quite a difficult blag to accomplish. Let's say I had legged it out of the place with a million pounds. It's not a huge bundle to handle, all vacuum packed in fifty grand packets – bricks we call them. So you make it to your car, get yourself going and... where exactly do you head for?

Der! The airport?

So, off you go to the airport with no passport eh? Think about it. Gotta head home first, grab the old passport, maybe pack some sun lotion and then head off to Terminal 5. Try to buy a ticket at the counter – most flights are fully booked unless you're heading to some far flung place like Bonga-Bonga or a war zone.

Bonga where?

It's not a real place. I just made it up. The point is, off the top of your head you have to decide where in the world you are going to head for. And visas! Maybe the place you're heading for needs a visa in advance. You'd be straight on the plane home again. Meanwhile, whilst all this is going on, you'd quickly be missed, two and two would be put together and the filth would be winging their way to your house, with blues and twos for excitement, and they'd no doubt find you fannying around trying to pack your talc and favourite teddy.

Filth?

Police.

Oh, okay!

Also, the airports and docks would be on high alert and at the first sign of your pretty little mush you'd be straight off to clink. I tell you, it's not as easy as it sounds, trying to get away with the perfect crime and I know, because I've thought about it – a lot! Like I say, a million quid wouldn't last that long anyway. At least not the way I spend it!

Anyway, what was I talking about? Oh, yeah, the million quid. As I said before, maximums are set and there is little deviation from these standards or the rules of play. However, sometimes, big time Joe Six-Pack comes in, giving it large and asks for special treatment. Like more than normal allowed on a number. So, this dude comes in, Emirati sort I think, son of some royal or other, a playboy if you like, living on Papa's wealth. He comes in late one night and asks for the Salle Privée to be opened up.

Salle..?

One of the V.I.P. rooms where a more private game can be played. These rooms are luxurious with a roulette table or two, a couple of blackjack tables and a mini Punto-Banco. The furnishings are very Middle Eastern with some tasty, original art scattered about the place. Very expensive, all expertly designed to make the top punters, snails we call them - the very wealthy, feel right at home. This Arab bloke wanders in, bold as brass, with the obligatory high class prossies...

Real prostitutes!?

I reckon so, why not? If not working girls then the sort of

gold-diggers that you'd pick up in any of the night clubs around Mayfair. These creatures we call slugs, because they are pretty disgusting, slimy individuals and of no real value to anybody or anything. So, the guy turns up in some super-charged Bentley if you please and three slugs, or girls to you, spill out onto the pavement. One of the girls is well drunk and can hardly stand on her own so her friends help her to her feet and she breaks the stiletto heel on her FMBs.

FMBs?

Fuck Me Boots! Knee high black leather.

Um! Yes, right oh! Err… carry on.

The Arab looks at her with total disdain, tosses a two and a half grand packet at her feet and tells the others to leave her be. Her friends quickly hail a black cab and she is whisked away into the night, which probably saved her from a jolly good rogering up the bum, I reckon. Plus, she's two and a half grand better off for the deal. Dog's dinner, everyone's a winner!

How d'ya know all this?

Car-jockeys. They stand outside as unofficial bouncers, the all-seeing ones who catch everything that happens on the street. They tell us everything and I let them in on the inside gossip. It's a nice bit of camaraderie. We're all good buddies and look after one another.

The Arab, forget his name, starts giving it large about wanting a bigger maximum on roulette, something like five grand on a number with fifty grand on the outsides. This we don't normally allow but punters like to ask for it to make out they are super wealthy and to show off. The duty manager calls the director and comes back with an answer. They tell him to show a million quid in cash and he can have the maximum he requested but, he must play for a minimum amount of time with a minimum bet for each spin.

What's the point of that?

The point is; the more he plays, the more he loses, in theory – I told you all this before.

But there's no guarantee he'll play the lot?

No guarantees at all but gamblers, being gamblers, if they have the money they can't resist playing it. The casino ensures they have a chance of getting the money from the player by stating that he must play a minimum of twenty-five grand per spin of the ball and play must be for a minimum of one hour, with at least three spins every five minutes. What the casino doesn't want is someone placing a huge bet, winning big from the off and then playing the minimum stake whereby the casino has no chance of recovering the loss.

But you said the casino will always win?

It will, in the long run. They always do. Imagine we give the player his maximum and he dumps five grand on a number. It comes in – remember it can and does – and he scoops a hundred and seventy-five grand for his trouble. He then decides to play the table minimum, one number at the minimum stake of twenty-five quid. You'd be looking at 7,000 spins of the ball, assuming he lost every single spin, before you could recoup your loss. During the subsequent days or even months, he would come in and take full advantage of the complimentary food and wine on offer, as well as all those other expensive inducements to ensure his patronage. This can add up to tens of thousands and it would all be in the hope that he might play big and lose big. It's a right bugger if he only plays and loses a couple of bob. In essence, he could eat and drink a couple of grand's worth a day but is only paying a couple of hundred quid for the privilege. It's just not in the casino's interest to allow that sort of thing to happen. It may seem like haphazard logic but everything is worked out to the '*nth*' degree in a casino. Nothing is left to chance, except the games of course, but even they are stacked in favour of the house. We're not a charity you know, it's a profit making business and we're bloody ruthless at it. Don't be fooled by the courteous manner, the complimentary dinners and drinks, the tickets to Ascot, the box at football, the centre court seats for Wimbledon finals - all these things are calculated to ensnare the punter and get him into the casino where he will undoubtedly lose. Relieve them of their wealth as some might say. It's a bit like licensed mugging if you ask me.

Back to the action then. The Arab now needs to save face as we have called his bluff. We think he is just bigging it up in front of his 'lady' friends. He leaves and we have a giggle at his expense. Tosser! Then, bugger me with a drainpipe, he turns up about an hour later with one of them aluminium suitcases and a small Egyptian chap. It's just like the movies and our side stands in a line with the Manager, the Pit Boss and the Cashier facing them and they stand opposite us with the Arab, the little Egyptian and one less prossie. The Egyptian opens the suitcase to show the other side, us, the contents, like it's some crazy drug deal or something. Inside the case, stuffed to the gills, are travellers' cheques and loads of notes of various denominations and currencies. The deal is agreed and the Egyptian sits down and starts pulling wads of cheques and cash out. None of the travellers' cheques have been pre-signed so Mr Cairo sits down and starts signing them, one after the other, continuously, like a little machine on full speed. The Arab starts playing and the Egyptian can barely keep up with the cheque signing fiasco. There was some very condescending wagging of fore-fingers as the Arab's patience began to wear thin. At the end of the day, the Arab lost his money, and a little respect, and we thought that would be the last we would ever see of him. A few years later he popped up again, out of the blue, a lot wealthier, incredibly wealthier actually, with a story that had us in awe. He had succeeded his late father to become the ruler of some far flung part of the Middle East, somewhere unpronounceable and way off the tourist trail. I couldn't say whether it was true or not but his wealth certainly was – he squandered it like there was no tomorrow and for several years this kept the casino in record profits. Anyway, it was during that initial play when I was tasked to deliver cash from downstairs to upstairs, which was in the region of a million quid.

The travellers' cheques?

Not entirely. There were some of those travellers' cheques and cash in my hands but there was also another big game going on upstairs and the punter was cashing out and he was insisting on taking hard cash, which was kept in the downstairs safe. All that money, it was very tempting but only for about three seconds. After that I just carried on with what I was doing.

What about the Arab?

Like I say, he became a regular and spent many, many millions. Most of the casino's profits over the following three or four years were solely down to his play. It was shameful really but I made some really good Christmas bonuses out of him during those times. I can't complain, I bought a house on it. Can't remember his name for the life of me but we did give him a nickname.

Which was?

We called him Bones.

Skinny then?

Yep! Scrawny fucker. He would always turn up with some stunner or other, picked up from one of the nightclubs in the area. I can't imagine any girl would actually go for a bloke like that, except for his money. But who knows, there's no accounting for taste – you ask my missus! Guffaw!

Another time, Bones rolls in with a mate. This guy, another Arab, is wearing some white gown affair and he literally wobbles in and, quite frankly, takes everyone's breath away.

A stunner then?

No way! He was fucking huge. Enormous! I mean he was B.I. fucking G! The biggest, fattest, widest arse you have ever seen in your entire life. He didn't play but hung around a lot whilst Bones did his thing. Now, with an arse that size, there was nothing to accommodate it so he took to sitting on a coffee table outside the Salle. The table was a chunky affair, had to be, but it didn't look right to management and there was always the chance it might buckle under those massive bags of arse blubber. Bones expresses his dissatisfaction that his mate has nothing proper to sit on and, quite rightly, he's embarrassed for his chum. He demands something be done. 'Of course, Sir,' we say. Nothing, and I mean nothing, is too much trouble for a player of such value. Wouldn't want him taking his business to a rival casino, now would we? So, they get a specially made, super arse size chair for him. It was in the same style as the other chairs in the lounge area but was clearly a lot wider. It looked like a shortened sofa or a stretched armchair. Solid as fuck it was and it really did the job. Sitting down was the easy bit though. It was the standing up that was hilarious. The CCTV room had videoed the humiliation on a number of occasions and it was a real hoot when it was shown at the staff party one Christmas. Once seated, the lard-arse would stay that way all night whilst his friend played in the Salle. His tubbness would tuck into sandwiches, finger platters, fried tit-bits, kebabs, fruit, dates and anything else that the kitchen sent out. Not once did he ever get up for a piss. Bucketful after bucketful of water and juice, as well as coffee and tea, were guzzled but not once did he ever manage to get his fat arse off that chair in order to relieve himself. Nope! He just did it where he was. That's wealth for you! Why get up to go to the toilet when you can just sit there and piss your pants. Oddly enough, there was never any visible sign of his bladder contents on his clothing and we just assumed that when no one was looking, he hitched up his robe thingy and sat bared-arsed on his special chair. Can't say for sure what went on but the seat was always sopping wet when he left and required some serious cleaning and drying in readiness for his next squat. Wealth, as they say, has its privileges. Dirty bastard we say, but it was nothing exceptional in the grand scheme of things, all those creepy things that go on in the murky world of casinos. You get used

to odd behaviour and then all of a sudden, it becomes the norm. Frightening really!
Well, time's knocking on so I best get going or I'll miss the night bus.

It's only last orders. I'll get you one for the road.

Twist my arm then. Get us some nuts... the honey roasted ones.

There you go. Enjoy!

Ta very! I am getting paid for this, aren't I?
Now, there was this one weird guy – proper weird if you know what I mean? He came from Belgium and it all started one dark and stormy night.

You're kidding, right?

Only about the dark and stormy night. The rest is absolutely, one hundred per cent, cross my heart and hope to die, all above board, true. What I didn't personally witness myself, the rest came from very reliable sources.

I don't doubt it.

One afternoon, late summer it was, an off-the-street customer walks into the casino reception. Now, this is one of the most prestigious casinos in the Western hemisphere and this bloke is looking pretty crappy, dressed like he's slept in his clothes and never had them cleaned or pressed. The reception staff, good as gold and never judging a book by its cover, eyes him up and down and decide to let him become a member. Later, I asked why this was and the receptionist told me that it looked like he didn't own shit, he smelt a bit like shit too but, it was noticed, he was sporting a rather nice Patek Philippe watch. A sixty-grand watch by all accounts. Very observant of the reception staff and they sure earned their money that day. So he applies to join the casino club then waits twenty-four hours to come in, as you did in those days.

Why?

It was supposed to be a cooling off period, to stop impulsive gamblers. Now, the next afternoon this dude walks in and we get his name as he comes down the stairs from the mezzanine floor. The phone goes and it's the receptionist on the other end telling us a Mister Bouchon was about to come onto the gaming floor. The casino was usually empty in the afternoons as it was one of the top end casinos and most players came for the evening only. As Bouchon came down the short flight of stairs, all the table staff eyeballed him, everyone trying to gauge his worth and possible style of play. Momentarily, he looks around and then he sits down at the end roulette table and asks the dealer to spin.

A free spin!

Very good! You're getting the hang of it now. So the dealer spins, the ball drops in and on goes the dolly. Matey boy writes down…

Hang on! What's a dolly?

A plastic cylinder that marks the winning number, about the size of a quarter length of a fat cigar. They come in various shapes, sizes and colours and are nothing more than markers. They should prevent cheats popping chips onto the winning number after it has been announced, although a proficient cheat can overcome this quite easily.

Tell me about the cheats!

Another time. It's getting late and I doubt whether I'll get to finish this story as it is. Bouchon writes down the winning number on one of the roulette table cards that are stacked at the head of the table. Punters use them to write down numbers, patterns of numbers and goodness knows what else. There is a picture of the wheel on it, the wheel numbers and a list of the basic bets you can make as well as their individual payouts. In a grid on the back, Bouchon writes down the winning number then looks up at the dealer in anticipation of another free spin. As the ball is hurtling around the wheel, Bouchon lifts up the back of his jacket and slides it over the back of his chair whilst still wearing it, then leans back to look into the wheel and writes down the next winning number. He took great care not to crease the back of his jacket but to look at his suit; it looked like it had come from a charity shop. There were lots of oddities about this bloke: there were some tell-tale signs of good breeding, he was handsome in a rough sort of way, a hint of wealth about him but more than anything else, there was this overriding air of mystery and slowly it began to consume us all. Managers had ring-rounds to see if any of the other casinos knew of this guy, but no one had ever heard of him.

You say he was Belgian?

We didn't know that at the time. We found out later on. He came in day after day, sat for hours on end writing down the winning numbers but never, ever placed any bets. Spinning the ball for no bets is a real pain in the arse for any dealer. Endlessly spinning the ball with no respite or any pause, endlessly reaching into the wheel and endlessly popping that ivory sphere around the track. It's enough to drive you crackers. I had my fair share of doing it but the Pit Boss made sure the chore was evenly distributed amongst us all. We groaned when Bouchon appeared at the top of the stairs, audibly groaned and wished he would pick another table, any table other than the one we were stood on. It was just like the nutter on the bus - when we all hope and pray that he won't sit next to us and how relieved we are when he sits down next to someone else. We mentally command him to sit somewhere else and that is what we all did with Bouchon, we literally willed him to sit at another table. Immediately upon sitting, he would look up at the dealer expectantly, wait for the ball to be spun, then lift his jacket over the back of the chair and having taken a table card from the head of the table, he would start writing down the following winning numbers. By the end of the shift, when we all handed over to the night shift, he would still be sitting and writing and we would hear stories about him the next day along with the anguish that he caused. This is how it went, day after day, week after week then one month after another. It was mind numbingly painful and still we knew nothing about this Bouchon fella. It came very close to a decision being made as to whether he should be politely asked to leave. Maybe he sensed this because on one particular afternoon, appearing at the top of the stairs, he glided down and chose the nearest roulette table at the end of the room, the very same table as his first visit. We, those of us on other tables, silently sniggered as furrows could clearly be seen on the forehead of the dealer at the table where Bouchon now sat. Carefully, he lifted the tail of his recently pressed jacket over the back of the chair, told the dealer to spin and reached for a table card. He placed a silver, ballpoint pen on the card, sat silently watching the ball as it began to slow on the wheel's track, then from nowhere produced a brick and slammed it down on number twenty with words that were barely audible. 'Twenty complete to the maximum, change on black."

A real brick?

Noooo! Fifty pound notes in a sealed packet. Fifty grand, remember? A brick?

Oh, yes. Sorry!

Bosh! The dealer is caught unawares and the Inspector is caught napping. It was a chipper watching from a nearby table that woke everyone up.

What's a chipper?

An assistant to the dealer who essentially picks up, or 'chips' up, the losing chips so they can be used again. They also assist in the dealing of the game and a good chipper almost runs the show, pacing it by getting pay-outs ready and advising the dealer of anything that they should be aware of. Quite often it's a good chipper that makes a dealer look great. Conversely, a shitty chipper can really fuck up a dealer's mojo.
'TWENTY, FULL COMPLETE TO THE MAXIMUM, CHANGE ON BLACK!' hollers the chipper. The dealer repeats it along with the Inspector and hearts everywhere are a pumping for the first time in a long while. Out of nowhere it came and where he was hiding that brick we never did fathom – it was game on. At times he would leave the casino for thirty minutes or so but then return to continue his play, brick after brick until, shortly before the change of shift, he had lost exactly one million pounds. Cool as a cucumber he stands up, jacket sliding up off the back of the chair, takes himself down to the reception and asks for a ride home. Most casinos have a club car to run valued punters around, usually picking up and dropping off locally. V.I.P. punters can also get a car and a driver to use at their leisure, often to take spouses

on shopping trips to Harrods or Harvey Nicks. It was not at all unusual for a player to ask for a lift home, especially if they had done all of their money and were pretty much without the means to replenish the Gucci wallet. Even if punters could get some more cash they would probably gamble it rather than spend it on a taxi. They'd walk home if they had to.

'Not a problem, Sir,' says the receptionist, waving to the driver to make ready. 'Where do you want to go?'

'Brussels,' says Bouchon.

'Brussels?' repeats the receptionist.

'Brussels,' confirms Bouchon, very matter-of-factly. 'Brussels in Belgium.'

So, with all due authority gained from the manager, Bouchon is driven home to Belgium, and in the Bentley if you please. It must have cost a bomb in petrol. I don't know what went on or what was said on that long, long journey into Europe but the driver had a very big smile when he returned and whenever he was questioned about any tip he may, or may not have received, there was a twinkle in his eye that was full of satisfaction. For a while after that Bouchon was not seen but stories began to circulate. I've always meant to research these stories but never quite got round to it. It was said that he had killed his first wife for the insurance money and had actually got away with it. Some say he gambled the insurance money which was, exactly a million quid. Spooky! What we did know for sure was, a few weeks later he was seen cruising up and down the street outside the casino in a pink Rolls Royce convertible. With the top down, he could clearly be seen sat on the back seat, being chauffeured by a female driver in full uniform, enjoying the close company of a couple of good-time floozies. Bouchon and the brasses were seen to be waving at passers-by and yelling at the top of their voices. Apparently, he was going up and down the road, again and again, showing off to whoever was in the vicinity. The car jockey told me about it. It was like the million quid he'd lost just didn't matter and he needed people to know it. Or that's what we initially thought. Later on, we concluded that he was making himself very obvious by letting everybody know where he was at a particular time on a particular day. Sort of an alibi, I suppose. A couple of months later, someone spotted a newspaper article, which I actually saw for myself, where an old biddy had reported Bouchon for tricking her out of a large proportion of her personal wealth. Allegedly, she had met him on a plane and being a real schmoozer, he started up a polite and flattering conversation. This good looking Gallic guy had conned her out of a fortune by masquerading as a very successful investment broker. The foolish widow had fallen for his charms and fascinating stories and she subsequently parted with an awful lot of money in order that he 'invest' it on her behalf. I mean, how naïve can you be, honestly? He had received a short prison sentence because of it and we knew it was him because his picture was all over the papers. Then, a little later, we all took an interest in a local murder, a ghastly attack that had been discovered just down the road from the casino. A lady of the night, a working girl so to speak, had been found murdered in one of the flats, down at the Parade which is a bit of a red-light area for your up-market desperadoes, if you get my drift?

Right with you on that one!

Said young prostitute had essentially been found battered to death in her bed-sit and there were no clues or suspects. Police were at a loss and asking for help. As it was later reported in the papers, Bouchon approached the police and stated that he was possibly the last person to see the young girl alive. Christ on a bike! We couldn't believe what we were reading. He had purchased some 'special time' with her but he claimed he had left her, after doing his business, without harm.

He simply pleaded his innocence and stated that he had only come forward to assist the police with their enquiries. We were shocked but not totally surprised by it. We all suspected that he would be discovered as the murderer, sooner or later, but low and behold he walked away totally scot-free. Last I heard, no arrests had been made. The last person to see the girl alive was Bouchon, who had handed himself in as a witness and was never considered a suspect. Incredible! You can check it for yourself if you don't believe me. The story didn't come to much else, as far as I know. Other things happened in our line of work and we soon lost interest in him. I don't think anyone ever heard of Bouchon again. Stories were always rife but none of them had any credible sources or evidence to back them up. The best one I did hear was that he had kidnapped a young man, a casino croupier, and it was all to do with an incident that went back a few years. Apparently, a greasy stain had been left on the lapel of his expensive suit during a clothes fitting and this had caused him much upset. It happened in some local outfitters, so I was told. The young man is thought to be Bouchon's prisoner now, a submissive sex slave, held in one of the flats around here. Some say they have heard the croupier screaming late into the night but can't actually trace the sound because it echoes around the buildings so much. Some say Bouchon is slowly eating him alive...

'TIME GENTLEMEN, PLEASE!'

Chapter Four

Behaving Badly

FOR ALL ITS GLAMOUR, casino life can be a solitary existence...
"What an absolute din! Yes, I am fully aware of a croupier's reputation."
There was a short delay as Veronique strained to comprehend the words that were being mouthed to her. The incessant thump, thump, thump of dance music obstructed the communication process, it made comprehensible conversation all but impossible. She paused momentarily to consider an answer then spoke with all the clarity one would expect of a honeyed, middle-class, Shires girl. A small, sweet voice artificially made loud, emerged from beneath the heavy cloak

of drum and bass to spit its saccharine venom.

"Personally," she began, pausing for effect then repeating herself, "Personally, I would not piss in your mouth if your throat was on fire!"

The recipient, her third sexual predator that evening, was the jack-the-lad pervert that was Floyd Dixon. Floyd, or Dixie as he preferred, jolted his head to one side to catch as many of the vilifying words that he could before they were quickly snatched away by the headache inducing bass rhythm of another dance track and all understanding disappeared into the alcoholic atmosphere that served to entertain London's young, free and foolish. Highly suspect alcohol kept the party rolling along but the ridiculously expensive prices were more than effective in applying the binge-brakes. Dixie took the opportunity to press his ear against the moving lips of Veronique in order to receive some small gratification from the encounter; where lips touched ear, it was considered a gratifying reward, befitting of Dixie's lecherous demands.

"You really are a fucking pervert," said Veronique. "If I see your shit ugly face anywhere in my casino I shall happily substitute my shoe for my mouth which, I can assure you, will make contact with considerably more force. Now piss off please!"

Being berated in a perfectly enunciated, middle class accent was so much more belittling, and immensely satisfying too.

Such eloquence served to reinforce derision and Dixie's weak and feeble parries were no match with which to retaliate. As it was, he didn't really hear a lot of what was said but the look on Veronique's face sent all the right messages - signals no less painful than a swift kick to the gonads.

Dixie mouthed his words in response,

"Your loss sweetheart!"

With the pretence of making himself heard, he tried to get as close as possible to the smooth curves and folds of Veronique's perfectly formed ear, hoping to steal a well-shrouded kiss which, if discovered, he could easily pass off as accidental contact. Were it not for the firm pressure on his left shoulder he would indeed have stolen that sensual moment and fantasized about it as being something real, something to savour, something to relish, rather than the 'unintentional' excuse he held in readiness. Veronique felt the pressure of his move and held him firmly in the pretence. Dixie would receive nothing but scorn.

"You are such a fucking sleaze-bag," she shouted, the pitch of her voice now rising with indignation. "Take your schoolboy fantasies elsewhere and leave the grown-ups alone."

"What?" boomed Dixie, who had perfectly understood the rejection but thought the chance to be up close and personal again was worth a try.

Veronique held Dixie tight, her right hand on Dixie's left

shoulder prevented him from leaning in. Slowly and very deliberately, she began to mouth her irritation to his face. "FUCK... OFF!"

Having lost the battle, Dixie spun on his heels and headed straight for the dance floor where a disorganised display of drunken youthfulness was manically gyrating to the shrill sounds of cold electronics with over-passionate, over-exuberant and out of key vocals.

"Fucking lesbian!" muttered Dixie to himself by way of self-consolation.

"He is such an arse-hole," shouted an exasperated Veronique to her friend, who had tried to listen in but could only watch the feuding couple. "Don't you agree, Jen?"

"I can't say," replied Jen. "He's kind of cute and I wouldn't say no if I found him rummaging around in my Christmas stocking!"

The two girls thought on the concept for a moment, then fell into each other's arms holding their bodies close and firm like lovers who are not afraid to let their emotions guide them. They laughed out loud in a vain attempt to drown out the vocal-and-synth duo which began belting out another synthesized chorus of some northern soul remix.

Jenny, or Jen to all her friends, was commonly known as a 'good time girl'. A little flirtatious in most cases but definitely not the total prick tease she was made out to be by most of the male dealers. She was a tad more choosy than most, did a fair bit of window shopping before gracing anyone's front doorstep with her playful, demanding presence, but she was definitely not an easy ride. She and Veronique had been good friends since training days and they didn't look out of place crammed inside the suspect nightclub that always welcomed dubious customers, especially those employed in the casino industry.

Most casino staff struck up early, in-house friendships which often lasted throughout their entire careers and physical distance was rarely a barrier to these relationships. Flat-mates often worked in different casinos, on different shifts, with separate days off but still remained loyal and caring friends. Flat sharing would often last for many years, right up to and often beyond the bounds of most serious relationships. Old friendships would develop in tandem with cohabiting couples and flat shares would remain unaffected where the third, fourth or fifth sharer might be the ex-partner of the new person moving in. In times of need and when suitably anesthetised with alcohol, old relationships were rekindled and inhibitions went out of the window as drink and drugs guided nature on its sinful course until everybody would, pretty much, be fucking everybody else in the dark. In the cold light of day, relationships would be terminated but friendships, true, unconditional casino friendships, they always remained strong and faithful. Like the camaraderie shared by those in whom you trust your life, casino employees have unwavering solidarity in their bonds.

Along with off-duty prostitutes, criminals, petty drug dealers, bent coppers and a whole host of other shadowy, underworld folk, croupiers, inspectors, pit bosses, waitresses and half the casino bar staff could invariably be seen loitering around nightclub toilets snatching a quick snort of cocaine or letting loose as they flapped around on the dance floor like an epileptic in the throes of a seizure. Entry to the preferred club was strictly down to the pleasure of the door staff who eyed up potential customers through an ironwork grill, cunningly placed at head height but only if you were five feet five inches tall in stocking feet. It allowed for complete inspection of those presenting themselves for approval. A series of knocks, three times exactly with a longer pause between the first and second rap, would be met with an unnerving wait until, from the other side of the door, a sliding panel behind the grill would snatch open and eyes would peer out, inspecting, scrutinising and systematically judging before snapping shut again with no word, indication or acknowledgement of presence. More often than not it was unclear which way the decision would go and were impatience to compel any repetition of the knocking process, the door would not be opened at all and no one would be able to enter or, quite unnervingly, leave for at least fifteen minutes. It was a respected entry procedure recognised by all the regulars and the knocking process was religiously adhered to however, it was all by way of blind compliance as beyond that, nobody really knew what the hell it was all about. Nevertheless, everyone loved the secrecy, the mystery, the forbidden fruits, the air of being on the wrong side of the law (possibly) and the clandestineness of it all; where a den of thieves lurked and an unspoken honour system prevailed but in all honesty, it was just a late drinking club that attracted most people. Chucking out time was in the morning, usually just as dawn was just about to welcome the sensible, sleeping folk of London but for the alcohol and sometimes piss soaked customers of The Honey Trap Club, it was off with a sprightly gait down to the meat market where taverns opened ridiculously early for the dawn traders of animal flesh. Like most drinking haunts in and around the city, casino staff were always welcome - so long as there were girls present.

The Honey Trap Club was the late night watering hole of choice; the name changed periodically but no one really knew why. One month it was the 'Sugar Cube' and the next it was 'Late Hours' or 'Early Times' and the next, well 'Greens' or 'Blacks,' Xela's or something else totally unconnected or indecipherable. This was all thought to be part of the mystique and lure of the place that brought in fast-living, fun-loving, cash customers and party people; a place where customers would, curiously, also change their names along with the establishment. It was never a dull venue no matter what day of the week it was and it was *the* place that Veronique and Jen would frequent to be seen enjoying themselves without restraint or criticism. Veronique was studying for a law degree and was far more interested in a legal career than anything a casino had to offer. She was merely covering some of her education costs but would cut loose from the restraints of work and study as often as she could - going crazy was the best stress reliever she knew and Veronique had an awful lot of stress to release. Jen was looking for social acceptance. She desperately wanted to be liked, to be loved more than anything else, and she desired acceptance but with the power of control over others in order to fulfil her every desire. She loved being loved but sadistically relished the heartless rejection she could inflict on those who had been enticed into her confusing, sad little world of love and loathing. She loved everyone and everything and loathed herself for doing so. She felt weak and ineffectual, feelings exacerbated by having experienced the worthlessness and despair from so many who had spurned her. With one unsuccessful suicide attempt forming a major part of her reputation and a very recent joint attempt associated with her, Jen was not the sort of girl to be taken too seriously. She certainly wasn't the sort of girl to take home to meet Mum and Dad for Sunday afternoon tea. In fact, she was the perfect girl to steer well clear of and no matter how many people tried to dissuade Dixie from a path that would eventually cost him his sanity, a perfect marriage, a successful career and an enviable golf handicap, he made the mistake of confusing lust with love and blindly strolled into the dragon's lair.

The unsociable hours that a casino was legally allowed to open allowed Jen and Veronique to operate on two, very different levels. There was casino life and then there was life outside of the casino. The two were rarely interchangeable as real life did not exist inside the artificially lit dens of iniquity, barely legitimised by giving them posh names with the suffix casino or club tacked onto the end; places where clocks were forbidden, time was never mentioned and staff had to pander to the absolute dregs of society's vain and selfish. Once outside the casino's salaried embrace, there were many, many more experiences to be had as well as studying to be done, feelings to suppress and self-esteem to nurture. Work was rarely discussed, if ever, during those off-duty escapades. Veronique and Jen were a formidable duo and when they were unable to balance their emotions, they found solace in each other with alcohol, cocaine and sexual fulfilment being preferable substitutes for the multitude of lecherous shits and other desirous leeches that tried to infiltrate their lives. The girls were both bad. In fact, they were very, very good at being very, very bad and just about everyone wanted to share in their magical world of wonder and naughtiness.

***

"A little bird told me that your friend fancies me?" Dixie spoke from the corner of his mouth as he chipped up chips for Veronique on what was the busiest game of the night. Veronique skilfully separated the losing chips from the winning number and guided the mountain of plastic discs into the chipping area where Dixie worked furiously to get them back into stacks. Veronique touched shoulders with Dixie but it was strictly accidental, a working manoeuvre to get everything from the apron into the chipping area with no ulterior motive in mind. Dixie stretched both his arms below those of Veronique and pulled the loose chips towards him where he began to assemble new stacks at lightning speed.

"Why would Jen want to be seen with a half-wit newbie like you?" gibed Veronique from the side of her mouth, hiding her indiscretion from an over officious table Inspector.

"I'm a god amongst men!" Dixie whispered back before Veronique had time to pull away to sweep in the next mountain of chips. "And I'm hung like a donkey!" he quipped as shoulders touched again. "I've got a nine inch tongue and I can breathe through my ears!" he added.

Veronique looked at him before stepping back to the apron,

that green area of baize where she would make up the winning pay-outs and exhibit her female charms. She gave him a sardonic smile of acceptance and began to assemble the winners' pay-outs, speaking only as she entered the chipping area where she reached into the float to grab the necessary cash chips. This area was an intimate zone reserved for professional purposes only but it was one where most relationships were nurtured or destroyed. Dixie tucked his chin down to hide his mouth and tilted his head to face Veronique and as she came in close.

"You out tonight?" he asked hopefully.

"Of course!"

"The Glass Bubble?"

"Of course!"

"See you there?"

"Piss off!"

***

As soon as Dixie got through the door of the pub he spotted Veronique and Jen sat in the corner at the back. A rush surged through his body; a warm, exciting sensation that reminded him of MDMA on the back of the tongue to herald bliss, where happiness rolled out the welcome carpet like an old friend coming in from out of town, pure ecstasy beckoning for an intimate embrace.

"What d'ya want?" Dixie casually asked both girls, eyeing Veronique first, then Jen.

"Two pints!" demanded Jen.

"Stella?" asked Dixie, already making headway towards the bar.

"What else!" shouted Jen, loud enough for those already at the bar to take unnecessary notice.

Dixie gingerly guided three pints of lager towards the girls then sat down astride a stool to deliver them. A puddle had formed on the table from an earlier spill and Jen ushered it across the smooth, polished surface with a beer mat where it trickled from the edge onto Dixie's lap. Dixie, sadly, did not notice the act nor did he notice the stream of liquid, now spilling on to his beige trousers to leave an embarrassing wet patch.

"You fucking idiot!" snapped Dixie, whose warm feelings of acceptance were now drowned by the cold, wet presence of beer about his groin. "What d'ya do that for, you moron?"

Jen laughed but it was neither funny nor clever, and she knew as much, but then again adverse attention was better than no attention at all, she figured. After all, wasn't she the one who had shown all the interest in Dixie that night at The Honey Trap? Now he was working in *their* casino, wasn't it only right that any relationship was hers for the taking, or torching? Veronique thought otherwise but it was never going to be something that would cause any animosity between the girls; more of a slight annoyance than anything else. Jen knew that Veronique needed a plaything as much as she did so she addressed her jealousy promptly.

"Sorry, shouldn't have done that," apologised Jen.

"Too fucking right. Fucking hell!" snarled Dixie, standing to brush the excess liquid from his lap.

"I'll take you shopping and buy you some new ones," offered Veronique.

The feeling of satisfaction that now washed over Dixie was immensely satisfying and Veronique could have done no more than had she offered herself to him totally naked, bent over double, wet and wanting. Finally, he felt his insistence was paying off.

"Don't be daft," he replied coyly, trying to stay casual although his heart was barely coming to terms with all the excitement. "You can come with me tomorrow, if you like, just to choose some but I'll be paying, of course."

"You're on," said Veronique.

Jen sat motionless then finally broke from her simmering frustration. Unable to prevent the outburst, she raised her glass to take several large gulps of lager before burping loudly for maximum effect and passing attention.

"Jen!" condemned Dixie and Veronique simultaneously. Both laughed out loud and Jen quickly joined in, her moment of disability quickly subsiding as Dixie shot her a look that could not be misconstrued as anything other than flirtatious. It was this lustful, exciting eye contact that quickly fuelled Jen with all she needed to get her machinery of nonsensical relationship building under way. For the initial hurt she had received, as well as all the pain inflicted upon her by so many others, she would make Dixie pay dearly and she would relish the suffering it would bring. She would need to be careful though, very careful, as she could not risk damaging the precious relationship she had with Veronique. It wouldn't be difficult, both girls had played this game many times before and they were well rehearsed in the unwritten rules of engagement.

The trio continued their seductive eye contact and were practically the last to leave the pub as the call came to finish up drinking and vacate the premises. Jen overheard a nearby conversation that had been going on between a couple and it reminded her that both she and Veronique had not eaten as yet.

"I just heard someone say that there's good eating nearby, I think it's a place called Bouchon's. Any takers?"

"Give it a whirl," said Dixie, alcohol dumbing his common sense and better judgement.

Veronique stood up first, quickly followed by Dixie and as Jen came to her feet, she bent over in a motherly fashion to brush down Dixie's lap where there remained an unsightly damp patch. She purposely brushed in a taunting, motherly fashion that suggested he had wet himself and should therefore be punished for it. As much as Dixie wanted to play this game, he did not want to pass up the opportunity to be out shopping with Veronique and possibly, maybe fulfil an immediate sexual fantasy of his. He laughed off the matter, pushing Jen's hand away with a jovial,

"Sod off, Jen," to reinforce the somewhat temporary rejection. Jen's lips pursed in anger and she added yet another dimension to the pain that she planned to inflict on Dixie for the rebuke and anguish she now felt consuming her. She didn't like rejection and Dixie would definitely suffer for it.

"Jen," interrupted Veronique, "Don't be such a pain."

The two girls linked arms and made their way out into the street with Dixie following close behind trying to disguise the wet patch on his trousers. Behind them they heard the baying of an antipodean barman who was desperate to be somewhere else.

"TIME GENTLEMEN, PLEASE!"

Outside, a black cab was hailed.

"Do you know a place called Bouchon's?" asked Jen.

"It's a restaurant, I think," slurred Dixie.

"No love," answered the cab driver. "Where do you want to go?"

The trio looked at each other and with barely any hesitation, collectively they shouted.

"Zerons!"

"That's the old Honey Trap, isn't it?" asked the cabbie.

"It surely is," replied Veronique.

No sooner had the cab completed its U-turn in the middle of the road, Jen slipped her hand between Dixie's thighs as he sucked and slurped away on Veronique's erotic mouth. With one hand he held Veronique's chin and with the other he surreptitiously fondled the large, firm breast that did not belong in this embrace.

Veronique broke away from the kiss and pulling back far enough to speak, she whispered into Dixie's mouth whilst looking him in the eyes.

"I know what you're up to you fucking sleaze-bag," she whispered.

She turned her head slightly and looked past Dixie to see his hand groping Jen's left bosom, squeezing it like an over-ripe melon.

"We share everything anyway, don't we Jen?" announced Veronique.

"We do my love," confirmed Jen and she giggled as Veronique

went back to the matter of snogging someone she neither desired nor wanted, but it filled her time, for the present.

"Make yourself useful, go and get something nice," ordered Jen.

Having made it into the confines of Zenon's back bar, Dixie was tasked to find the drug dealer and procure something chemical to start the weekend with. Veronique had yet to return from the cash point so Jen made her way outside to see if she was safe. Dixie looked around as if searching for an old friend, a familiar face and then, having spotted the purveyor of dreams and the odd nightmare, he jostled his way through a small crowd of squabbling prostitutes. Squatting down face to face with the angelic looking Oriental that he had often, but only in his unnatural dreams, masturbated over, he hoped for so much more than what he had on his shopping list. Half Chinese and half Vietnamese, Cherry was more of a casual drug runner than a drug dealer proper. For some freebies and a loose connection to one of the notorious Chinese gangs in London, Cherry dished out small quantities of Class A drugs and took in the tendered cash. She was herself feared as much as she was revered, her looks were unbelievably well proportioned - porcelain skin layered upon a beautifully balanced bone structure, jet black hair hanging in a conventional oriental style with a fringe that could not have been any straighter had it been scribed with a blade and ruler, she looked every bit the Chinese baby-doll that Dixie, plus a hundred or so other testosterone fuelled young men, desperately desired.

"Nay Ho Mar, Lang Loy", offered Dixie, in his best Cantonese.

"What d'fuck ya want?" replied Cherry in her distinctive, South London (of Chinese origin) drawl.

"Err… Charlie, Mitsubishi, Happy 5s, anything?"

Beautiful, long slender fingers held out a red and white wrap, an intricately folded portion of paper formed from a lottery slip. Not quite origami but if folded right, it made an envelope in which to conceal portions of illegal substances.

"Twenty-five!" demanded Cherry with her other hand held out, pristine palm waiting to be dirtied with cash.

"Ta very," thanked Dixie, taking the goods with one hand whilst simultaneously handing over twenty five pounds with the other.

It was going to be a bit of pot luck as to what he would actually get but he had not been disappointed in the past and was forever hopeful of a very good night ahead. Such was Zerons, discretion was neither needed nor expected as tolerance was afforded to the particular clientèle that frequented there - the undeniably, rebel rousing, hard drinking, hard playing, drug abusing happy souls of the world.

In expectation of something very special, Dixie was already high on anticipation and started to move in an endless, flowing motion to a dance track that thumped from two oversized speakers in the corner of the back room. Hands acting like the tips of flames, they licked the air above Dixie's head as arms of fire held the image aloft, snaking their way towards the sky, twisting and turning, tying themselves in knots. The ashen, limp body beneath swayed to and fro, hidden by thirty or so other bodies performing exactly the same movement.

"What d'ya get?" whispered Jen into Dixie's ear as she got up close. Veronique had sidled up to his other side and mirrored his exotic movements that were unbecoming of a man on a dance floor but somehow acceptable, in this particular situation at least.

"I think it's some coke and a couple of Happy 5s," said Dixie, his movements continuing to mimic that of fire, flames or possibly agitated snakes.

"You look like a right cunt!" announced Jen, in a lighthearted way that she hoped would coerce Dixie in handing over the drugs without starting any, 'I should go first,' debate.

"I'll go first," said Dixie, having stopped gyrating now and fully alert to the pecking order that was all part of the ritual. "Buyer's prerogative!" he added.

"You're such a twat!" scolded Jen before the three wandered off in search of a hidey-hole in which to imbibe their manufactured fun.

In a corridor that led from the back room to the toilets, in a small alcove, somewhere at the end of a long, fairly intimidating, dark passageway, Jen and Veronique hustled around Dixie as he carefully opened the envelope to show off a fine, white powder. Veronique was the first to hook some granules onto her fingernail, followed by Jen and then Dixie who snorted the remainder straight from the paper up his nose, one nostril at a time, evenly matching the amount as best he could using nasal vacuum alone. All three rubbed the remnants in and around their gums and stood expectantly, looking at each other, waiting for confirmation that the purchase was good and the night would be exciting, wild and free.

Nothing! Nothing happened. There was no tingling sensation, a bit of coughing and spluttering and some serious sniffing, but no hit. They waited a while longer, eyes darting between eachother, all looking into each other's stare for some semblance of hope that they hadn't been taken for suckers and ripped off. Dixie was the first to speak in the hope of saving some reputation.

"We've been done people. Fucking teething powder!"

A great rip off and an undeniable favourite of those dealers who could no longer 'cut' their drugs with other crap to make it go further – they simply sold pure crap. Sometimes it was ground aspirin, sometimes teething powder which would numb the gums and fool the buyer into believing the test dab was the real thing, and sometimes it was just plaster dust - in fact, anything that was white, powdery and did not have a recognisable smell would suffice for ripping off unsuspecting buyers. It was a cheap, despicable trick and one that caused many an argument that had, on occasions, resulted in a stabbing or two.

"Cheeky whore!" declared Veronique.

Dixie barged his way past both girls and made a beeline straight for Cherry who was idly leaning against a stair post. At the top of those stairs, a girl in a pink tutu was dancing to the hypnotic beat of a compilation soundtrack engineered by the resident DJ.

"Fucking rip-off," Dixie said, straight into Cherry's face while trying to look hard and menacing, but really he wanted to hold Cherry and take her for himself, for his life, forever.

"Crareful boy," said Cherry in a subduing voice, "Chop, chop, chop!"

These three words were definitely not a reference to being quick. As Dixie knew all too well, as everyone knew, this was the threat of having some part of one's anatomy, usually a hand, an arm or finger, removed by a meat clever wielded by a member of the Chinese gang. It was also common knowledge that Chinese girls would openly flirt with Caucasian men only to report the men's behaviour to their Chinese boyfriends so they could sit back and watch the resulting fracas. Proud Chinese boys would wade in with steel flashing, slashing and slicing at the delicate, pale pink skin of simple, Western boys. "Something decent by way of compensation at least?" begged Dixie, with a tone of assertiveness in his voice but fear showing in his eyes.

Cherry handed over another carefully folded envelope of white and red print, placed it in Dixie's waiting palm and then pressed another envelope on top of it. Dixie quickly curled his fingers into a fist, snatching the goods and feeling pretty good about the whole deal. Cherry held out her other hand and, just for a moment, Dixie began to offer his in order to give it grateful shake. Before he could make a fool of himself, Cherry spoke.

"Fifty, geezer," she demanded.

"Fifty? Fucking rip-off!" complained Dixie.

"Chop, chop, chop!" warned Cherry.

Dixie took a folded fifty from his trouser pocket and held it out for Cherry to take. As he did so, he decided it would be now or never.

"Would you like to go out sometime, somewhere, with me?"

As if it was an everyday occurrence, Cherry stared back at him expressionless and Dixie anticipated rejection and maybe a darn good kicking with a bit of chop, chop, chop for good measure.

"You fink I'm some sort o' prostitute? You gimme fifty quid 'n' ask me out..." protested Cherry.

"No, I didn't mean it like that," apologised Dixie.

"Jokin' init," replied Cherry. "Okay, crawl me."

"Seriously?"

"Seri...us...ely."

"Sure, cheers!" was all Dixie could muster from his appreciative repertoire.

Hardly believing his good fortune he strode back to the alcove and with his head somewhere else, he handed over the procured goods.

"Oh! Fuck me. That is it," were the words that brought Dixie back down to earth from his daydream of Cherry.

"That is fucking kicking!" said Jen, and she offered the envelope to Dixie who leant into the huddle to take two, sharp intakes of breath through his nose then watched the world light up before his very eyes.

Feeling good was one of nature's natural highs but feeling outstanding, well that could only be achieved through drugs and it was everything, absolutely everything, that the trio had hoped for. The night was just beginning to roll, there was hope, there was enlightenment, there was everything that ever was and it was all good – it was outstandingly good and there would be no need to pause for sensible reflection and definitely, definitely no regrets. Cherry had watched Dixie disappear out of site but hoped that she would catch sight of him later, while he was still appreciative of what she had done for him. Somewhere in the mish-mash of Dixie's head he was determined, dead set upon and would not take no for an answer; shagging Jen and if that wasn't at all possible, then Veronique but hopefully, both of them at the same time. Cherry was also waiting for his attention but she would have to wait until the not too distant future because, as luck would have it, the second envelope was just as potent and astonishingly poetic as the first. The Happy 5s from the first purchase gave a brief, ecstatic peak just as euphoria was beginning to wane and then it was finally lights out as Dixie's dodgy knee finally gave way and he fell to the floor in a miserable, crumpled heap of clammy skin and damp clothing.

"The Dorchester please driver!" sang Veronique and Jen as they bundled themselves and Dixie out of the club and into a waiting taxi.
"Not really mate," interrupted Dixie with a laugh, "Peckham, please!"
Wide eyed, grinning and grinding teeth, wagging jaws and incessant talking, were all obvious signs for any cab driver to quickly interpret. Knowing his fares better than they knew themselves, he chipped in with his tip encouraging comment.

"Had a good night then?" he gruffed from the corner of his mouth. "Interested in a bit more?"

One hundred and twenty pounds worse off, fare not included, Veronique had given up the last of her money to get the three of them back to Jen's place where the partying would be brought to a sudden halt by something totally unexpected and quite disturbing.

"Glasses," shouted Dixie, as he detached a clear bottle from its icy embrace in the freezer compartment of a tall, upright fridge in the kitchen. "Who's for Wodka?"

"Vodka," you dumb ass," admonished Jen. "You got some weird speech impediment or something?"

"No wucking furries," giggled Dixie before shrieking, "MIRROR AND CREDIT CARD, WAITRESS, IF YOU PLEASE!"

Dixie struggled to sit upright on the body absorbing sofa so Veronique leant over and chopped the white crystals into a fine powder, then sorted the mound into six, fat, white lines of pure bliss. Following usual protocol, Veronique rolled a twenty pound note, taken from Dixie, into a thin tube and positioned herself in front of the frameless mirror that lay on her lap, twelve white lines staring back at her. She lowered her head, exhaled gently and then cocked her head to one side. Partially inserting the tube into her right nostril, she sniffed vigorously whilst keeping the left nostril closed with the middle finger of her left hand. She briskly swept the tube of paper along the path of the white line and two lines quickly disappeared from view. Veronique caught her own reflection in the mirror as she changed position to repeat the procedure with the other nostril. When she was done, she whipped her head back and using two fingers to intermittently open and close both nostrils, she snorted the powdery remnants, along with some nasal debris, hard into her lungs.

"Move over honey," said Jen, giving Veronique a friendly shove with a pointy elbow as she heard Veronique announce,

"Fuck me... that is... fucking 'A'... number... fucking... one!"

Veronique slewed sideways and sat back; head resting hard on a heart shaped cushion she closed her eyes and laughed out loud.

"Fucking, kicking my sweet darlings. This is so sweet."

Jen carefully placed the mirror on her lap and snorted her two lines then, having watched four more white streaks vanish, Dixie grabbed hold and quickly followed suit.

"Music Dixie, you dick head," laughed Jen, "Put something on."

Dixie leant over the arm of the sofa and with a protruding finger jabbed at a bright, silver button sitting proud on the front of the music tower. Almost immediately the panic stricken beats of a techno music track filled the room; heads, minds and entire bodies were instantly consumed by electronica. Dixie was first to his feet and began gyrating to a rhythm that only he could sense, dancing around the coffee table upon which the mirror now lay. Having been cleaned with a stealthy, swabbing forefinger, all trace of the smooth, white powder had disappeared onto someone's greedy gums. Jen jumped to her feet and started to weave her body in a juvenile and seductive manner, displaying her intimacies before Dixie but it was not solely for his pleasure. Veronique eyed the pulsating body and the inviting hips that jerked back and forth and Jen gently rotated herself for Veronique to admire. She looked directly into Veronique's eyes as she brought both her hands up to her own breasts; slowly smoothing her dress as she went, following the contours of her body, traversing the floral pattern of red roses and green leaves on white polyester, she cupped two, full mounds, one in each hand and squeezed them gently. Jen blew a kiss at Veronique and smiled the smile of a malevolent seductress.

"You are so naughty," said Veronique, in a theatrical tone.

"Get up and get your kit off, now!" ordered Jen, in the manner of a dominatrix.

Veronique stood up and joined the flaying duo of arms and legs that belonged to Dixie and Jen. After a short period of temptation, Veronique finally pushed herself into Jen's arms to hold a firm breast for herself, her other hand circling Jen's back to pull her in close as she tried to absorb her body. Succulence secreted itself simultaneously, both girls moving in time to the music, the beat increasing to one hundred and twenty psychotic, pulsating beats per minute. The air was thick with tension and full of promise. Jen dipped her torso then leaned down to reach under Veronique's skirt, her hand rising up along her smooth, silky thigh where searching fingers sought out delicate underwear and the rapture that lay beneath.

"You tart!" whispered Jen, discovering there were no lacy garments to negotiate.

Veronique tightened her lips as Jen spread her fingers across the shaven pubic area before probing with a middle finger. There she found the soft wetness between a small mound of flesh where she played and pleasured before fully inserting a slick digit.

Dixie slumped back onto the sofa, sweating profusely he undid his trousers and pulled the waistband down past his knees. He spread his legs apart, as far as his trousers would allow, then reached into the opening of his underwear to take hold of his firm cock that glistened in the light of a blue lamp that shone from the side of the room. Having watched Dixie collapse onto the sofa, Jen and Veronique stood statue still. Both girls looked at him with incredulous eyes as he began to work himself with a great deal of fervour and an admirable amount of dexterity.

"You fucking pervert!" reprimanded Jen.

"What?" replied an indignant Dixie.

"What are you doing?" quizzed Jen.

"Joining in," whimpered Dixie, sounding very unsure of himself.

He quickly coerced the phallus back into its hidey-hole; still throbbing and wet with self-lubricant, it felt uncomfortable against his inner thigh, a stringy gel-like trail marking its retreat.

"No! No! No!" encouraged Jen, "Let's get this out in the open. Don't be shy, big boy!"

Kneeling down in front of Dixie, she slid her searching fingers under his loose underwear and grabbed at the now flaccid tool; roughly pulling at it, she began to cajole and caress the life back into this object of her desire, her hand working firmly with dedication and lustful devotion.

"Sort out some gear," murmured Jen to Veronique.

But Veronique sat in the embrace of a voluptuous armchair writhing to the tempo of another techno beat and she cared little as to what was going on between the two, over-sexed degenerates. As the music faded out, then back in again with a more sedate dance track, Veronique emptied an envelope onto the dazzling mirror that lay on the coffee table and began chopping, sifting and lining up several big, fat lines of mood enhancing white powder. Two heavy snorts in quick succession and Veronique signalled to Jen that she should dive in. Jen, without interrupting the handiwork she was exercising upon Dixie, leant over and took a wisp of white powder on her finger nail then tipped it down the hole of Dixie's penis, squeezing the head as she did so to enlarge the opening before relaxing her grip to close it up again. She leaned heavily to one side and without letting go of Dixie, she took two long, sustained snorts of the divine, white powder. She turned back to look at Dixie but his head was thrown back, face to the heavens, eyes shut - he had no place to go and nowhere else he wanted to be. Jen turned and winked at Veronique but Veronique could only look without seeing. Crystals of light twinkled in Veronique's peripheral vision and intermittent flashes of colour pulsated to the sounds in her head as she drifted mindlessly in her personal pleasure dome. Jen leant over and took another line of coke, which would have been one of Dixie's, before handing the rolled note to Veronique so she could be a party to this act of theft and selfishness. Veronique was unresponsive, so Jen cleared the bright reflective surface by herself to leave it clear and clean, save a few specks of wonderment that she dabbed at with her tongue. Then, returning to the matter of Dixie's cock, Jen bent forward with the intention to take in her mouth that which she held in her hand.

"Fucking hell, Dixie!" screamed Jen, "You're a fucking Cavalier!"

"What?" moaned Dixie, somewhat oblivious to what it was that Jen was so obviously pointing out.

"I only like round-heads," said Jen, with mock rejection.

Jen fumbled in her handbag and passed a cigarette packet to Veronique. Veronique clumsily opened the flip-top packet and slid a smooth cylinder of tobacco from its communal bed. The cigarette hung limply between her clasp of rosy red lips as it waited for ignition so the cancerous fumes could be carelessly imbibed. Jen fumbled around in her handbag.

Another heave to the side and Jen sucked on the remnants of some white powder from a discarded wrap that she spied on the floor; lovingly she looked up at Dixie whose soul was full of contentment, his face a picture of pure bliss.

"We'll soon sort out your little problem my darling," whispered Jen, in a comforting manner which Dixie failed to comprehend but heard nonetheless. "No one likes a Cavalier!" she proclaimed.

A piercing, blood-curdling, high pitched squeal and sickening cries of sheer terror began to fill the room as Jen's hand quickly became covered in warm, sticky liquid.

Dixie's head jolted forward, his whole body convulsed and curled around its centre as horror filled his face. Jen held up her prize and Veronique, shaken back to consciousness by the tormented screams, gasped out loud. A small, wrinkled piece of blood soaked skin was pinched between Jen's thumb and forefinger and as she held it aloft, she stared at it like an inquisitive scientist. Dixie held his bleeding member in his hands, screaming and gasping, panic filling his racing mind. Jen giggled with wicked delight as Dixie stood up, desperately trying to drag on his trousers in a panicked attempt cover his recently performed circumcision.

"YOU FUCKING CUNT! YOU IDIOT! YOU FUCKING BITCH!" cried Dixie.

"Oops!" apologised Jen with schoolgirl silliness. "The thing about this job is..." she smirked, "... the wages are lousy, but the tips are huge!"

There was an eerie silence before Veronique and Jen started to howl maniacally with uncontrollable, drug-induced, sardonic laughter. Dixie tried to stem the flow of blood with a sofa cushion that was rough to the touch but served its purpose in stemming life threatening leakage. An embroidered penny-farthing bicycle on a white background scattered with blue flowers was slowly turning a deep red colour. Dixie jabbed the cushion hard into his groin and curled his body around it for comfort. He pulled out his phone and fumbled the dialling process, touch tones appearing louder than the music that still pounded away in the background, none of which did anything to ease the chaotic situation.

"Don't be daft Dixie," spluttered Veronique. "They'll only call the police and we'll all lose our jobs. Best we forget about it and just accept you've lost a bit of your willy."

Veronique and Jen were contorted in uncontrollable laughter while Dixie slumped back onto the sofa, the blood flow practically halted by the penny-farthing and corn-flowers.

"Shall we get a cab to the hospital? I'll call one," offered Veronique, through a sharp intake of breath that was interspersed with more rapturous giggling.

"My fucking missus will go mad!" proclaimed Dixie.

Both girls were immediately silenced and then, with utter astonishment, they spoke in harmony.

"You're fucking married?" they asked.

"Probably not anymore," shrieked Dixie, in fear as well as agony.

A pair of scissors lay on the carpet, bright and shiny, bloody and cold.

Chapter Five

A Life on the Ocean Wave

July 12th

Dear Dad,

Well, I finally made it! The roads were busy as hell but it wasn't so bad getting to the port once in Southampton. It was pretty amazing really; the ship is an almighty piece of engineering and seems so much bigger when you're standing on the quayside waiting to embark. Luckily, I didn't have to traipse along with the passengers as my crew pass allowed me to go straight up the *gangway that is reserved for ship's personnel only. I was met by one of the casino staff and shown around my new workplace. It's quite small really, only three roulette tables and three blackjack tables with a cash-desk and a cocktail bar close by. There are two slot machines with $1000 dollar jackpots. The casino area is movie themed with actors and actresses of old, black and white pictures are dotted around the walls and there are even some old movie actors onboard too. You would love it.*

Well, the first week shot by. The sailing to New York, a dream come true for me, was pretty amazing. Yes, I was sea-sick all the way and continue to be so however, I have just been told about an antihistamine pill that might stop it. I'll try one and let you know how I get on. I expect the sail back will be much the same although I can't help feeling excited by it all and keep thanking my lucky stars that I'm finally here and getting to experience everything. Just looking out of my porthole, as we cross the ocean, is something in itself; the mountainous waves, grey and bleak, lick, lap and crash against the thick, round glass as the ship pitches most unnervingly with its constant battle against the ferocious north Atlantic waves. I could sit all day just watching the sea roll by. Passengers have paid thousands to be onboard this cruise and here I am, being paid to do it. Brilliant!

Work is, well, as usual really. The casino opens for a few hours in the afternoon and for five hours each evening. We get one day and one night off per week but it's not like hard work or anything. The hardest part at the moment is keeping my dinner down! If the pills don't work then I hope I'll get my sea-legs by the time we dock in Southampton next week. We have a big punter with us called Loi. He's Malaysian I think. Our casino back in London, where he usually plays, paid for him and his wife to take this trip. Obviously, we are hoping that he will lose some money in the casino – speculate to accumulate, as you always say! He's a nice enough punter, not too demanding, although he is obviously indifferent to us and reluctant to lose any money. I think he's down about fifty grand at the moment.

I was dealing blackjack the other night, which is not my preferred game. Remember I told you about my emergency Blackjack training? Well, learning Blackjack in just a few days is hardly a good grounding for me to be dealing with any degree of competence. What with my nausea and inexperience, I can only just about manage to bumble my way through at the very best. I do what I can but had a little trouble paying out 3 to 2 on a really odd amount last night. I don't think anyone noticed as the alcohol was flowing freely and some of the staff appeared to have partaken as well! Not me, I hasten to add.

With my one night off I went to the cabaret show. The theatre is comparable to the best in London I reckon and the shows are very professional, very American and very, very glitzy. As we are employed as concessionaires and not crew, we basically travel as passengers; we have passenger cabins, eat in the restaurant, drink in the bars, sign for our drinks and can watch the shows, take part in the entertainment and even enjoy the celebrity lectures. We have crew status too for certain things so it's a win, win situation in that respect. Of course, the customers always come first but there is very little that we are not allowed to do. We are forbidden anywhere in crew quarters but then there's no reason I'd want to be down there myself. Our cabins are made up for us every day, twice a day in fact, everything cleaned and our beds made nice and cosy for us. Our laundry is done in the Chinese laundry below decks, which is a whole different world. We are allowed to go there just to collect our laundry and I can tell you, it's like little China Town down there. It appears to be a self-contained environment and the Chinese guy told me they never leave the laundry, except for disembarkation to go on leave. They eat, sleep and gamble next to their washing machines. It's just like the Chinese Kung-Fu movies we used to watch. Unfortunately, they put your clothes on a skewer and it joins the process line of dipping and washing. This means all your clothes have little holes in them where they are, quite literally, skewered. Back in our cabins, we have a bath and even a duvet on the bed. I share a cabin with a guy from one of our casinos in London. Jewish fella he is, fairly decent chap.

Well, I guess that's all for now.

Love you,

JVW

July 12th

Simon,

How goes it geezer? Finally got here although it was a real bugger in the traffic. The ship is fucking huge man – I mean you see pictures of it but, standing there on the quayside, it just towers over you like a metal goliath. Inside is like a whole town, massive and a sod to find your way around. The casino is bloody small by comparison to the one in London but then that's a good thing; not too much work to do! I work with a couple of nice girls and another bloke who I share a cabin with. He seems okay although he is a four-be-two. One of the girls, the cashier, is a right old dog so I think I might use her for some comfort shagging when there's nothing else on. The other cashier is called Katie but he's a bloke. Not quite sure what's going on there because he doesn't seem to be a poof or anything. Maybe it's not his real name? Maybe a nickname? I'll try to find out and if he is gay and I get buggered senseless, it'll be your fault. The punters are strictly out of bounds for us, if you know what I mean? There are other rules of course: like passengers are not allowed in your cabin and you are not allowed in theirs, no going below decks and the crew are not allowed up unless they are working. They say that we must stop where the carpet runs out – and there is no carpeting in crew quarters! It doesn't leave too many options for shagging but I think I might be on for the occasional 'al fresco' job if all goes to plan.

I've found a spot on the top deck where nobody seems to go in the evenings. It's up front and fairly dark although the ship's police (yep, coppers here too!) do patrol that area but not very often. Failing that, I'll get the Filipino room maid to give me a hand-shandy next time she plumps-up my pillow. I'm sure she'll be glad of the extra cash.

The sail to New York was grim as I chucked up most of the time. Not sure if it was sea-sickness or too much alcohol. It seems everyone has a fully stocked bar in their cabin. You get cheap alcohol from the 'slop chest' (which is the crew shop) as it's discounted for the staff. We are allowed to visit it once a fortnight but that's always under supervision as it is deep down in the maze that forms the crew's domain. There are loads of other things to be had cheap, not just booze – there's chocolate, soap and other cosmetic bits and bobs. I got a bottle of Bacardi for next to nothing and have been getting into that after work. American chocolate is nothing like what we're used to but it does the job when you fancy a nosh on something sweet. Guess that could be one reason for throwing up all over the place – alcohol and chocolate?

We have a big player with us called Loi or Hoi or something Oriental. His missus is stunning and while he is playing in the casino she is blatantly putting it about. She was hanging around the night before we hit New York and I finished early because I felt a bit queasy. I thought I'd get a beer from the bar (which we sign for then pay at the end of the month) and try to relax a little before going to bed. We have a TV in our cabin which the Jewish bloke bought off the croupier he was replacing and it came with a video recorder and some old movies. We often kill a few hours watching porn. Anyway, on my way down to my cabin, I come across Mrs Loi so I stop and make polite conversation and see if there's anything I can do for her. You know me lad, all polite and courteous! Well, bugger me if she doesn't suggest that I assist her back to her stateroom as the ship's swaying a bit and she feels unsteady on her feet – right!? They have the Royal Suite up on the top deck, cost a fortune and beautifully furnished. Now don't get me wrong, I'm only a few days into my three month contract and I'm wrestling with my conscience, as well as my memory, trying to figure out whether I am doing any disservice to the casino, the ship, Mrs Loi or even my moral fibre. Funnily enough lad, I somehow seem to be unable to stop myself! One thing led to another and I now find myself sitting here recounting the most sordid of sexual episodes to your good self. Really mate, it was absolutely blinding. Man, she was lush; incredible silky skin, shaven where it mattered and she gave the sweetest, high-pitched yelp in order to express her satisfaction for my enormous effort and even enormous-er bell end! Too right, I knobbed her good and proper because it would have been downright rude of me not to. Admittedly, I did feel some guilt but only in as much that if I got caught then that would be the end of my first cruise contract which is still in its infancy. A huge risk but sometimes you've just gotta say, "What the (F...) heck!" You know how much I don't want to lose this opportunity to travel but to have something like that offered to you on a plate – well, I'm only human. Anyway, best keep that one to yourself me old chum. Luckily, the Loi couple got off in New York and headed for the Waldorf with no immediate plans to return. The bloke was about SP so it'll have to go down as a loss and a waste of time for the casino but not for me, I hasten to add. I dread to think what might have happened if I'd got caught though. Apparently, there are no laws on the high seas, just the Captain in charge and what he says IS the law. Oh yeah! I nicked the writing folder from the Royal Suite as a memento. If I ever get back in there, I'm going to get the matching pen set too!

Well, I'll finish up now as I want to get this posted. I hope you and the lads are okay? If you want to drop me a line then use the address at the top and it will get passed on by the shipping agents.

Ha'way me hearties!

JVW

August 4th

Dear Dad,

Goodness! Time sure does fly. It'll be almost a month since I last wrote. How are you?

For me? Well, I'm just plodding back and forth across the Atlantic, doing my thing, watching the sea and sky as we sail. It's a bit like commuting really, the same journey to and fro, to and fro, to and…well you get the picture. My cabin chum is a nice guy and we hang out a lot. As we lie in our bunks at night (early in the morning by the time the casino shuts and we get cashed in), we have a chat and find that we have quite a lot in common. We have the same sense of humour and are very much into charming the female passengers. Don't panic, I'm not doing anything I shouldn't. The casino bumbles along as most passengers are not considered to be hard and fast gamblers. There's a lot of Americans onboard but they don't really understand our style of gaming. They are used to the Las Vegas style and cannot understand the quiet, reserved manner in which we conduct our games. They don't usually stay too late and most of them just play the slot machines for amusement. Of course, once they get to know us they cannot help but talk to us at every opportunity and it doesn't matter whether we are on or off duty - in the restaurant, at a show, in a bar or wandering the corridors - even the library isn't safe. However, we have developed a ruse to keep them at bay. We put our Walkman earphones in but do not connect the jack plug to anything. We just tuck the loose wire into our clothing and the Americans, in fact all annoying passengers, are duped into thinking we are listening to some music. As such, they believe we cannot hear them so they don't bother talking to us, we're deemed to be too preoccupied to give them the attention they so crave. It's a neat little trick that works surprisingly well and a polite way of saying, 'DON'T TALK TO ME!' On the occasions that I have engaged with them in some polite conversation; well they ask the most stupidest of questions and at first we thought they were joking but believe me Dad, they are not, such as: 'Do you sleep onboard or do you go home at night?' and 'Do these elevators go up as well as down?' and 'Can you tell me what time the Midnight Buffet starts?' and get this one, 'How do you manage to get fresh milk onboard, do you have cows down below?' Honestly, these are genuine questions from our Yankee-Doodle-Dandy cousins.

I'll write again soon. I did some shopping in Southampton and it was weird because I was falling about all over the place. It's like the feeling of still being at sea, you get so used to rolling about because of the waves so, by the time you are back on dry land, it feels as though you are onboard a moving ship. Just like after you've taken off roller-skates – it still feels like you've got them on for a short while afterwards. I got some very strange looks as I was rolling about the aisles in Marks & Spencers!

Right, that's it then. Love you and leave you.

JVW

August 4th

Simon,

How are you dear boy?

I, myself, am sailing back and forth across the cold, menacing seas that are known as the North Atlantic. Bloody brilliant it is too. I have recently discovered American beer and the 'lite' aspect of this amber liquid. Of course, the less sugar there is in it, that being the lite part, the more alcohol there is. I managed to acquire a rather nasty hang-over the other night. Signing for the drinks, as we do, means they go down far too quickly and everyone jumps up to get the next round in. I dread to see my bar bill at the end of the month. There's not much action by way of shagging at the moment although I keep my hand in with a little mutual masturbation with a couple of the waitresses. Word got around about the Loi woman so I've been labelled as a bit of a bastard at the moment. Naturally, I denied everything but what a bloody cheek judging me. I was merely assisting a valued passenger with her immediate needs. So, it's back to sniffing around and relying on the pleasures that one provides for oneself. A man's got to have a hobby! I have made a further discovery in as much as American girls don't do it like our old slappers in the UK do. They are more than happy to give you a blow-job but there's no sticking it in the good hole. Not even just the helmet, (and that old chestnut always used to work for me). I think it's something to do with preserving their virginity or something or maybe word has got around that I'm just too big and it'll stretch their fannies beyond repair? Ha bloody ha! Ah well, it suits me fine. More amazing discoveries: the chamber maid doesn't do extras, one of the entertainers (a bloke I might add) has the hots for me, the secret to not being sea-sick is to eat well and always have a full stomach and finally, wanking in public is no longer a crime. I made up the last one but the rest is true. My comrades are an okay bunch and my cabin-chum isn't too bad, however it's a little disconcerting at times as the cabins are quite small and when you're both getting ready for work or dinner at the same time, two male bodies fresh out of the shower in a confined space makes one feel a little uncomfortable (or excited?) to say the least. Anyway, don't be alarmed, I would only ever take it up the dirt-box from you, big boy!

So what have you been up to? Have you managed to sort out your business idea yet? There'll always be a market for second-hand cars, I suppose.

Back to the Americans. Last week we had a group of girls onboard, a debutante party by all accounts and it was all paid for by some rich chick from Texas. She paid for thirty of her friends to cruise to the UK and then they all flew back after a knees-up in London. You would think there was enough totty to go around but sadly, there seems to be a pecking order for this sort of thing. Either by the choice of the interested parties or by the strict hierarchical order that is clearly apparent, the top bloke for shagging is the Captain himself, obviously! The next in line is the First Officer and so on and so forth until all the white uniforms have been spoken for. Next in line, wait for it, are the male casino dealers and this is the one, rare occasion when males have an advantage in this industry. Hanging around the bars, in the evenings, during a break or having finished a shift, wearing our dinner suits and bow ties, well, apparently we all look a bit James Bond(ish), irresistible and apparently the premier choice (after the officers) for those lone girls who want/need a holiday romance. I met (and got a nice blowy) from a pretty Latino girl and she said she was from Atlantic City. So I said, 'Don't speak with your mouth full, you dirty whore!' Guffaw! Not really. I mean I did get the blowy and all that but I never said that to her. I do have some scruples you know. I've taken to posing in the disco now, playing the part... "Call me Bond, Basildon Bond."(or is it Brooke Bond?)

Maybe not!

Guess that's it then.

TTFN

JVW

October 22nd

Dear Dad,

It was so good to talk to you and the telephone charges are really reasonable too. There are special booths on the quayside for crew to phone home. Anyway, I thought I'd drop you a line this time. At last the sea-sickness has gone and I quite enjoy seeing new passengers suffer the way I used to. You can see them walking around with plasters stuck behind their ears, some method of preventing sea-sickness that is issued by the ship's doctor. If it is severe sickness then they can get an injection but that makes you very dopey for a while. It doesn't seem five minutes ago I was writing to you after my first crossing and here I am now, looking ahead as we come towards the end of my stint. I can safely say I have enjoyed every single moment of it. But what next? I can now confidently say, this is DEFINITELY the life for me.

Our casino cashier left a cash box out on one of the tables the other night. The cash was still inside come the morning, thank goodness, so it just sat there all night until the cleaner found it. It probably had several thousand dollars in it but nobody touched it. Maybe nobody knew what it was. Maybe they didn't care. Suffice to say, said cashier will be disembarking in Southampton. I too will be getting off but not for anything I've done. My time appears to be up now and it feels like the end of an era – a very short era at that. Will you be there to meet me or not? To tell you the truth, I'm pretty sick of it on here at the moment so I'm looking forward *to getting away from these bloody Americans. They really do drive you bonkers with their over gregarious greetings. We had a big player onboard one time, a really nice bloke and I got talking to him. I met his wife and they pretty much offered me a job in California. Apparently, he owns a company and they would like me to be the 'nanny' for their two, young boys. He said he wants a man to raise his boys, take them to football, wrestle and do men stuff. He doesn't want a woman bringing them up and turning his boys into namby-pambies. He said, when I wasn't doing the nanny duties I could help out in his business – real estate - and I would have an apartment and a car to use. He said it would pay, including commission from working in the business, about $250,000 per year. You know dad, it all sounded too good to be true and for some reason I thought it was. I said no in the end because something didn't seem quite right about the whole thing and I still have a lot of travelling to do yet. I've already applied to another ship company as I expect to leave the casino when I get back home because I really do want to find a permanent job on the ships. I've managed to get a lot of contacts and I love this life. I'm fed up at the moment but that's because I just need a break, then I'll be fine. I'll speak to you about it when we meet. Are you going away to work again or are you settled now?*

I've probably put on a bit of weight since you last saw me as the food onboard is very rich – all restaurant dining on lobster, veal and beef where everything is cooked and presented in very rich sauces. It's played havoc with my constitution I can tell you. Sometimes, we just cry out for egg and chips, something plain and simple. My kingdom for a cheese sandwich! No more spinning trays, big smiles, high fives or empty wishes to have a nice day!

We should dock about 6am so I'll wait for you in the customs shed. I don't have any more luggage than I left with so the small car will be fine. I'll look forward to seeing you in Southampton but let me know by ship-to-shore telephone if you can't make it and I'll get a lift into London with someone else. Tired as hell now so I'll sign off.

JVW

October 22nd

Simon,

It's been a blast lad and I can only think about doing it all again somewhere else. I don't think I can settle back in a London casino now so I've decided to quit my job and get a permanent job on the ships. I've made a few contacts and have been for an interview already. I expect to hear by the time I arrive in Southampton next week whether I have got the job or not. New York was brilliant and I pretty much know the place like the back of my hand now. The Atlantic is a fun kind of ocean but I need more adventure, more sunshine, more shagging. The job I've applied for is on a cruise ship out of Miami which sails regularly down to the Caribbean and back. All American punters but the cheaper end of the market. It sounds good to me though and the money is more than I'm getting now.

I fell in love with an amazing girl from Atlantic Beach. Rolling in money she is, a real dream. We have spent the last two weeks together as she did the return trip to New York. We went shopping in Southampton. I know how to treat a girl, right!!? Seriously, she is incredible but she has gone home now. I said I wanted to stay in touch and maybe it could be something more. I think I was just the bit of rough that every girl needs at least once in their life. I love her so much though. I'm already devastated. Best I go to sea and forget my troubles.

I see you had an almighty storm where you are, trees uprooted and everything. We read about it on the news ticker-tape that is pinned to the notice board outside the Purser's Office.

I got offered a mad job by some rich bloke who wanted me to look after his two boys in California. He said he didn't want them growing up to be faggots. He wanted a man to look after them, take them to football, play baseball, do men stuff, talk cars and hockey and whatever else makes men out of effeminate boys. In my down-time he expected me to help out in his real estate agency and he promised $250 grand a year. I considered it but I don't want to be somebody's slave and you know how much I hate kids. Bloody horrible things and I should know – I used to be one! I think it was a pucker offer but I turned it down because I have the travel bug in me now. It'll probably turn out to be another of life's classic mistakes but from where I'm viewing it all, I can't see me settling down anytime soon. Not unless that gorgeous American babe from Atlantic Beach makes me an offer. Her name? Like I'm going to tell you so you can rib me about it forever and a day. You are not worthy to breathe her name for she is pure and belongeth to me and me only. Seriously, an absolute cracker but she is an uptown, up-tempo girl and I'm just a downtown, downbeat shit-fer-brains! I tried to put on my jeans the other day – jeans I haven't worn since coming onboard and I can barely fit in the bloody things. My jeans must have shrunk in the humid atmosphere onboard! If the truth be known, I've turned into a right fat bastard and only a determined sweat-up in the gym will move the huge beer-gut I now *possess. I thought it was the booze but I'm drinking lite beer so it must be the food, right? I've had the terrible shits of late too and if I see another Swan Chantilly or Lobster Bisque then I'll fucking explode. I've eaten far too well of late and done naff all to burn it off. I had an episode that required a visit to the ship's doctor. My insides seem to have fallen out of my arse. Sore as fuck, I had to go and see the ship's surgeon. With trousers round my ankles, he bent me over a leather topped bench, injected my arse ring with something that stung like a wasp and proceeded to cut out a blood clot. Yeo! A fucking blood clot – right out of my arse - right there and then, on a moving ship, with me awake and feeling it all. I nearly passed out. He showed me the blood clot, presented it to my face in a nice, shiny steel kidney dish and told me stories of life-threatening danger should said clot have broken lose and travelled around my system. With a clumsily inserted pad of heavy gauze and a swift pat up my crack, I was sent away to slowly bleed to death on my bunk, where I whimpered ever so slightly. I was told that the ship's surgeon had been struck off from practising in his own country so was now working as the ship's doctor onboard. I think he was Chilean but I can't say for sure. Worse thing was, he claimed it was my homosexual activities that had caused the protruding vein from my anal orifice. It's the bloody rich food I told him. I could have lumped him one. I will need to get it checked out when I get home. Get a proper English doctor to have a look at it - Doctor Singh or Patel! Maybe you could have a look at it for me? You're probably into that sort of thing, what with you being an old queen and all that. I always had you down as a shirt-lifter and I've seen the way you eye up my arse when you think I'm not looking.*

That's it then. My dad's picking me up in Southampton and I'll be at his after that. I'll call you and we can take in vast quantities of beer and a decent ruby. Hopefully, I'll get the job I've applied for and then I'll have a few weeks before I shoot off again.

Smell you later!

JVW

November 5th

Dear Audrey,

I guess, having heard nothing from you, I was no more than a plaything for your holiday romance? What can I say? I hoped for so much and the love I said I had for you was absolutely genuine. Maybe you were being honest about the so called 'arranged' marriage your parents had made for you. Sadly, I have none of the things that would make me a fine suitor for you in the eyes of your parents. All I have is my profound and undying love, a love that I so much want to give and share with you. I don't want this to be a sob letter but I am deeply disappointed and saddened. I shall be working on the Star cruise ship out of Miami from the 12th November. I'll be on the Caribbean run. If you ever want to meet up I could always make my way to NY or you could always come down and see me in sunny Florida – maybe take a cruise and rekindle something special? If it's not meant to be – then I can only wish you well.

I will always love you.

JVW

December 1st

Dear Dad,

All bit of a disaster really! There was no one to meet me at the airport so I had to make my way to the Coconut Island (sounds very glamorous but it isn't) office of the company I'm supposed to be working for. It all got sorted in the end but they are a bit lax really and what's worse, they have decided to alter my contract so my pay isn't quite as much as I was expecting. They have introduced a tip scheme with a complicated method of calculation that no one thinks will work. We don't expect to be getting any of the tips any time soon. First of all, the casino onboard has to show an overall win and then tips are calculated as a percentage of that win but determined by how much is given over in the first place. It's all very odd and obviously designed to rip us croupiers off! Still, I'm being paid to cruise the Caribbean so it can't be all bad. We stop off in The Virgin Islands, Puerto Rico and of course Miami; it's a lively ship, a good atmosphere and the work isn't too taxing. The casino has five roulette tables and seven Blackjack tables with fifty or so slot machines. We are concessionaires so we are travelling as passengers, we have very nice cabins and we eat in the restaurant. At the moment I am applying myself at work to see if I can get some sort of promotion. There is a quick turnover of staff so anyone with half an ounce of sense can make it to management quite quickly. Hey! I have at least half an ounce of sense?

The food is good but very rich, as you would expect on a cruise ship, so we often make up something ourselves from the kitchenette. We are allowed in the crew area this time although there really is nothing of interest down there in that warren of sheet metal and piping. I went down there the other day and it's like being in a submarine with endless corridors, no carpeting and pipes all over the place. Grim being a crew member! Most of the crew seem to be foreign; Filipino or Indian by the looks of them. The other day, I was wandering through the staff canteen, which was closed, and two Indian chaps were cooking up their curry over a meths tin on the floor. In a tin bucket they had a Vindaloo bubbling away and they invited me to join them. It was one of the best curries I've ever had. Didn't get poisoned so that's always a result. I have found my colleagues to be okay and we go ashore as a group and enjoy ourselves. We shall be in St. Thomas tomorrow so I'll send you a postcard from there.

Hope you are well.

JVW

December 1st

Simon,

You old land lubber-you! Thanks for the send-off pressies, they'll come in handy. As it happens, knob-rot cream was actually on my list of things to get. Cheers! As for the haemorrhoid cream – how very droll!

The ship is a lot smaller than my last one but my cabin is bigger as it happens. I'm sharing with some Turkish guy who seems to be okay but I have my doubts about his sexual preferences. You know what these Johnny-foreigners are like? Especially from that part of the world – all men together enjoying each other's company! Best I keep my hand on my ha'penny. His name's Ahmed and he told me that he and the other Turkish guys are working on the ships to avoid their National Conscription. They are supposed to be doing a couple of years military training but are blatantly avoiding their service to King and country. I don't think they actually have a king but you get the idea. One of them, Zeki, says he used to be a coiffure before being a croupier so he cuts all the girls' hair. He asked me if I wanted my hair cut but I declined. I'm like a faggot magnet!

We are allowed down in crew quarters although we still travel as passengers, with all the perks but without the hassle. We get the best of both worlds – like getting off first with the crew (before the passengers as they take time to organise) then coming back late with the passengers (as crew have to return to their shifts before the passengers get back onboard). Passengers are abbreviated to pax, both in writing and speaking. We have several other names for them but that's another story. The pax are all Americans with some tasty girls about. The cruise is a cheap fortnight jaunt so nothing posh, just good time girls looking to enjoy some Caribbean partying. I was gutted about Audrey, as you are well aware (sorry about that), but I have managed to get over her by knobbing one or two of our local beauties. Good thing is, the turnaround is one or two weeks so there is always fresh meat coming onboard. The one weekers stay in hotels wherever they disembark and the fortnighters return with us to Miami.

I found out when I got here that the company I now work for have stitched up all the staff over some stupid tip scheme. When we get tips, we can play them alongside the punter's bet. The more we win, the more we are supposed to get but it actually goes to the casino. The casino then decides whether we have reached some ridiculous target or other, which is seemingly impossible to calculate and even more impossible to achieve. I have concocted a scheme to help myself… Mum's the word!

I have been a bit of a crawly-arse-bum-lick of late. Why? Well, I want to be seen as enthusiastic and a good worker, helping out and all that. I want some promotion and maybe a better cruise ship to work on. The company has seven cruise ships that they operate casinos concessions on and some of them are amazing. Anyway, at the end of the night I always volunteer to take out the cash drop boxes and put them in the safe, ready for the count which takes place in the morning with the Purser present. The casino is nothing like London as there are no Pit Bosses, no Inspectors, no cameras, just a manager (who is usually in the bar pissed), some punters and the dealer. You can do pretty much as you like when you're dealing, there's no real procedures and the punters expect to be entertained – after all, they've paid good money to be on the cruise and they don't want to be upset by rules and procedures. When they first sit at my table I have a real laugh with them as I chat away and they lay their dollars down on the table waiting for me to exchange them for chips to play with. I remember where everybody has their money and they usually buy-in with hundred dollar bills. I sweep up all the cash, fold it up and 'hide' it in my top pocket. We don't have our pockets sewn up here, not like in London. I then ask the punters if they are ready to play and if so where's their money to buy-in with. They look a little perplexed at first but soon realise I am having a joke with them. I cut out the chips relating to their respective buy-ins, carefully remembering who bought in for what, then I place the chips in front of them. Once that's all done, I take the bundle of notes from my pocket and post the notes down the slot into the drop box, except I don't use the paddle to do it, I literally post them long ways down the slot. Now, the box doesn't really fit the holder it's in, there is quite a gap at the top. If I push the box right in, the slot in the table doesn't quite marry up to the slot in the box below, there is a lip or *ledge. As I post the dollars down, some catch the lip and instead of going down into the box below, they slide on the lip and come to rest on the top of the box. When I remove the box from the holder at night, I simply take the dollars resting on top and pocket them. I don't do it too often though, I pretty much take what I was promised originally as salary, plus a bit extra depending on what I'm doing on shore. It has paid for me to do my SCUBA training so far. Genius! I should have been a master criminal. I'm quite sure that everyone is having something away on this ship as we spend our evenings in the casino when we get into Puerto Rico and I see some of the other dealers gamble a hell of a lot more money than they earn. I can only assume they are up to no good as well. It'll probably all end in tears. We will see.*

Blimey, I've written loads. Getting ready for dinner now then it's a long night before we arrive in St. Thomas.

It's funny really but I still kind of hope to hear from Audrey. I just can't get my head around the fact that we're not meant to be together. Why doesn't she love me? I'm adorable!

Right then, must get on. Let me know how things are with you and how the business is going. I'm always ready to invest but only if it's successful first!

Hope you and the lads are all good?

JVW

December 23rd

Dear Dad,

Just a quick letter to wish you a Happy Christmas. What are you up to? I suppose you are at your club for the day then at the bar most of the night? Usual Christmas for you then! I shall be working but I don't mind. We have a secret Santa thing between us casino staff and a special dinner with the passengers. I'll have a quick drink and then head for bed probably. I have New Year off so I'll be in the disco for that.

Everything is going fine and I'm managing to save a bit of money. We all keep our savings in the casino safe. One good reason for this, apart from the obvious, is that it stops us impulse spending, especially when we get into ports that have casinos. As the ship's casino is closed in every port, we cannot get access to our money so there's no chance of anyone getting drunk and doing anything stupid. Just about all of us gamble but only small amounts, five dollars a bet with a maximum of a hundred or so. We usually win a bit and are quite sensible.

I'm working on getting promotion as I hear one of the manager's will be leaving soon. I think it might be a bit too early for me however, I have heard stories of people getting promoted only a few days after they've arrived. Staff are at a premium, especially when you are just about to sail and someone hasn't shown up for their job or a member of staff hasn't returned. Fingers crossed eh!

As I say, it's only a quick letter and I'll call you from Miami.

Sorry about last time but the quarters fell on the floor, I couldn't get them in the slot fast enough and we got cut off. I'll try the crew telephone booths next time. It's like before so it should be easier and better, I just need to find out where they are.

Take Care, have a great Christmas (don't drink too much) and a Happy New Year.

Love you,

JVW

December 23rd

Simon,

Christ on a Christmas tree! I saw my career flash before my very eyes. One night I didn't get to put the boxes away, I was sent down to get a telegram from the radio office and by the time I returned all the boxes had been done. There was a bit of a ruckus as the dealer doing them identified a fault, an issue you might say, with the drop boxes where the money didn't go down properly. I nearly shat myself! The box holders have all been altered so there is barely any gap at the top now and no margin in the slots marrying-up. I've sort of got used to the extra money, I mean, I have an expensive lifestyle to maintain. Not to be outdone, I've concocted another method to finance my lavish lifestyle. It's the same as before but when I take the money out of my pocket, I leave a bill or two in there. It's a lot more risky of course; if I get caught with money on me then it will be tricky to explain although I could always say it was a genuine error. They'd probably be a severe bollocking in it but it wouldn't be seen as theft, I hope, which is exactly what it is of course. It's a bigger risk but it has to be done! Now then, on to plan B…

I was dealing to this drunken pax who actually sold his jacket to another punter to get some money to continue playing. After a while, it was just the drunk player and me and I sort of felt sorry for the guy. I made a couple of payout mistakes, paid him on a losing bet and not once, but several times. I was knackered and not *concentrating. It then occurred to me that I could do it even if it wasn't a mistake so, if you ever fancy going on a cruise, as a passenger, you could play in the casino and we'd make out we didn't know each other. When appropriate, you could play alone at my table and I just pay you out as much as we want. If it's too much then alarm bells will start ringing but there's no reason anyone would suspect, say $1000 dollars a night with a big win before your departure. If nothing else you'll get a cruise for free as I should be able to get that money across the table to you without any suspicion at all being raised. Actually, I could give you a very big win on the first night and you could return occasionally and play big with the money I passed over to you. That way you're gambling the casino's money and not your own. You up for it?*

Let me know and if you want to bring your lady along then that will look even more convincing. Drawback is, we cannot let on we know each other although towards the end, we could pretend we are having a professional relationship. I meet punters all the time and all over the ship and it's expected that one should chat and be polite. I have a few drinks or tea or lunch with them so why shouldn't we act the same way? What d'ya say?

Right then, apart from that brilliant idea, not much else has happened. It was a bit of a frightener at first, the drop-box scam being foiled but I think my new method will be safe enough. Have a Happy Crimbo lad, New Year's wishes and all that crappola. Tell the lads to have a beer for me. I'll be working and shagging

my way through this particular festive season. Get some in!
Have a good one!
JVW

January 31st

Dear Dad,

How are you? Happy New Year!

I was just thinking, at what point is it no longer appropriate to say 'Happy New Year?' I mean, if you haven't been in touch with someone since New Year then it's fine to wish them a 'Happy New Year,' right? But does that extend into February or March? What about saying it in June or July if you haven't seen someone since the New Year? I think I have too much time on my hands!

I've been asked to move to another ship. I'm still with the same company but one of their assistant managers has gone home early and they need a replacement. Of course, there are not too many of us out here who have worked in London so I am in demand. There are lots of northerners and foreigners but only an elite few with the much revered British Gaming Licence and some London experience. It's a similar ship to this one and on a similar route, a bit more upmarket, less tables and a bit more money. I still have to share a cabin, which is a bind but it's another step up the ladder to being a Manager. I will transfer ships next time we are in Miami, in about five days' time. By the time you get this I will be well in to my new itinerary. We stop off at Martinique, St. Kitts, St. Thomas (Yawn), Puerto Rico (bigger yawn) and Barbados.

I had a sort of steady girlfriend for a bit. She is from Canada and was a passenger on here with her parents. Her name is Darlene and I still write to her. I said I may go up to see her during my vacation. Real love? Who knows? We spent every moment together whilst she was onboard - she would wait for me to finish my shift and we simply couldn't bear to be apart. It was tough when she flew home but I'm encouraged by her words – she says she'll wait for me and we can be together when my contract is finished. Here's hoping. Until then, I have a new adventure to embark upon. Sadly, it's still in the Caribbean but I can call myself Assistant Manager now, which has a better ring to it than dealer.

Look after yourself and don't forget to write. Make a note of the new ship's address. Don't write to the old address anymore otherwise it won't get to me.

Love,

Your son,

JVW

January 31st

Dear Simon,

Thanks for the pictures. Why has Stoaty got that truncheon thing stuck up his arse? Is that really a knob in his hand? What on earth is that boy up to? He's sick, I tell you, SICK! I liked the picture of you though. New Year is always a good excuse to fancy dress and put on some women's clothing. You looked very much like my mother. I've put the picture up on my mirror. It's to remind me that wanking is bad and I should refrain.

I've been promoted so all that crawling and arse-licking has done some good. I am now, or will be very soon, Assistant Manager. I'll let you know what the system is like on the new ship to see if our idea (wink, wink) is still viable. One of the land based office ladies came to see how I was doing. She was onboard for a couple of days and I was pretty much on her for all that time. Guffaw! Not overly enjoyable, more a means to an end really. Christ she was hairy. An enormous bush (in which I fully expected to find Livingstone) with hairy inner thighs that were a most disconcerting sight and something that will remain particularly troublesome to my psyche. I kept thinking I was with a geezer – I thought it was you, then I really did get a hard on. Hahahaha! Not really, you gay bastard!

Next week I shall be in the Caribbean stopping at Martinique, Puerto Rico St Kitts, Barbados and a few of the other usual places

I've already been too. I met a real lovely on here although she has buggered off back home now. Her name is Darlene and she lives in Canada. Boy, I tell you, she is soooooo sweet. I am in love, man. The real thing this time! She is lush to the hilt. Bugger the fact that I only spent two weeks with her - it was probably the best two weeks of my entire, miserable life. She would wait and watch me deal in the casino every night, couldn't take her eyes off me and when I finished my shift, we went down to my cabin (I had to pay my Turkish cabin mate to vacate first) and we spent the night just making love. NOTICE I didn't say shagging or anything else derogatory? Real love! Ah, I miss her sooooo much. I said I would go to Canada for my vacation although I can't say when that is. I have a new ship and position to sort out first so I don't suppose it'll be anytime soon. Love will overcome all – time and distance, even age and money. I can hear you laughing now you heartless son of a...

Rather see ya than be ya!!

JVW

February 5th

Dearest Darlene,

I'm heartbroken. Seriously! I haven't heard from you for ages and when I phoned, your Mum said you were out. Really? I hope you got the flowers I sent? Guess I was nothing more than a holiday romance to you and I'm disappointed because I gave you my heart. I know that the time we spent together was very short but didn't someone, somewhere, say that love is timeless? I had so much more to give you, so much more to share. I cannot but hope I have made a mistake and your letters have been lost with the shipping agent and that you really were out on an errand when I called. Your Mum also said that an old friend from school had visited and you were meeting up with him. Yes, she said **HIM**! *I don't want to be the jealous kind but I can only think the worst. I hope with all my heart that I'm wrong and there is still a spark of romance between us; it was that spark that ignited the inferno of our love, didn't it? And, I believe this lights the way for our future together. I can only think it is all but lost, although I will still try and work for what I believe in, and that is* **US**.

I shall shortly be changing ships and will have a different schedule. Take a note of the address at the top of this letter as this is where you should write to me and if you look at the itinerary, you will be able to see where and when I will be in port. Maybe, I can only hope against all hope, to find you one day waiting for me at the end of a gangway somewhere in the Caribbean. Remember where we first made love? Remember the restaurant where I just couldn't eat anything, where I just couldn't stop looking at you? Remember the words that I spoke and the promise I made to you? I still keep that promise but you need to let me know if I have anything to stay faithful for.

I hope to see you again.

My Love, Always,

JVW

xxxxxxxxxxxx

March 29th

Simon,

You salty old sea-dog you,

I can't believe you bought a boat without me. Mind you, we talked about it often enough so it's no surprise you've finally gone ahead and done it. Maybe my sea-shanties and tall tales of four mast square riggers got you all jealous and stuff? Oh, didn't I mention I was now on a tall ship sailing the world? I wish! There was a replica of a tea-clipper in one of the island bays out here and I just thought wouldn't it be great if... I'll dream on, but you never know, dreams do, sometimes, come true. So what you been up to?

I never heard any more from that bitch from Canada. A real bugger 'cos I really, really, really truly, deeply, really loved her. I can't help myself but I get all loved up every time I think of her.

I spent a great week with the new gift shop manager before she transferred to another ship. She is Swedish and a darn good shag. A bit spotty, greasy skin like but very pleasing to be in the sack with. I learnt a bit of Swedish, all the important things like, 'I love you' and 'Hello, how are you?' and 'Will you marry me?' We meet up every third week in St. Thomas so it's an odd sort of relationship but it serves a purpose, if you get me?

If you are still interested in having a cruise, probably free, then it'll still work as the operation on this ship is about the same as the last. In fact, it is the same layout and the procedures for the casino are exactly the same too. I suppose they would be as it's the same company. Let me know a.s.a.p. though as you never know when I might get transferred again. I have just heard that some dealers on another of our ships have 'jumped ship' and gone to work for another company. Quite simply, you get off one ship and get on another one – it's really that casual. Contracts are broken but there's not much a company can do about it as we're all at sea and jolly hard to pin down. Casino staff are in great demand everywhere so there is a lot of poaching going on. I'm just waiting to be head-hunted myself.

I've just had my first run-in with staff, as Asst. Manager, with a lad who took exception to me telling him off. He was playing the slot machines during his free time. I bollocked him for it and said it was against company policy and it just didn't look right and then the next thing, he is seen playing the slots again but this time he has hooked up with some female passenger. He is sitting on a stool in front of the slot machine and she is sitting inbetween his legs on the same stool. She is feeding the money in and pressing the buttons but it's obviously him 'playing' the game. I bollocked him again and a big argument ensued. I tell you, I nearly floored the twat; giving it large he was and then his girlfriend joined in too. It's thin ice dealing with pax though as they can't be upset, they're paying guests you see, so I had to walk away from it. I expect to get negative feedback from her when she gets off. I sent a telegram to Head Office recommending he be taken off at the next port. Let's see how he likes those reels! I can see why he was tempted to play *though as some jackpots are over $5,000. He would sit there, watching players pump money into the machines and when they walked away, in he would jump. Not cool! Practically theft! And you know I won't tolerate theft!*

Another scam I discovered was the 'lost items scam' which is worked in the casino all the time. Whilst in the cash-desk, I discovered some cameras, purses, jewellery and goodness knows what else. It appears that when things are found in the casino by other passengers, cleaners, staff or whoever, they hand the stuff into the cash-desk and when the owner appears asking if anything has been found – the cashier simply replies, 'No!' Then, the finder (or cashier) gets to keep the item at the end of the cruise after all the pax have gone home. Bloody dishonest I say. In fact, it appears that when people have walked away from gaming tables and the dealer can clearly see that they have forgotten to pick up their camera, bag or whatever, it is not pointed out to them so they are left to walk away and the item is delivered to the cash-desk. I've left a note to let my staff know that I know what's going on. Is there no honesty left these days?

What else? Had a spot of bother with my arse again and it seems I am to suffer from Farmer Giles for the rest of my life. I don't know whether it's my age, the food or what but it's a real pain in the arse. Hahahaha!

Here's a couple of photos for you and the lads. The fat pig in my bunk, though she looks dead, she's not, she's pissed as a fart and that dark, wet patch you can see in the foreground is some of my manly love juice. Hmmmmm, tasty!

The other picture is me all kitted up to go diving. I am now a qualified open water diver although funnily enough, I'm not that keen on it. I get a bit panicky down there. I was diving at 100 feet and my mask started to flood. I had real trouble staying in control. Not pleasant! The photo of me with a beer is the best one. Why look! I have two ice cold beers. One is for you. Take it, enjoy! Cheers!

JVW

April 18th

Dear Dad,

How goes it your end? All well and good here. In fact, it is very good here. We cruise up and down from Miami to the Caribbean and back. The islands are all much of a muchness really - swaying palm trees, golden sands, turquoise seas, etc, etc. After a while, it all becomes a little bit samey but then everything does in the end. We mostly take to the bars and restaurants or hang out where passengers aren't likely to be. We have found, on one particular island, a nice lagoon where there is a little restaurant and a water-skiing business. We have barbecued prawns, ice cold beers and muck about on water-skis all day. I can water-ski quite well now but can't quite manage it on a mono-ski just yet. I had a nasty tumble that literally ripped my swim shorts right off me. Not an image you want in your head, I know. One of the entertainers that we hang out with can bare-foot ski but when he takes a tumble, he really does flip over and over. The evenings, if we are overnighting, are spent in a restaurant or back on the ship. The restaurant on the ship is always operational and we use it like a floating hotel. I can see the attraction for passengers and think you would actually enjoy a cruise such as this yourself. Might meet the woman of your dreams; you never know? We also do a little bit of sightseeing but generally, the order of the day is to relax or, for some (definitely not me), to get blind drunk.

A week ago, the manager turned up just before we were due to sail.

He had been out somewhere and got completely drunk. He turned up on the ship a lot worse for wear. His clothes were torn, he was all scuffed up and he had cuts and bruises everywhere. His face was bleeding and he looked a real mess. We all thought he had had an accident but when we questioned him he said he had been kidnapped, taken somewhere to be tortured and then thrown out of a moving car. He's a bit of a character anyway, stories of derring-do and ex-military stuff but this seems a bit too far-fetched, even by his standards. If it is true then I for one am gob-smacked and if it isn't, well I'm not surprised. We all think he got drunk, tried to buy some drugs (we think he is a cocaine addict) and got beaten up for being an idiot. Point is, he is laid up in his cabin, has been for a few days now and I have assumed the role of Casino Manager. I have let head office know the situation and they are coming on board when we reach Miami.

I like Miami a lot. We usually do a bit of shopping, buy cigarettes from the mall (you can't get decent English fags out here) but there is one shop that sells cigarettes from around the world. Sometimes they are out of date, dry and stale but we still buy the favourite brands we know and love to choke on. I generally stock up on Silk Cut myself. We return our rental videos and get new ones – the shop knows we are on the ship and we get a two week rental deal, then we head for 'Tug Boat Annies' which is a bar at the Venetia Plaza hotel. The other afternoon we listened to a really good band called The Miami Sound Machine. We all sat there at the bar, eating chicken wings with our chilled Budweisers and singing along. Ah! The good life.

Nothing doing on the love-life front but then that's probably a good thing for me. What have you got planned for your summer hols this year? I guess you're not going back overseas then?

I'll try to call when I'm in port but until then,

Take Care Papa, love you lots,

JVW

April 18th

Ahoy Simon!

I was hoping to see you turn up one day ready for embarkation. You really ought to because it'll be fun and free! The shipboard life is a good one but jolly dangerous as it happens. Once a fortnight, when we anchor down in the Caribbean, we have to do life boat drill. It is the most rudest of awakenings, especially if you've been out on the lash the night before. The alarm sounds and staff have to muster at their specific posts. You can tell who is suffering a hang-over as they are the ones in dark glasses standing in the shade looking decidedly jaded. My station is next to the upper deck bar and I wait there, feeling like death and regretting the alcohol I guzzled the night before. It is 7 a.m. and all is not well. The real crew, the proper sailors, man the lifeboats then lower them down onto the millpond that is the Caribbean Sea. They test the winches, the engines and all that stuff, the crew then take the lifeboats, all of them, once around the ship before being winched back up. It's a fairly routine but precarious ritual. Last week, as usual, I stagger from my bunk, the siren giving seven short blasts followed by one, long blast, feeling particularly nauseas; head pounding, I make my way to my muster point. It's a beautiful day, the blue, green, turquoise sea sparkles in the morning light, welcoming and most inviting under normal circumstances. The island is a majestic sight with hills of green in the distance and a warm wind gently blowing away the cobwebs of excess. Stepping out of the shade, a warming sensation travels up my forearm as the sun creeps its way across my tanned flesh, soothing and enveloping my body as I emerge into the glorious sun to look over the side at the lifeboat action. A high pitched whine pierces the air, tranquillity shattered and confusion elbows its way to the fore of consciousness. What the fuck! One of the pulley systems on the lifeboats has broken and the cable has snapped leaving one end of the lifeboat swinging wildly just above the sea below. It is being held up by the other pulley, a single wire straining to hold all the weight. Some of the crew have already fallen into the water, two I think, or maybe three, and four more souls are clinging on as best they can to the dangling lifeboat that is bashing the side of the ship with reverberating thuds. There's a panic on; the deck is quickly becoming overcrowded at that particular muster point and the officers on the bridge are calmly observing the proceedings from the Pilot's observation deck. There's an odd sort of roar, a whipping thunder, something I've never heard before and then an almighty crash. The other cable has given way and the life boat is in the water, bobbing the right way up but men are everywhere, both in and out of the water. There's an obvious anxiety but there's something more going on. Someone seems to be missing and people are duck-diving under the surface of the sea and coming up stricken with concern and distress. A couple of absolute nutters swallow-dive from the upper decks of the ship and then there are pointing fingers from the watchers lining the ship's rails. I follow the direction of brown arms and directing fingers with my eyes and focus on an officer, still in his whites, hauling in a man from below the surface. He is joined by two others as they help the submerged man up onto the surface of the water. There are gasps whispered in that warm, morning breeze. The submerged man, held by the waste to one officer's chest, doesn't have a head! The rescuing officer, it appears, doesn't realise this as he frantically tries to bring the man in for resuscitation. Only after several attempts of trying to placate the adrenalin fuelled officer does he relent; all effort was in vain. I tell you man, it was the most surreal thing I have ever seen. It seems that when the pulley failed, the crewman had been looking into the engine housing, poking his head in to look at something and as the lifeboat went down and hit the water, the edge of the engine housing sliced his head right off. Oddest thing though, no one could find his head. Divers spent most of the day going down but nothing was brought up. Later that evening, there was a ceremony which I didn't quite understand but they auctioned off everything that belonged to the crewman. His shoes are still outside his cabin as some sort of mark of respect or something. It was like a jumble sale of the dead man's belongings. Totally weird but I hear it is traditional back in his homeland.

I have a new leather belt…

Well, that's my day matey. What about yours?

L.J. Silver

April 25th

Dear Dad,

Tada!

I am now the Casino Manager. The last one got thrown off and we all know why that was. I will be receiving a new assistant as well and I don't mind admitting, I'm a little nervous as well as excited. My money goes up and I have my own cabin. No more sharing although I'll miss the camaraderie one has with fellow cabin mates.

There was a nasty accident onboard a while ago and one of the sailors died. It was an accident to do with the lifeboats and so I hear, it isn't that uncommon either. Poor bloke! There was a collection for him and I gave a few hundred bucks on behalf of the casino. They sold off all his belongings too to raise money for his family. I bought his trouser belt. I don't know why. Macabre? I suppose his family needs the money more than they need a leather belt and in a way, it's the most sensible thing to do. I feel as though I have contributed, in some small way, to the survival of his family. Not sure what to do with the belt though, so if you get it for your birthday present, try and look surprised and grateful! Everything else is pretty much the same.

I was shocked to hear that you are heading for Ethiopia, especially, having seemingly settled back at home. I now know what the itchy feet thing is all about and quite frankly Dad, I can't blame you on that one. I hope you get this before you leave. Let me know where I can write to you over there. Maybe I could come and visit you when I get a vacation? I have no plans for vacation as yet although I am told that you must take at least one vacation every year. 'But this is a vacation!' I tell them. It certainly doesn't feel like work. I have heard that it's possible to walk off the ship to start your vacation and then turn right around at the bottom of the gangway and walk straight back on again to sign on as a waiter. It's like a working holiday and apparently it satisfies the criteria for taking at least one break every twelve months. I might do that if I have no other holiday plans. I don't feel exhausted or drained. In fact, I feel fully refreshed and ready for action. The sea air and hot weather does me good. You can feel the goodness melting into your bones.

I won't write any more in case you don't get them.
But at least let me know you are okay in Africa.
Let me know you are safe.
I'm worried about you.
Love you,
JVW

May 12th

GEEZER!

Where you at boy? What news of the Cotswolds? I haven't heard anything at all from you lad. Maybe letters have been held up or gone astray? I sort of look forward to your letters mate, keep 'em coming if you can. Maybe you're dead!!??? Blimey, that would be a blow.

My old man's buggered off to Ethiopia on one of his 'save the world' campaigns. As for me, I am now the official Casino Manager of the good ship Lollipop. I was in a care-taker position for a while 'cos the last manager got sacked. Bit of an old druggy I think he was. Anyway, with no other managers to choose from I got the permanent position and have a cute little thing as my assistant. I don't know how to tell you this, I don't know if I can ever live it down myself, I don't know if the world is ready but... I'm in a relationship with her. Yes, I know, nothing special about that BUT... she's a bloody ginger!!!!!!!! A true cheeser mate, a real carrot-top. As gingery-ginge as they come and to prove it, her pubes are ginger too and I've put some in the envelope for your delight and delectation. You can thank me later. Her name's Sharon and she bangs like a shit house door in a storm. She is a real screamer too and on a ship with paper thin partitions, that's not a good thing. I stuffed my sock in her mouth the other night, to shut her up, but she seemed to enjoy it rather too much, as it goes!

Someone asked me if I had a drink problem. I said, 'NO! I drink,

I get drunk, I fall over – No Problem!' Really though mate, I'm hammering it big time. Every night, every single night, the dealers and entertainers take turns to host bedtime parties and these turn into riotous affairs which are usually visited on more than one occasion by the ship's police. Of course, we are in passenger accommodation and with cardboard for walls, twenty drunk people packed into a small cabin with U2 blaring out, well, I'd complain too if I were a paying customer. I mean, I'm supposed to discipline my staff for such things but I'm usually involved in it all. I remember when I first came on the ships and someone offered me a drink – they had Bacardi but no mixer so I refused as you can't drink it neat, right? Now, I drink it straight from the bottle and sometimes first thing in the morning after a skin-full the night before. Thing is, it's seen as the norm so it's not considered socially unacceptable, like it would be at home. Being an alcoholic is almost a badge of honour for long service on the ships. In all honesty, I need to control this beast but not quite yet. I'M HAVING TOO MUCH FUN!

What you got planned for the summer, anything good? There's still the offer of joining me onboard for a week or two?

I had to put on my serious hat the other day. A cleaner, Jamaican lad, turned up at our cash desk with a stack of blacks. That's $500 worth! He said he had been given them as a tip a few cruises ago. When I checked back through the records, I saw the chips were taken out of service because a stack had gone missing without *explanation, possibly nicked. Thing is, that was over a year ago. The blacks had been replaced with a different design and the matter pretty much forgotten about – 'til now. So, I saunter down to the crew mess to interview this guy, Samuel his name is. He's a little, skinny bloke with dry, flaky skin stretched over a scrawny frame – no threat whatsoever, or so I thought. I give him the good cop, bad cop routine – I play both parts but get nothing from him. I tell him I won't pay out any money to him and he seems a little annoyed by it, as though his claim is genuine or something. After a bit of to-ing and fro-ing, I walk away only to be stopped by another black bloke. He was really friendly and wanted a quick chat. This bloke tells me a story about a crew member who had upset another crew member a while back, once upon a time sort of thing. So the protagonist in this story is laying in his bunk, fast-a-boo-boos and in storm five men in the middle of the night. They wrap the bad guy in his own bed-sheets and chain him up with some ships metal work. Then they carry him out to the back deck (where they usually chuck the rubbish overboard in the middle of the night – beats paying for rubbish disposal in the port!) and they lob him over the side. In the morning, everyone denies any knowledge of his whereabouts and he's presumed over the side, suicide. I listen with all due attention and I'm thinking, what a load of old bollocks but then this bloke gives me a weird sort of look that says, 'Your life, your choice!' He then walks away and I'm left thinking about all this shit. I have enough weird shit going on in* *my head at the best of times and this is an obvious warning. I return to the scrawny one and state that I cannot pay him out as that is company policy, it's out of my hands and all that sort of stuff however, I do agree to give him $200 dollars in free casino chips (the ones we give to players when they first arrive; you can't cash them, only play them). I tell him he can sell them on to a passenger and he seems quite happy with this and I feel somewhat relieved. I can honestly say lad, I was quite concerned about my well-being at the time. On a ship, in the middle of nowhere and something like that happens – who're you going to call for help? In fact, had he not been happy with the offer of the free chips, I would probably have given him the $500 out of my own pocket just to be on the safe side. Better a few dollars out of pocket than sleeping with the fishes, eh?*

Take Care buddy,
JVW

June 30th

Dear Dad,

How are you? I hope this gets to you. The address you gave doesn't even look like an address. There's only two lines to it so how on earth, I wonder, will it get to you in deepest, darkest Africa? Here's hoping, as always…

I don't know whether you are receiving these letters at all now as I am not receiving anything back from you. That's a little bit disconcerting as it goes. I hope you are safe?

I shall be on vacation from July for four weeks and intend to return to the UK to stay with my mate Simon for a bit. Don't make me have to come out there to Ethiopia to look for you. You better write to let me know you are okay. **<u>Okay?</u>**

I have a, sort of, girlfriend called Sharon. She is my assistant on here and we have been together for a few months. It's nothing too serious but we seem to get on well. She's a red head and quite feisty at times. She certainly doesn't take any nonsense from me or anyone else for that matter. On a couple of occasions she's stood up for me, in a fisty-cuffs sort of way, when confronting irate players. Very lively indeed! She will only be on this ship for a few more weeks before vacation but we hope to meet up in Vermont, of all places. I want to see New England and she has relatives there. I'll be scratching those itchy feet some more then!

I have been told, well someone let it slip, that I will have a new ship when I return from vacation. It's much bigger and is doing the

Mexico run, so that'll be cool. I will be the General Manager of the casino and I hope to get Sharon on as my assistant. It's nice to have a permanent bed-warmer on hand, don't you think?

Look, let me know you are okay otherwise I really will come out there and track you down. I'll call the agency when I get home to see if they can give me any more information as to where you might be. For goodness sake be careful, stay safe wherever you are.

Love you Dad

JVW

July 4th

Boy!

Happy Independence Day!

Yep, means little to me either but all the Americans on here love the occasion.

Right then, where the fuck are you? I've heard <u>nothing</u> from you for ages now. I'm a bit worried to tell the truth. I reckon you must be dead, in prison, in the nut house, held hostage or a quadriplegic. Seriously mate, where you at?

I go on vacation in a couple of weeks and I was looking to come and stay at your place. I shall be going to the States afterwards to meet up with Sharon – my, sort of, girlfriend and we'll hang out in Vermont for a while just to see stuff. My Dad seems to have gone AWOL too, somewhere in Ethiopia I think. Maybe you two are together, up to no good – a coup perhaps? Stuck out here on my lonesome, no mail for months, it seems like the rest of the world has forgotten me. Boo-hoo! I haven't said anything to offend, have I? Sorry if I have mate. Let me know buddy 'cos last thing I'd want to do is piss you off about anything.

Well, you only have a matter of days to write something and get it to me before I go on leave, otherwise there'll be a strange, tanned hunk of an alcoholic banging on your front door real soon – and it'll be ME!

Call me on the ship's phone if you have to or send a telegram.

Let me know something, anything!

I'm going crazy out here.

Someone speak to me. Pleeeeeeeeeeeeeeeeease!

Arghhhh!

Your most humble a loyal servant,

Cap'n Pugwash

July 23rd

Dear Audrey,

Thanks for nothing. I was prepared to give you my all. I would have married you if you'd asked me to. You ungrateful bitch. You <u>USED</u> me. I hope you have a miserable life. Don't ever try to contact me, <u>EVER</u>!

J

July 23rd

Mate,

Don't know why or what's happened but I've heard nothing from you. I go on leave today and I can't say I'm at all happy about it. Where do I head for? I was coming to see you, take in some beers and make some plans. Guess I won't be now.

I'm going to head for the States. I can't give a forwarding address or any contact details as I'm going in cold. I'm off on an adventure.

Come on geezer! I mean, fuck me man, you can't be doing this to your old pal. No letter, no nothing. Your only excuse will be that you're dead because there is no other reason you could've stopped writing to your old chum. Fucking hell! I'm really annoyed now.

Maybe catch up some time in the future.

Take Care buddy,

J

July 23rd

Dear Dad,

I'm like, really worried now. Nothing, nothing at all! Christ almighty. I rang the agency and they said you had crossed the border into Sudan or somewhere but couldn't give me any further information due to security reasons. So, you can help the refugees in this world but it's at the expense of your own son, is that it? I hope not. Maybe mum was right after all?

Well, there's no point in me trying to find you as I don't even know what bloody country you're supposed to be in right now. Bloody hell! Doesn't anyone ever consider my feelings?

I'm leaving on vacation today and heading for the States. I shall be staying in some motels and then with Sharon and her relatives. I guess I won't expect anything from you then? I'll send this to the agency and maybe they'll get it to you.

Can you blame me for being angry?

Take Care,

Love you,

J

July 23rd

Dearest Darlene,

I know it's been a long time but I felt the need to write to you. I still have the same feelings for you as when we first met. I'm not sure why I'm writing this but I just needed you to know that I will always love you no matter where I am or what I'm doing. I suppose you already have a boyfriend by now – maybe you are married? I cannot help my feelings and maybe someday, somehow, we will be together because, I believe in destiny and destiny says we were meant for each other.

*I believe in **us**.*

My love, always and forever,

JVW

Chapter Six

Cruise Diary

November

Dear Diary,

FUCK YOU!

Only kidding...

In case I die in some freak yachting accident or I get eaten by cannibals, this is a record of my adventures which, I hope, might make its way to my dear old Pa, wherever he may be – last heard of somewhere in Africa. Also, for my oldest, bestest bum-chum of a pal Simon, who I have not heard from in many months and now I must presume him to be lost in space or lost in mind. Also, for the one true love of my life, Darlene, where 'er she may be and if she has married, then I hope she is happy, but I also hope her husband drops dead. So here goes...

Back from hols which was darn good. Went skiing, did some hunting, met a nice old biddy at an antiques shop called the 'Chocolate Barn' on Route 101. She made her own chocolates. Crazy dogs there, big and menacing. Bought an outrageous full length fur coat in town. I look like a trapper but regret it now. Cost $1000 and a bugger to drag around. Sharon's gone to another ship and we parted as good friends.

Back onboard where I belong – cruise ships! The MS Viscount is bigger than the last ship and I have a staff of twenty under me. Sailing down the coast of Mexico with an overnight in Acapulco. Visiting: Mazatlan, Puerto Vallarta, Ixtapa and Zihuatanejo. Let the good times roll...

Issues onboard already. Seems the casino isn't at all welcome on the ship. The casino closes at 2 am but there is a curfew for all concessionaires – that's us, which starts at midnight. Difficult to get to our cabins without being seen in a public area! Had ruck with Officer. Notified Head Office. They say to tread carefully.

December

Things no better. Staff on breaks are not allowed to use any public area. Even I have to hide away during a break. Most staff stay in cash desk or sit on an empty Blackjack table but not ideal. This is Stupidville.

New pax arrived and all heads of dept. introduced at welcome night in theatre. I was left out! Waited in wings on stage to be introduced but not called. Something definitely wrong here.

Now been told my staff can no longer eat in restaurant. Now have to eat in crew mess. Also, have to use crew bar instead of public bars. Yeeha! Outrageous parties in crew bar. Crew take turns to run the bar. Cheap as chips and some serious drugs going on down there.

Rumour has it that sniffer dogs are coming onboard. Crew stashing their illicit items in channel underneath handrails along passenger corridors. Clever!

Called to Captain's office regarding late party held in casino last night. Party for players which went on to 3am. Told that it is unacceptable and complaint will be going in. Met a nice girl from Washington, Amy's her name, and spent the night with her in another passenger's cabin. A couple allowed us to use their spare bunk so while we shagged they watched and listened. Bloody weird Americans. They had some 'Red Leb' and we inhaled it from the pin of a lapel badge, capturing the smoke under a plastic cup, smouldering and potent. Utterly trashed! Faceless! Had to make way back to own cabin in morning, along corridors still dressed in wrinkled tuxedo. Risking it!

Called to Captain's office. Been reported as being in pax accommodation. Not the night that I was actually in pax accommodation but another night when I actually wasn't. Captain and First Officer wouldn't listen to reason. Loads of shit about insurance cover. It was a Captain's Court apparently! Been told to get off the ship at next port. HOLY FUCK!

Can't get through to Head Office. Shit and corruption – what to do?????

YOU MUST BE FUCKING KIDDING??!!! Turns out, Amy was on a previous cruise some months ago and the First Officer was doing her – some sort of relationship they had. Jesus, Mary and Joseph! He be the jealous kind then.

Next port: Mazatlan.

Spent day packing and about to disembark. In Amy's cabin now. Had a few drinks to calm my nerves. She has been to see the Captain and complained bitterly – so she said. She has offered to pay my fare as a passenger to the end of the cruise. He refused. I'm sat, angry as fuck. Have to disembark at 4pm.

Totally bizarre but watch stopped and ship's police came looking for me to escort me off the ship. It must have looked like I was trying to stay on or refusing to go. Head Office called and said not to worry. Will spend night in Mazatlan before flying to the U.S. Amy has disembarked with me and insists we head back to Washington.

On plane to Washington. Head Office said take a break. Waiting for new ship. MS Viscount was always trouble they say. Don't feel so bad now. Had the mother of all hang-overs, vomited violently. Thought eyeballs were going to pop out of head. Amy very cute.

Christmas here.

Christmas gone.

Fuck Christmas!

<u>January</u>

Silver lining or what? Washington was cool but Amy disappeared back to some former boyfriend. I even cleared out her stuff from his apartment for her but now she is back there. Strange people. Been offered new ship. Emergency posting. Heading to Miami now and waiting for plane.

How exciting!

I love Tug Boat Annies. Chicken wings to die for and Miller Lite to wash it down. Dreamy. Cloud nine. Seventh Heaven.

Got rotten drunk and called Darlene. She still loves me. I love her. She wants me to go to her. I've been offered the position of dealer on the current WORLD CRUISE! Dilemma or what! Darlene? – World Cruise? – Darlene? – World Cruise? So drunk last night I burnt entire fag into pillow on bed. Fell asleep with fag on the go. Burn marks all over sheets. Lucky to be alive, probably.

Heading to airport. Joining the World Cruise in Fiji as it's already set off. Unbelievable! Darlene wasn't happy but she loves me and understands – I think. Will travel via Houston, Los Angeles and on to Fiji to pick up ship. Previous dealer been caught with cocaine in cabin – silly boy. Ship only on first week of world cruise. Fiji second port of call. Silly, silly boy!

Arrived in Fiji, minus luggage. Will wait to see if it turns up.

NO fucking luggage and setting sail now. Have to borrow some clothes from my German cabin chum. Luckily had hand luggage with smalls in. Will have to claim and buy clothes on route. Don't need much really, suit and casual gear.

Casino is tiny: one roulette table and three Blackjack tables and two slot machines plus cocktail bar. Three female dealers, me and a German. Nice little dark girl with us but she fancies the German. The manager appears to have broken his leg! He's Welsh, you know!

Read itinerary: Australia, New Zealand, China, Singapore,

Borneo, Philippines, Thailand, India, Africa, a number of obscure islands, South America, Columbia, Salvador, Panama Canal and finish in San Francisco. Loads of places in between that I've never even heard of. Three months touring the world. THIS IS IT!

Work for two hours in the afternoon and four hours in the evening. One day and one night off per week. Always off in port though and a lot of ports to visit. Have amazing tan already. Most pax are old. The ship is amazing. Very few players in casino, ever, and it's nothing more than a minor distraction for most. Casino tucked away at pointy end of ship and difficult for pax to find. Suits me. Endless games of backgammon with girls. Made up mind to limit alcohol. Doing well so far.

Different atmosphere here, no partying - much more sedate and relaxed. God I love it!

Casino girls, Cathy, Roxanne and Petra do extra work accompanying shore tours so they get to go on the tours for free – follow the umbrella! No boys wanted – surprise, surprise. I help the ship's photographers develop and print photos. No wages but I can develop all my photos for free.

New Zealand – Cold and wet. A bit like a colourful, candy cane seaside town with English weather. Vintage cars everywhere. Had to hang out with the German, Hans. No one else to go ashore with. I hate not knowing anyone or what the routine is supposed to be.

Australia – Nice and sunny in Sydney. Sailed past the Opera House with sister ship alongside. Fireworks and pageantry. Saw sights, took photos. Sailed across the Great Australian Bight heading west. The waves are HUGE! Sea came crashing right up to the top deck windows. Furniture everywhere. Unbelievable!

Round other side of Australia for The America's Cup yacht race but arrived too late in Perth as race is already finished. Pax very annoyed. Some came on this leg of cruise especially for race. Oh Dear! Winner won straight legs apparently. Bought souvenirs as most shops selling stuff cheap because of it. Perth a very happening place. Lots of young people and loads of live music. Nice atmosphere and the weather is very agreeable too. Love this place.

Girls always get an invite to the Officer's Ward Room. Boys never invited. Wonder why? Crew are mainly Scandinavian and horribly drunk when not on duty. They call the bottles of beer, 'little green men.' They crazy fuckers! Mostly big, blonde geezers with googly blue eyes and rubbery, red faces.

Fancy the dark girl, Petra, something rotten and pretended to be asleep on her so I could touch her tit without getting a slap. Nice and pert. What a waste. Fucking German. Literally! She's fucking the German!

Heading up to Asia.

China is awesome. Went around on a private bus, like royalty we were as foreigners don't usually come here. Chinese folk stared at us as they not seen 'round eye' before. Broke away from the pack and got amazing motorbike tour of town from a local boy. Paid with special vouchers that only us tourists are issued with, which buys luxury items the locals cannot get. Boy is very happy. He will buy soap and shampoo he said. I bought some Chinese money (notes) for my collection. Walked a bit and saw real poverty. Took millions of photos. Met soldier with young son – they posed for photo which will be an award winner someday.

Been told off for printing too many personal photos. Eight rolls of film in one go a bit excessive. Ship's photographer's bosses back in U.S. are livid. Accounts didn't add up. Oops!

Had Singapore Sling in Raffles (outrageously expensive), saw banana trees in Borneo, nothing much in Manila but Thailand is pure magic.

Did tour of temples and stuff with casino gang. Rode around in Tuk-Tuk. Filthy dirty. Slid off quietly and joined some crew for jolly jaunt down to red light district. Shown the ropes by old hands and picked out girl number 22. Sat in bath whilst watching porn on overhead TV. Tried to get a stiffy. Nothing! Had to knob girl without protection whilst temporarily hard (ish).

Fucking Crazy or what? Mad, Mad, Mad! Just heard all about this Aids shit spreading like wildfire. MAD! FUCKING MAD!

Thought of Aids driving me insane. Will need to get a test.

February

Fuck Aids, fuck the world, fuck everything – live fast, die young. Came to terms with it all and just hoping for the best. Have heard that a break in the skin is needed to catch the disease. No break in my skin. I'm safe. Hooray! Will get test though when back home.

Thailand is brilliant. Promised to go and rescue prostitute someday. Meant it too. She is so sweet. Name's Daen. Had amazing, out of body experience, after hubbly-bubbly pipe in market square. Daen stayed with me until re-embarkation. No souvenirs bought and hope none acquired.

Trip to docs to see about itchy knob. Fearing the worse.
Hoorah! It's only fungal – quite normal in this heat and humidity. Hip, Hip Hooray! Just a tube of anti-fungal cream

advised.

Asia all much the same really. Eating out a lot, taking lots of photos. Nice bamboo raft ride down some river and right under a waterfall. Emotions rather taken over by six foot three Austrian girl with great hair. Rafting and romance got to me. She's lovely but not too keen on the short-arse English type that I am.

Note to self – try to look taller.

Show dancer, blonde gay lad, attracted to me and won't leave me alone. Girls think it's funny. I don't! Needs twatting but can't do anything to jeopardise my world cruise. Camera bought in Hong Kong has been dropped already and zoom lens broken. Can't stop taking photos of Oriental girls. Love the slitty eyes they have. Rather partial to Oriental ladies at the moment. Met an Oriental girl called Nong on board. She's doing short leg of cruise. She says her father owns the biggest beer company in China. Extremely wealthy. Asked for blow job but she refused. I offered to lick her out but she refused that too! What does a girl want these days? Spent day with her chatting up on deck. Yawn!

Gay dancer getting on my nerves now. Asked entertainment manager to have a few words.

Work is almost non-existent. Worked out plan to prop up poor salary. Literally taking chips off table now and exchanging them whilst on cash-desk duty. Working with one of the girls. Shhh! We rotate between a sit down in the cash desk and standing at the table. Chips secreted about our person as we change over. Cash straight in pocket. Sweet!

Caught the bitch taking chips but when I asked for my share, she denied taking anything at all. Grassed her up. Teach her to cheat me.
Feel guilty about Cathy being removed from ship. Still, she deserves it. Stopped helping myself – for the moment, at least.

India is unbelievable. People dead in the street! Shit in the street. A little man will pick dirt out of your ears with a little spoon for a few Rupees. The noise, the dust, the smells. Mental place. Toured streets alone and met nuns doing charity work. Went back to the school they run. Chatted to kids about England. They couldn't understand me. Gave all the money I had in my wallet to the nuns. Took pictures of me and kids.
Gate-crashed a wedding. Given ice-cream but didn't eat it – thankfully remembered the warnings of no water, ice or ice-cream, no salads or anything unpeeled. Nice gesture though. Took pictures of newly-weds and promised to post them.
Threw away address for posting photos - feel guilty now.
Having a curry.

Went to the embassy to enquire about war graves. Chatted with the ambassador, who is obviously ex- public school and bit of a laugh. Hired taxi to take me to cemetery but now realise I can't get there and back in time before ship sails. Took tour of 'the cages' where women prostitutes are chained to beds and live behind bars. Sex slaves for real! Saw them with my own eyes and took photos against advice. Dodged big missile thrown from one of the cages. Insane, absolutely insane. I've seen it all now!

Stopped off in Sri Lanka and took train to nowhere along the coast. Wandered about at night and was the object of curiosity for many. Loads of photos. Caught train back. Compared notes to those who went ashore to have dinner in a nice hotel. Suckers!

Rounding the pointy bit at the bottom of India.

Went to crew party on back deck. Amazing! Guys from the bands jammed together. Beer and drugs flowed freely. Guy offered to spray my hair green. Thought it a good idea at the time. Paint turned out to be deck paint!! Hair turned solid. Chased guy through crew quarters and he barricaded himself in his cabin. Screaming and furious, I told him to get off at the next port or I'd kill him. Quite a crowd gathered to subdue me. Hairdresser onboard took me to salon and washed paint out with Acetone. Nightmare that took forever. Thought I was going to have to shave my head. Offered to take hairdresser out. She accepted. Silver linings!!

Went to Mahabalipuram – great sandstone sculptures. Met a family living in straw hut by side of the road. Got invited in but then saw father sleeping in the corner so quickly crept out again. Went in search of the Bombil fish and got trapped in a time-warp village. Young kids threw sticks at me. Only trouble so far. Legged it pronto.

Africa – Zanzibar - a bit like time travel as well, backwards of course. Tanzania the same.

Kenya a real blast – on safari.
Dressed up like a twat in pith helmet, shorts and safari shirt, went to Tsavo National Park to see animals. Saw a couple of lions, zebras and giraffes, gazelle things and an elephant but nothing close up. Camera on its last legs, I think. Too hot for animals, we were told. In town, bought elephant hair bracelet (and you can tell it's real by burning a little bit of it – it smells like burning hair as opposed to burning plastic). Tried to take photo of Masai man walking down street but them fuckers get violent unless you give them cash first. Tall bastards too.

Masai women walking about town but NO bare breasts, unfortunately. Bummer!

Expect to come across dad somewhere out here...

South Africa – had to do a little 'helping of selfing' in the casino to fund the hire car. Went with Roxanne and toured about. Came across shanty town and drove to the edge. Too frightened to go any further. Petra staying on ship because of apartheid. Big celebration on the quayside as cruise ships don't come here too often. Went to night club. Did my weird dancing and won bottle of whisky. Dropped whisky outside club.

Going on vineyard tour in Stellenbosch. Getting it on with Roxanne, sort of.

Went to the top of Table Mountain to look down at where we had just been. Cable car ride to top. Took photo of history on plaque so as to read it later. Saw the oceans meeting at Cape Point. Looked out onto the Cape of Good Hope.

Exhausted – dinner and bed. There's still work to do.

Hosting themed night in the casino tomorrow. Supposed to be like a carnival but it'll be the same as usual with bunting hanging up and balloons scattered here and there. Put on some Samba music and hey presto! Carnival time. Yawn! No one cares. Sometimes we make three or four hundred dollars a night, that's all and that's on a good night. Mostly, no business whatsoever. Hopefully it'll be a dull night tonight and we can play backgammon.

The Manager has the cast off his leg now. Still haven't got the full story on that one. Drunk I expect. He's still Welsh, you know? Long haul across the South Atlantic so time to recuperate.
Will write to Darlene. Living in hope now that we've rounded the Cape.

March
Stopping off at Tristan Du Cunha. Weird little British island inhabited by the descendants of shipwrecked sailors. Not allowed to go ashore –they're fearful. Some will come on the ship to sell us stamps and souvenirs however.
Blimey! They all look alike. Talk about inbred. All dark skinned with black, curly hair – all of them, women, men and the children. Dogs too I suspect! Very strange.
Only here for a few hours.

On to South America.
Captain has closed the show lounge to hold party for CREW only. Unbelievable. No pax allowed. Pax all for it to show appreciation for crew. Bands will play, a cabaret show and free

bar. Captain will be there so it'll be an orderly affair. Bloody good on ya Cap'n.

Can't make Captain's party as a dodgy tum has got me. Bad case of the shits. Can't be more than three steps from toilet – just in case. Lying in bed with a flock of seagulls in my guts. Just water coming out – bit like emptying an old radiator. Will have trouble with the old Farmer Giles after this episode. Roxy just been down to check on me and tell me I won the crew photography competition. Got nice bit of glassware for first prize. My first ever photographic prize and I wasn't even there to receive the accolade. Oh no! Got a gurgle going on... here it comes again...

Brazil – Rio de Janeiro, Sugar Loaf Mountain, Corcovado, Christ the Redeemer, Ipanema.
And it's pissing down with rain...
Made it up to the statue but most of it obscured by the low cloud. Worked my muscles on the parallel bars on Ipanema beach, in the rain. Returned to the comfort of our lovely ship and just heard some horror story about pax being mugged. One guy was mugged on his way out of the port and again on the way back. He went out with an expensive camera around his neck, Rolex watch on show, gold necklace and matching bracelet. Might mug him myself! How stupid can you be?

Having been mugged, he made his way back to the ship and got mugged by another gang only this time they took his shoes and shirt. That's all he had left. Always dress down I say – don't make yourself a target!

Salvador – was tempted to buy a Marmoset monkey from a street vendor. They cost $1. Thought better of it. Took photo and endured wrath of the vendor for doing so. Air of danger about the place. Found ship's photographers and hung out with them as safety in numbers.

Columbia and the Panama Canal – We're being towed through the canal by mules – mechanical trains that pull you along. Not very wide in places but in other places it's huge with water as far as the eye can see. Looking over the side right now and there is barely three feet to spare either side. Phew!

Columbia - Cartagena is a nice town and the place to get the best cocaine in the world, or so I'm told. Not risking my career for that though. Can get a blast for free in the crew bar if I want. Wandered the town and took photos.
Pretty much the long haul back to Frisco now. Where has the time gone?

A sad affair and something I didn't expect. It is fairly common, I am told, but still shocking nonetheless. A number of passengers, three is the current rumour, have gone overboard. As we headed towards San Francisco these passengers jumped overboard. The reason being – these are suicides and it was all planned. Jesus! People plan to have a last blowout, a 'fuck the cost' world cruise because they have no intention of paying for it – paid by credit card I suppose. They fully intend never to arrive home – not alive anyway! On the last day or days of the cruise, they simply end it all by jumping over the side, into the murky waters, to drown. I'm shocked but I'm not sure why. A very clever idea actually.

Apparently, there was one other death onboard but I was not aware of it. The body has been kept in the freezer all this time.

On a lighter note – I heard the Captain refused to marry quite a number of couples. They just don't do that anymore. It's amazing what you learn at the end of a cruise.

Been told to get off in San Francisco for vacation. It's the rules!
Just heard the ship is going up to Alaska for its next cruise. Why would I want to get off then?
Will ask to stay on.

STAYING ON!

Sitka, Ketchikan, Juneau and Skagway. Can it get any better?

You can feel the weather changing. I have nothing warm to wear.

Ketchikan – buying some clothes today, sweaters mostly.

And a hat!!

Amazing scenery. Seen whales breaching, ice-flows drifting and glaciers breaking off into the sea, which is surprisingly loud. Lots of cruise ships up here. Bit touristy as it happens. Pax called to Port side to view Polar Bear captured by crew. Life boat heading for ship with man dressed in comical Polar Bear outfit. Not sure of the point myself.

Went into a bar in Skagway. Gang of us there but no one realised it was a gay bar until we began reading the safety notices about 'anal fisting' that were on display on all the tables. Quick exit stage left.

Went bowling instead.

What are the chances... I met Sharon in Sitka this afternoon. She's working on the MV Empress. Rekindled an old romance but nothing too serious. Good to see her. Miss her a lot. She says she is on regular run.

Asking to stay on for one more Alaska cruise, to see Sharon again.

GET IN!

Given okay to stay on for one more cruise.

I love Alaska, although it is quite intimidating. Not used to being surrounded by mountains and all that snow. It has a wild feel about it – lawless and threatening.

Met up with Sharon and brought her onboard to look around. Got guest pass quite easily. Couldn't help ourselves but fell into each other's arms and into my bed. Have horrible visions of AIDS disease and feel terrible now. I need a test. I should tell Sharon too.

Been told to take vacation, everyone on the world cruise must take a vacation - it's the rules!

Just heard the ship will make for the Amazon on next cruise. How can I pass up an opportunity like this? Will ask to stay on.

REQUEST DENIED!

No getting back on as a waiter either. SHIT!

I always wanted to be taken up the Amazon. Ooh, Err, Matron!

Will hang around San Francisco for a bit.

San Francisco – Staying with Ed the musician. Saw the prison island from a distance but no desire to visit. Love driving up and down the roads and riding the trolley bus. Going to Gay Pride march. AS A SPECTATOR.

Have booked ticket to UK.

WHY?

So... Here I am, back where I started. Heathrow bloody airport.

Don't know where to go now. I'm lost. What do I do?

POST SCRIPT
August

Arriving at Heathrow airport was the worst day of my life. Nowhere to head for, no friends, no family, essentially homeless and jobless with very little money. Hour upon hour was spent at the airport trying to think of what to do or where to head for. The casino dream behind me, I felt abandoned.

Here I am reviewing my sparse notes on what will, undoubtedly, be the best years of my life. I wish I had written more but time was always short and with so many things to do and see, scribbling notes became a chore and any excuse not to do it was quickly embraced.

Memories are still strong and the pain of having to let it all go just too unbearable to contemplate.

What do I have to show for it all?

Nothing but a head full of memories and a suitcase full of photographs.

Chapter Seven

The Long Game

A SINGULAR, £1000 chip sat forlornly on number seventeen and as all eyes starred at it in anticipation, Buckley, an experienced dealer of dubious intention, stood on an empty table nearby shuffling chips. Red and black flashes melded together into one, sickening blur as the wheel spun anti-clockwise. A small, white ivory ball rattled and spun in the opposite direction upon the wooden track. Buckley had been keeping a discreet eye on the cabbie since he started winning a while ago; he had watched his transformation from nobody to V.I.P. and then back again. After examining his play strategy, he would now focus once more to watch the wheel and the fate of this bold, final wager. Slowly, he began to appreciate the secrets of wheel bias.

Buckley had started his career in one of the 'cheaper' casinos somewhere up north. He had been trained in-house by an older, experienced dealer, unlike everyone else in London who had attended a bona fide training school. He always felt second best, just a second rate dealer and his prospects of promotion were practicably negligible. However, he had one saving grace; he was stunningly handsome and engaged to an incredible beauty from Laos. Buckley stood a little over six feet tall, six-three, six-four perhaps, with dark hair, permanent designer stubble, emerald green eyes and a swarthy complexion; most females preferred to look at Buckley than watch the gaming tables. He was definitely male model material and he cut a fine figure being young, handsome and very full of himself. Unfortunately, he was a little too partial to experimental drug taking which involved those many elements, compounds and mixtures that were readily available to those in the know, back in the day before it all became mainstream. Such handsomeness was all but wasted on him for he was no more than a boy who failed to mature into a man. He had a son from a previous relationship and paid dearly for that privilege, both financially and emotionally. In another time and another place, he could have been anything he wanted to be, the epitome of charisma and good looks, but in this life he was a no hoper who was forever hopeful.

"Tel, Tel... you been watching that cabbie?"

Terry was Buckley's contradiction. He was a wiry, unwashed looking individual who did not possess any endearing qualities and was equally unsuccessful with everything he turned his hand to. It appeared as though his face had been constructed by an inadequate drunken artist who had thrown together some materials and hoped for the best after a heavy night on the booze. Nothing seemed to match in his looks department. He even had one leg slightly shorter than the other and with no arse to speak of, there was a hideous ballooning in his trousers where some fulsome butt cheeks should have been. His nickname was Treasure, due to his underdeveloped rib cage which was concave about the sternum; a sunken chest was the reason for the common quip. He was a prime candidate to have sand kicked in his face and when stood next to Buckley, the joke would often be that they were a 'before and after' picture. Terry, five feet four in bare feet, was a self-taught dealer who had learned everything he needed to know about dealing roulette from a friend who had attended a respectable training school. The simple idea was that the two would club together their savings in order to pay the extortionate training school fees and then one could teach the other what had been learnt that day. As schemes go, it was a good idea but it came nowhere close to the scheme that

Buckley was about to present.

"Who hasn't?" said Terry, pushing his plastic cup against the lever to eject some juice from the machine.

"Do me one!" ordered Buckley.

"Okay!" replied Terry.

"What d'ya think then?"

"About what?"

"The cabbie, of course," said Buckley, beginning to show signs agitation.

"What about the cabbie?"

"De...err!"

Buckley recounted everything he had seen and suggested they do something about it.

"Like what?" Terry asked, curiosity getting the better of him. "What you got in mind?"

Buckley began his coercing speech, recited once already in his head, he now felt sure he would convince Terry to form a partnership with him.

"Let's become professional gamblers?" he suggested.

"Oh, you fucking idiot!" snapped Terry. "Like all the other mugs before us, yeah?"

Watching games played, day in and day out, many a croupier believed they had found a winning formula. Unlike punter's winning systems, which were based on number patterns or card counting, witchcraft or even lucky trinkets, croupiers believed that with a proper staking system, maths and a resolute discipline, a career could be made out of gambling. It was always in the early stages of a croupier's career when they had this 'Eureka' moment, along with the honest held belief that they could live off the proceeds of casino gambling. After two or three years, when the big winners had been personally witnessed, admired and the mistakes of the losers identified and theoretically rectified, croupiers felt they knew what was what in terms of winning and losing. In fact, they never did or ever would. Beyond those years, croupiers quickly became aware that only the house ever won and to think otherwise was nothing more than pure fancy. A surprising number of naïve dealers, usually in pairs, set off on their professional gambling paths to fame and fortune but not one of them, not a single one of them, ever heard or spoken about, assumed or otherwise, ever made it to the big time. However, those who were brave enough to return to the fold, applying for their old jobs back, were silently admired for their courage. Others disappeared without trace, going onto other menial jobs or fading into obscurity, rather than face the ridicule of returning broken and poor.

Buckley had decided this would not happen to him, he had a plan and he needed Terry's help to put it all together. In fact, he didn't really need any help at all but projects always felt safer when there was someone else to share the decision making process with, especially when it came to quitting the security of a full time job. Get rich quick schemes, businesses and the like, were always being bantered around the casino staff room with people signing up for the most unusual of alternative careers. But, when it came to the crunch, when it got to the point of having to give notice to terminate secure employment, that's when it would all fall apart. Nobody wanted to step out of their comfort zone. Nobody really wanted to give up their regular income for some hare-brained scheme that had only been worked out on the back of a fag packet and discussed over copious amounts of alcohol. Buckley, it turned out, was indeed just that sort of person and all he had to do was to get Terry enthused enough to join him on the misadventure.

"No, Tel. It's not like all the other mugs before us. Listen, I've been working on this for some time."

"Go on then, give us a laugh," mocked Terry. "Go on, I'm all ears."

Buckley paused for a moment to build some tension but more importantly, to get it right in his own head.

"What, you forgotten it already?" taunted Terry.

"Tomorrow, they're taking the wheel off the table," Buckley began. "They're bringing it upstairs to test. I heard a couple of the security guys talking about it. The manager wants it put it in the staff room and if we are not doing anything, as we come in and out, they want us to spin the ball. They want to record the winning numbers over ten thousand spins to see if there's anything wrong with the wheel. You know the cabbie that won all that money?"

"Yep."

"Well, they reckon the wheel he played is dodgy or something, like it keeps bringing up certain numbers or sections of the wheel."

"Really?" said Terry, his interest very much aroused by this revelation.

He was partial to a mystery; be it a murder mystery or even invading aliens, he loved the chase, the elusive answers, the red-herrings and the final reward of being the hero who would uncover the truth.

"Too right," continued Buckley. "Look, I've been watching the cabbie since he started winning. I've mostly been put on a table near him so, I've had the chance to watch everything. Without writing anything down, I got the feeling that certain sections of the wheel kept coming up most of the time."

"But they moved the wheel around and put it on other tables, didn't they?" questioned Terry.

"Yeah, they did and when they did, I noticed where they put it and I kept my eyes on it. I reckon it brings up the same numbers all the time. Well, not all the time but more often than not."

"What, like magic or voodoo or something?"

"You fucking twat. Are you taking this seriously Tel because there's a queue of people who want in on this one?"

"Really?"

"The wheel seems to favour certain numbers in certain sections. At first security thought it wasn't balanced properly so they checked it out. They changed the balls, even used new ivory ones, but still it seems to favour these particular numbers. When I had the chance, I could see that the cabbie mostly won on these numbers."

"What are they then?" asked Terry, already straining to receive the incredible disclosure.

"It's sections of the wheel, you knob. You interested?"

"Yeah, sure!" affirmed Terry enthusiastically, a little frightened he might be left out if he didn't register his interest quickly.

"We'll do the wheel test, like management wants us to, when the wheel comes up tomorrow. Don't do anything just yet though."

"Okay!" said Terry, going back to the sandwich that now hung loose and unappetising in his hand, one side limply hanging over his knuckles to reveal sweaty cheese and a thick, dark brown pickle.

***

At the end of the gaming day, after all the cash had been counted, the manager finally left by the back door along with the Pit Boss. Daylight was just beginning to break outside and Londoners were waking up to their miserable existence in the rat race, ready to continue their chase of the unreachable dream of financial independence. Another bright and sunny morning awaited such normal, sad people. Passing on the back stairs as they left the building, the relief security officer dragged himself up each rung in the opposite direction, as though he were climbing Everest without supplemental oxygen.

"Rough night?" enquired the manager.

"And some," came the mumbled response.

"You moving the wheel today?" asked the Pit Boss.

"Gonna do it now, while there's two of us here. Not really up to it though," said the security officer.

The stench of stale cigarettes and alcohol drifted out of his mouth and into the morning air, fortunately bypassing the noses of the manager and Pit Boss; it merely dissipated into the sky to further pollute London's already contaminated atmosphere.

"Have a good one!" wished the manager, although it was more directed to the outside world of London folk rather than the fumbling half-drunk that made his way towards the back door.

"Cheers!" came the faint reply, along with an even fainter, "You too."

A slam was heard and the Pit Boss instinctively looked behind to find the space where the security officer had been now eerily empty. Like a spectre briefly seen, the security officer disappeared inside the building where he made his way to the girl's toilets in order to force a vomit. There was something so much nicer, even a little perverted, about using the girls' toilet when no one else was about. A fun distraction for the male security staff was to have the biggest shit they could manage in the girl's toilet. They would leave the shit sitting proudly in the white porcelain bowl, half submerged with a menacing look about it. No flushing was allowed. It was intended to be a fun surprise for one of the female dealers, a girl, any girl, to find and be amused by. Photos on the security office wall were a testament to the biggest and best turds ever produced. Some beggared belief and one could only stare in amazement at just how anything so long and thick could be expelled from a human arse-hole. Some were massive and others oddly misshapen, no doubt by protruding piles, and all the various shades of brown and green were there with one, curiously, being an albino jobby that defied all sensible explanation. All security officers, both male and female, being ex-military or police, found this sort of joke highly amusing; such is the mentality of ex-services personnel, one surmises.

On a disused card table, with sturdy legs to carry the weight, the wheel would be mounted just outside the staff room where dealers were instructed to do proper spins of the ball, at least three revolutions, as they entered and departed. The numbers were to be recorded in a notebook and if a dealer wanted to spend their entire break ball-spinning, so much the better. A notice to this effect was laminated and placed on the staff notice board.

Two security officers, one over tired and the other hung-over, carefully and methodically dismantled the wheel on AR5 according to procedure. A sharp spin of the wheel and a secure grab of the turret snapped free the thread and as the wheel continued to revolve, so the fine thread wound the turret loose to finally be lifted up and off the inner post. The turret base was lifted off the inner spindle and then the height adjuster removed and carefully wrapped in an oiled cloth. The wheel-head was lifted out by both men, who gingerly brought it up over the inner spindle so as not to damage it, the thread or any of the adjacent chrome or woodwork. A quick wipe over with a dusting cloth and the wooden bowl was ready for hauling upstairs. For a part of the journey, the bowl would have to be presented on its edge and that would require some careful and precise juggling if safe delivery was to be assured. Had someone the foresight to retain the CCTV footage of that journey, from gaming floor to staff room, it would have made riotous viewing at any Christmas party, possibly comparable with the classic, 'Punters Losing Their Tempers,' video. Sadly, no one thought to do just that so the whole affair was carried out without any appreciation or applaud. The wheel was in one position one day then, somewhere different the next. How this was managed, no one really knew or cared.

The novelty of performing endless spins soon wore off and it was just too much effort for anybody to perform this critical part of the investigation. It looked as though it would take forever to get ten thousand spins done but then there was a sudden revival of interest. Buckley had done some investigating and had found a niche that would utilise skills even he did not know he had.

In order to prove Buckley's system as being a viable business proposition, he encouraged, cajoled, bullied and pleaded with anyone who would take notice of him, to spin the ball during their breaks. It was mostly Terry and Buckley that were doing the spinning but every so often sympathisers would join in and there was also a little gambling on the side to make it more interesting. On occasions, Buckley would lose his temper when he caught dealers messing with the procedures – those who thought it funny to use two balls at the same time, those who wouldn't reverse spin, those who merely picked the ball up and placed it in another number and those who constantly put their snack rubbish in the wheel. For Buckley, it was a serious matter but for everyone else, it was a management direction that they chose to ignore. Buckley even threatened to get CCTV put on the wheel so the matter would be taken more seriously but everyone, except Terry, laughed him out of the staff room. It was only Terry that knew the real reason behind Buckley's obsession, everyone else thought he was just plain bonkers.

It seemed like forever and Buckley had no way of knowing how many spins had been performed or whether it was showing any bias. He would have to make discrete enquiries later, be seen to be showing a keen interest in order to get the results on which this scheme would rely. In the meantime, he spun the ball at every opportunity and even stayed late one night to get some extra spins in. It was a very serious business, at least to Buckley. He felt it was probably the one and only thing he could finally apply himself to, the one thing that could be the making of him, the one thing he might say he was good at.

The results of his further investigations had revealed, from a supplier, that the wheel had been made in a factory in Ireland. There were five others delivered at the same time and all with sequential serial numbers. Messrs' Murdoch and Finch, the manufacturers, had even supplied a high resolution photograph of their wheels, a bit like a police mug shot where each wheel was truly individual in character and design. At home, Buckley sat in his favourite chair, the one which had

had the legs sawn off so the seat was at floor level. With a huge joint between his fingers, sucking in hard and exhaling only the second before he felt his lungs would burst, Buckley studied the glossy A4 pages that described each wheel; the pin sharp picture accompanied by a column of specifications: '*diameter – 828mm, bowl with feet – 195mm, height with turret – 334mm, shipping weight – 73kg, configuration – single zero, ball track – solid surface.*' They were works of art, fine pieces of traditional craftsmanship that were too often and unjustly regarded as nothing more than objects for gaming. Just look at that beautiful workmanship, Buckley thought to himself. Just look at that beautiful wood, the colours, the grain, the knot...

A small explosion erupted in Buckley's head, a moment of enlightenment, an intense moment of illumination where a beam shone brightly – but only for a second or so. Eyes opened wide, pupils abnormally dilated, Buckley drew the page up close to his face and studied the glossy image of the European roulette wheel in front of him. Some remnants of marijuana smoke drifted from his nose, like writhing snakes they made their surreptitious break for freedom to escape the dark confines of two, debris filled cavities; lines of wispy blue-grey curling up around flared nasal wings to finally dissipate into the haphazard haze of previously expelled smoke that hung apocalyptically from the ceiling. Like a dark, low cloud, the living room threatened to erupt into thunder and lightning. In those black streaks of wood that formed the rim of the wheel, within the natural patterns that separated bible black lines from bloody browns, there was a misshapen sphere where once a young branch had sprouted from a living tree. Nothing big or obvious, not like one might find on natural pine, but a delicate swirl of Indian ink black that could easily identify this wheel from any other wheel of the same size and design.

"Get in you beauty!" Buckley screamed.

***

There was a small puddle of lager on the table top and Terry studied it intently before wiping it away with the back edge of his hand.

"Look at that!" he said with amazement, "Look, it's turned white where the wet was. Why's that then?"

"What?" said Buckley.

"It's turned the varnish white but it'll be brown again when it dries. Why's it do that then?" asked Terry.

"You're a fucking idiot Tel, do you know that?"

"No, I..."

"I fucking give in, I really do," despaired Buckley.

"What then?"

"Every wheel has a different pattern, just like a fingerprint, they're individual, just like you and me. No two wheels can ever be the same. The pattern of the natural wood makes each one unique, just like people and that's what makes them, and us, so easily identifiable. You could give them individual names if you wanted to because you could identify each and every one of them individually. Got it?"

"We're going to give roulette wheels names?" asked Terry cautiously and instantly regretting the question.

"You're fucking winding me up!" spat Buckley. "Err... yeah... right. Individual, like fingerprints. Got it. You spat on me!" said Terry.

"I'll twat you in a minute if you don't stop it. Now, for fuck's sake, listen will ya!" says Buckley and he drew out the word 'listen' to a prolonged drawl, over-accentuating the mouth movement for further effect. "There were five wheels made in a particular batch so we can expect that a flaw in the wood or manufacturing process has produced a bias in all of them. Our job is to track those beauties down and play the bias."

"Not quite sure what you're on about Buckley," quizzed Terry.

"Look, no one said it would be an easy ride," replied Buckley by way of an inadequate explanation.

"You've changed Buckley. You're different. You've gone all OCD with this thing?"

"You haven't changed Tel, you're still a tosser" said Buckley and he tapped his forefinger against his forehead. "Up there for thinking, down there for dancing," he instructed.

The forefinger was now pointing at the floor and Terry dutifully looked at the pub carpet noticing how the strange, black, sticky smooth bits stood out from the red colours and formal patterning of woven material.

"Oh, yeah!" agreed Terry, looking up at Buckley. "I've got it now, I know what yer on about."

"You clever lad, Tel. Now get that down ya and I'll get the next round in. We're in business boy."

Buckley reached for the two glasses with one hand and with a finger in each he snapped them together to produce a sharp clink that was reassuringly friendly and satisfying.

"Lager, Tel?"

"Yes please!"

"Well, get me one while you're there," laughed Buckley at the deception, whilst passing over the glasses.

"Right you are," acquiesced Terry, feeling inadequate and subservient.

As he stood at the bar waiting for two pints of Stella to be drawn from the tap, Buckley eyed up his surroundings. He looked with a slightly cocked head at a fading picture that hung on the wall in front of him – a group of dogs were playing cards around a table and one of them appeared to be in the process of cheating. Buckley laughed out loud but then, having realised what he had done, quickly tried to hide his embarrassment with an over enthusiastic cough. This caught the eye of a young lad nearby who gave a nod to acknowledge someone he only knew by sight. Buckley recognised him as a colleague but didn't know his name. The lad returned to face the older woman who sat opposite him and, as it appeared to Buckley, she seemed to be writing down everything that the two said. Buckley wondered why anyone would want to do an interview in a pub but then again, Buckley wondered about a lot of things.

With eyes fixed firmly on two lagers, Terry manoeuvred himself through the crowd trying to avoid any spillage. He took a long sip from the rim of each glass, a small collection of tiny bubbles appearing as foam on his top lip, then presented Buckley's pint for him to take. Buckley looked at him in disbelief.

"You been drinking my beer Tel?" he asked.

"I had to, it was spilling everywhere," explained Terry.

"You dirty, horrible little cunt. I hope you haven't got any diseases. If I catch something I'm going to cock-punch you so hard you won't be able to wank for a week. Now sit down and listen. Hang on! Where's the nuts?"

"Sorry mate!"

"You're fucking useless Tel. I bloody despair with you sometimes!"

Terry sat down with a heavy thud, the weight of a useless soul hitting a useless stool, both badly in need of refurbishment.

"Right then," began Buckley, "I reckon we could start by visiting the London casinos looking for the roulette wheels. We'll study the patterns and get round as many casinos as we can to try and find them."

"What about our one?" said Terry, in his most serious, enquiring tone.

"Good one Tel. We won't be allowed in our old casino, not as professional gamblers anyway. We'll have to forget that one. Once we track down one of the wheels we can start noting down some numbers and get this show on the road. Between us it might take a few weeks to get the number patterns but if we buy in for a big amount, we should be able to live off the complimentaries for a while. We can always play a little too, subsidise our observations, so to speak. We'll take it in turns to get the numbers down and analyse them after we've got ten thousand or so. You'll do the night shifts and I'll do the days..."

"That's not fair!" interrupted Terry.

"Look! I'll be doing lots of investigations and stuff, organising and running about during the nights, as well as trying to get some sleep, so it'll be up to you to be in the casino at those times. Sorry buddy, no option on that one. If we're going to make this happen, it has to be this way. Okay?"

"Suppose so," agreed Terry, reluctantly.

It was two days later when Buckley received another letter from the wheel suppliers. Having posed as a potential buyer, they had dutifully kept this new client's details in order to keep him up to date with information as per his initial enquiry. As a matter of courtesy, the suppliers informed Commodore Buckley (the title he had used to give himself some credibility) that the five wheels in the batch of six, as detailed in previous correspondence, had been returned to the manufacturers quite recently and decommissioned due to an unidentifiable fault. They had been dismantled and the parts used for the refurbishment of other wheels. Buckley sank into his legless chair and felt his spine jar as it came to rest on the insufficient foam padding that covered the base over the concrete floor below, "Fuck it! Fuck, fuck, fuck, fuck and FUCK!"

There had to be a way round this problem, so Buckley began to assemble a joint, a three paper job with a nice roll of soft cannabis resin running down the middle – a dangerous affair where great caution would be needed, lest those inevitable hash burns do damage to clothing, carpet or skin. A long, drawn out, sumptuous suck on a feeble roach of thin card ushered Buckley's brain into a neighbouring dimension, that very special place where colours are brighter, sounds sharper, contrast more defined and inspirational thoughts come thick and fast. Unfortunately, short term memory loss was the unwanted side-effect. A prolonged consideration as to the workings of the internal combustion engine held Buckley's attention for an inordinate amount of time; two stroke, four stroke and even the Wankel rotary engine went round and round in Buckley's drug addled brain, which did no more than present more questions than answers. Mount an engine onto a skateboard and with the right amount of thrust, maybe from rocket boosters...

Buckley remained motionless and desperately tried to remember what it was he was supposed to be thinking about. He sniggered to himself. A small laugh burst from his lips then subsided just as quickly. Bit peckish, was the thought that rose from the depths of his mangled subconscious.

He gave a last, long, hard think...

"Nope, haven't got a fucking clue!" he said out loud.

"FOOD!" he shrilled, struggling to stand but falling flat on his face.

***

"What you done to your face?" asked Terry, with a derisive degree of compassion.

"Shut up you gay!" snapped Buckley, without any compassion whatsoever.

Like most projects, it was the fun of planning that spurred the boys on. Buckley believed that Terry did not have the heart to quit his job and Terry thought the same of Buckley. At most times it was no more than pie in the sky planning, a challenge, the thrill of the chase, something to focus on, but then at other times it almost seemed as though they might actually pull it off. The wheel outside the staff-room became a permanent fixture but rarely did anyone bother to spin the ball as they should have done. Towards the end, the ball got nicked and the wheel filled with plastic cups and other staff debris. As is usual, it's not until something disappears that you realise it was there in the first place. Like a gaping hole in a wall that wasn't there before, like an enormous hole in Buckley's plan and an even bigger hole in Terry's intelligence - one day the wheel was there and the next it was gone. Buckley grabbed Terry on his way into the casino staff room and held his skinny chin with a masterful, clenched hand to direct his gaze towards the great void where a wheel had once been.

"What, what is it?" panicked Terry, confusion welling up in his inadequate chest.

"It's fucking gone mate. G...O...N...E!"

"Oh yeah, so it has," said Terry, before breaking free of Buckley's grip to sit and watch a football match on the staff room TV. Manchester United was one goal up but Buckley cared not for such insignificance.

"Where's the wheel gone?" Buckley shouted into the packed staff room. He got some puzzled looks but no one responded, eyes immediately turning back to the extra time struggle that Chelsea had before them. Buckley then made his way down onto the casino floor, another night ahead and another night of mindless dealing to mindless punters. He had to find out about the wheel. He desperately needed to find out about his future. His life and sanity depended on that bloody wheel. With all the good things going on in Buckley's life, especially his prized possession from Laos, foolishly he considered the missing roulette wheel to have more importance than anything else. He was determined to find it at any cost.

***

"Merde!"

A stubby, gnarled finger was wedged between a cream coloured door surround and the reddish, brown bowl of a European roulette wheel. More careful manoeuvring allowed for the thick digit to be released without serious damage to either and with a quick adjustment of green delivery aprons, one man and three youths continued their struggle to make their delivery via an inordinately tight passageway. Finally, one chubby finger still throbbing with pain, the wooden bowl was placed upon the roulette table in its new home, midway down Avenue de la Violette, Aix en Provence, Southern France. A tall, olive skinned man with a fabulous moustache that was pinched and waxed at the tips, assisted by a shorter man in an open-necked formal shirt, dark suit and carpet slippers, assembled the wheel-head, height adjuster, turret base and turret before the wheel was sharply spun and the chrome turret grabbed so firm it would wind itself firmly onto the thread of the spindle. A spirit level was centrally placed atop the turret and a slow push given to the wheel so it travelled smoothly upon its bearings to prove a fine balance that needed no adjustment at all.

"C'est bon!" exclaimed the owner, as he ceremoniously placed a few, crisp cash notes into the waiting hands of the four manual workers.

They quickly secreted the tip into their tight, front pockets that were sewn onto the front of their fabric pinafores. A bead of sweat ran down the forehead of the older delivery man, "Merci beaucoup, Monsieur," he thanked softly, dabbing his brow with a ragged piece of cloth that he held in a clenched fist.

Arms folded, the owner admired the latest acquisition to his exotic club, carefully examining the smooth, lacquered surface, the craftsmanship and the fine detailing of the roulette wheel that was undoubtedly the product of a master craftsman who took a great deal of pride in his work. He considered whether it was indeed hand-made. Definitely! But then again, it could well be made by a very clever machine. "C'est pas grave," he said aloud.

Bending forward and with a slightly wetted left thumb, he gently rubbed at a black mark on the rim of the wheel; a coal black spherical swirl that at first looked like an ink stain but was, on closer inspection, a natural fault in the wood that was probably once a ring of youthful attachment to a living tree. Upon realising this, the owner rubbed over the smear with a dry finger, to smooth away the marks of saliva, before turning on his heels to call out with great control and authority, "Elisé, Elisé. Allez!"

Elisé would prepare the gaming chips for the night's newest entertainment feature - the recently acquired, second hand, one previous owner, European roulette wheel purchased from a local supplier by the name of Monsieur Petrucci - purveyor of second-hand gaming equipment in Provence. Tonight would see the first, slightly illegal, game of roulette played at Le Kitty Kat Klub and this new side attraction, it was hoped, would bolster the falling revenues of the outdated, titillating cabaret show that relied on over-priced liquor and highly questionable adult entertainment.

The air in Le Kitty Kat Klub, or Le KKK as it was better known, was thick with the scent of cheap perfume and sex on discount. Outside, a steroid induced, muscle bound, ex-military time bomb explained the wares of Le KKK. He called to passers-by to try and entice in anyone who looked as though they were good for some hard cash.

"Hello, Sher today!"

A high pitched Netherlands accent rounded off every word to produce a sing-song tone that would be practically impossible to match to the immense muscular body that it emanated from.

"Corm on hin. Corm inside. Shmoking and poking, shucking and fucking, licking and dicking, heducational show, jusht for yoush."

This man-monster knew, by sight, all the local police, both uniformed and plain clothed, so would adapt his style accordingly so as not to appear confrontational with them, or any of the prospective customers, who might bring the might of the law down on this social necessity of a nightclub. To a certain extent it was tolerated but then it would be, the money flowed freely, especially into the pockets of the gendarmerie and the local mayor. Bribery is truly an international occurrence and one that shouldn't be avoided if business is to flourish, so believed the club owner. Stepping inside, for the very first time, were two of the most unlikely punters Le KKK had ever seen but they walked straight in without challenge, a brief show of wealth was their entrance ticket and it was immediately accepted and welcomed. Buckley looked at Terry as the faint sounds of gaming drifted into the narrow hallway.

'Faites vox jeux!' a voice called out.

Then there was the familiar rattle of ivory on wood which was quickly followed by a young female voice.

"Rien ne va plus!"

The bets were down, the ball was slowing and no more bets would be accepted.

"Rien ne va plus, merci!"

A faint gasp of surprise was heard as the dinkedy-dink- dink of a roulette ball fell upon the number separators, followed by a definitive clonk of ball landing in a numbered compartment. Terry looked to his left to see a single roulette table with half a dozen people standing opposite a scantily clad dealer.

"Trois. Rouge. Impair a passé!" she announced, before sweeping the layout with outstretched arms and caging hands. There was a rattling and crashing of table chips and when Terry turned back to look at Buckley, he could clearly see a satisfying smile creeping into the corner of the master's mouth and a glimmer of hope shone in those wide, sparkling, drug drenched eyeballs.

***

Buckley and Terry sat together at the canteen table, both writing their letters of resignation; they both thanked the casino for the opportunities afforded them over the years and wished the management and staff all the very best for the future. The reason that Buckley gave was 'personal' and Terry's was sadly misspelt as 'personnel.' Terry's wishes were 'very breast' and his regards came, 'With Love' and rounded off with a trio of Xs

Buckley looked over at Terry's written resignation attempt and smirked his superiority. Terry looked at Buckley's letter and had no idea that his own was in any way inferior. With slightly sweaty palms, both walked down onto the gaming floor and handed their hand written, un-enveloped letters to the duty manager before walking into the Pit to be assigned a table on which to deal for the very last time. Management took the immediate decision to pay-off both dealers rather than risk them working their notice. They were considered loose cannons and neither could be trusted to behave until the time of their official release. With two weeks' notice money, holiday pay and the rent that they would conveniently forget to pay before moving out of their respective flats, they set off on their path of adventure; Buckley would leave behind one of the most important assets he would ever own and Terry had nothing whatsoever to lose.

"So what now?" asked the duty manager. "You going after it?"
"Sure am," replied Buckley. "Both me and the milky-bar kid

over there."

"Well," continued the manager. "As I told you, the wheel was sent back because it was probably biased. I mean, over those six thousand spins we did, it was showing a bias towards the Tier so it couldn't be risked having it back on the floor. Maybe four thousand spins more would have told us something different, but I doubt it. You saw the cabbie hit us hard and it was pretty much down to those numbers... quick, what are they?"

It was an automatic reaction to stream off the series of numbers that made up the French bet Tiers du Cylindre. "Five-eight, ten-eleven, thirteen-sixteen, twenty-three-four, twenty-seven-thirty, thirty-three-six," came Buckley's quick response.

The manager spoke with all sincerity, "You're pretty good Buckley, you know that?"

"At my worst, I'm better than anyone I know," he offered with cock-sure confidence.

"Steady boy. I mean, you could still make it to Inspector or Pit Boss if you worked hard. Do you want to give up a good career for some half-baked, wild goose chase?"

"Gotta dance," sang Buckley as he headed back to the staff room for his very last break before being released early.

Buckley was popular with one particular manager who had certain, emotional leanings towards the green-eyed Adonis so anything Buckley wanted, well, Buckley pretty much got with this particular line manager. The doe-eyed manager had relayed what he knew about the wheel and this had given Buckley enough impetus to take the initiative and strive for freedom. The supplier had sold on the wheel rather than break it down and it had been shipped to France. There was an address, which was presented as a parting gift to Buckley, and also included was a printed analysis of some six thousand numbers with a detailed bar graph highlighting the frequency of the Tier. This confirmed what Buckley had believed all along, what he had mentally noted during those games with the cabbie - the wheel had a bias and now it had been confirmed. The chase was on.

"What about Tran?" enquired Terry, as they both walked, for the very last time, out of the casino's staff entrance and onto the streets of West London.

"I don't think I was any good for her," replied Buckley, solemnly. "I mean, I loved her and all that but I think I was just bringing her down."

"Was she upset?" pressed Terry.

"Of course she was fucking upset, you moron. What girl wouldn't be upset with me walking out on her?" he snapped.

"Yeah, right," agreed Terry.

"Anyway," Buckley whispered from the corner of his mouth.

"I owed her quite a bit of money anyway, plus she was getting all loved up and talking about serious shacking up together as well. I mean, you buy a girl a ring and she thinks you're her property. Bloody hell Tel, I value my life too much to be tied down to just one girl. Why buy a book when you can join a library, eh?"

"I like her a lot too," declared Terry, with far too much affection in his voice for Buckley's liking.

"Well you ain't fucking having her, you creepy little git! What you having to drink?"

The pub door snapped open and the two walked in to celebrate their unemployment by drinking as much lager as their bellies could manage, without regurgitating first, and they planned their assault on France, the French and all common decency.

***

"Gentlemen. Bonsior!" welcomed the owner as he stood proud before Buckley and Terry with his right hand held out for them to shake. "I am dee owner, Monsieur Blanc and I welcome you to Le Kitty Kat Klub."

"Ta very much,' replied Terry, feeling very welcome and relaxed.

"How did you know we were coming?" questioned a paranoid Buckley. "Who told you about us? What have you heard?"

"Why noth-ing," replied Monsieur Blanc apologetically. "I

merely greet you to my establish-a-mon and wish you *bon chance* should you wish to play a litt-le roulette?" He then added, "Peut être?" by way of an afterthought.

"Absolutely," uttered a slightly confused Buckley. "We'll have a beer and look at the girls for a bit first though. Maybe play later on." He then added, "Poo tet error," by way of an afterthought, but more so in ignorance.

"Garçon! Deux bière, s'il vous plait," commanded Monsieur Blanc to a nearby waiter.

Buckley and Terry were led into a side room that was divided into a number of smaller, private cubicles with each containing a round table with two, red velvet covered chairs.

"Asseyez-vous," said Monsieur Blanc and he gestured to the chairs for Buckley and Terry to sit on.

"And you too my good man," replied Terry, not quite understanding the language but feeling the warmth of Monsieur Blanc's sincerity.

Monsieur Blanc bowed his head in servitude and backed away from the room before disappearing down the narrow hallway to welcome another punter.

"Bonsoir, Monsieur Picard, entre, entre s'il vous..." and then his voice was lost to the sound of Terry's.

"This is a bit of alright, ain't it Buckers?"

"Don't call me that you cock-sucker. Don't you bloody well show me up either," warned Buckley.

Terry turned his head in embarrassment at something he had not yet done but knew he would – embarrass himself as well as Buckley and then have to suffer the consequences. He focused on the crimson, flock wallpaper and traced his forefinger between the lines of fluffy fabric, imagining a car negotiating the fine flowing patterns as it made its way to the centre of a pineapple.

"What the fuck are you doing Tel?" asked Buckley as he caught sight of Terry tracing a path around a Fleur du Lys pattern.

"Nothing," sulked Terry. "Stop having a go at me all the time... otherwise I'm going home."

"Don't be such a gimp. I'm only mucking about with you. Come on, here's our beers."

A somewhat dated waitress in a somewhat out of date Bunny uniform presented two small glasses of amber liquid, both only half filled but topped with a tall head of froth that rose above the brim. Buckley felt Terry's enthusiasm beginning to wane so he decided to lighten up, lest he find himself abandoned by his one and only true friend and business partner.

"Bloody hell, Tel, look at this," he said, holding up the beer glass in front of his face. "We won't be getting pissed any time soon on these!"

Terry smiled back and held up his own glass, "I know I like

good head but this is ridiculous," he quipped.

Both glasses were then promptly emptied of their contents. Terry held his upside down glass to his raised mouth as he drained the last of the foam which slid slowly, graciously and inevitably into his expectant aperture.

A short moment of silence passed before Buckley leaned forward to whisper his plan.

"Right Tel," he started, "This is the plan. We'll go into the casino bit, all casual like, have a mooch at the wheel to see if it's our one then when I confirm that it is, by nodding my head, then you can take over."

Terry strained to hear the rest of the plan. A new found sense of importance, found in Buckley's few words, gave him renewed fervour and direction. Terry was once again eager to get down to business, their business, the business of being professional gamblers.

"What do I do?" asked Terry enthusiastically.

"Your job mate..."

Buckley looked around before continuing.

"Your job is to note down the numbers for as many spins as you can without rousing suspicion. Get them down on a roulette card and if someone starts noticing you, buy in for a couple of hundred Francs, then carry on getting the numbers down as though you're waiting for your lucky number to come up or something. Don't start playing though. Wait until I get back before you play anything. Order another beer if you like, look casual."

"Okay, got it," said Terry, reassuringly.

"Do not start playing though. I mean it Tel, not a centime."

"Got it!" reassured Terry once again. "But what will you be doing?"

In his best secretive voice, Buckley lent further forward and whispered into Terry's ear, "I shall be doing some reconnaissance."

"What are you going to reccy?" whispered Terry, in his best secretive voice that was more comical than clandestine.

Buckley pulled away quickly and sniggered his response, "The inside of a fanny with my bell-end!"

With that, Buckley laughed himself to his feet and flapped his hand several times at Terry to get him up and out of the room.

"Can I come?" asked Terry.

"Not anywhere near me I hope, you dirty bastard!" mocked Buckley, his compassion for Terry having now dissipated.

Terry began to laugh too but it wasn't long before Buckley had disappeared into the gaming room to leave a young man standing alone in a very narrow hallway laughing to himself and looking decidedly moronic. Buckley casually observed the gaming room, the added plaster relief to the white-washed ceiling, the Louis XIV replica mirrors, the cheap chandeliers and the even cheaper clientèle. He made his way over to the roulette game and from the back of a small crowd he peered over their heads onto the layout. It was number twenty-two and Buckley rolled his eyes in a fake show of frustration, as though he had lost either by way of playing another number or not betting at all. He added a few huffs and puffs for effect but then, quite unexpectedly, he felt the desperate need to skin up a joint so he could get his head straight. He knew he had to concentrate because this was business, they were businessmen and things had to be serious otherwise it would be the walk of shame back onto the casino floor in London with peers lambasting them for being utter failures. Buckley moved up towards the head of the table where the Chef d'Table sat in dominance over a slow moving game. Buckley looked at the wheel, appearing to mentally question the winning number, tutting and shaking his head to further act out his covert role. Terry stood at the back of the room admiring the intricate patterns in the wallpaper, the deep reds and gold which formed intricate, flowery forms that if scratched with a fingernail, would bleed and leave a stain on the skin. Terry scratched at the wallpaper then looked at his finger in amazement as the cheap print left an indelible stain on his finger. Buckley, meanwhile, got a little closer to the roulette wheel and looked down onto the wooden rim; following the circumference with his eyes he tried to pick out any familiar marks or shapes. He thought he recognised a couple of patterns in the wood then, practically jumping out to assault his eyeballs, a raven black swirl, almost spherical in shape, hailed him like a biblical revelation. He turned to find Terry, searching the room with excited eyes, only to find a skinny runt looking closely at his hand and sniffing at his own finger. Instinctively, Terry looked up and Buckley gave the agreed nod. Terry spoke quietly in return, mouthing his words in an exaggerated, slow motion drawl.

"The...fucking...wallpaper... comes... off... on... your... hand!"
Buckley gritted his teeth, frustration now exacerbated by the fact that he really needed a joint but couldn't have one. His eyes informed Terry that he was a useless, mindless, half-witted, numb-skull of a cunny hole. Terry received the look and interpreted it as, 'Wow! mate. That's amazing.'
Buckley over-exaggerated his nod. Terry over-exaggerated a nod in return and then added a thumbs up to confirm that the message had been received and understood. Terry turned on his heels and left the gaming room to find solace between the legs of an experienced but inexpensive prostitute.

His heart pumping and sweat sitting heavy on his skin, adrenalin searing through his veins, muscles aching and sleep beckoning, Terry was feeling the effects of several small beers and the concentration that required him to note down all the numbers without being too obvious. It made him feel like he was about to keel over and die, ashen white and feeling decidedly giddy, he turned to look behind him as a hand pressed firmly upon his left shoulder.

"You alright mate?" asked a concerned Buckley.

"I need to go," slurred Terry, "I feel like shit, let's go home."

Buckley tipped the contents of a small, ornate glass down the back of his throat then cheerily sprayed some comforting words at Terry.

"Right you are spunky, me lad. We've done enough for one night. It's showing the bias, right?"

"Yeah, I think so," confirmed Terry.

"Tomorrow night then, we'll kick off the action with some serious play. It's all there boy, all there for the taking. This is our chance Tel, our time, our moment. C'mon, let's get you to beddy-bye's."

"Yeah, right," confirmed Terry, a pounding in his head now distracting him from any plan whatsoever or even asking Buckley about his time with the prostitute.

"I'm fucked Buckley, really fucked."

"And I, my little sausage-jockey, have been...well and truly!" announced Buckley with boyish glee.

Out in the street, to shouts of annoyance from an abnormally well-defined gorilla of a doorman, Terry spewed the contents of his stomach onto the smooth, slightly damp cobblestones of Avenue de la Violette. Buckley walked ahead, relieved of all physical and mental stress, he disassociated himself from the person projectile-vomiting behind him.

It was late morning when Buckley awoke and went downstairs to order some croissants from Ms Sharpe, a widower from South London who was now running a bed and breakfast two streets away from the Le KKK.

"It's a bit late! Breakfast finishes at 9.30," she explained indignantly.

Buckley worked his charm and with good looks to match, it yanked hard at Ms Sharpe's maternal heart-strings - how could she resist those puppy-dog, emerald green eyes and that athletic physique.

"I'll do you a baguette and some cheese, how about that?" she offered.

"That'll do very nicely," accepted Buckley, before returning to his twin suite to find Terry standing in his underpants in the middle of the room.

"I've been thinking, Buckley," began Terry.

"Oh dear!" sighed Buckley.

"I reckon we ought to at least see the sights while we're here."

"Too right me old chum, we'll take in some tourist stuff after breakfast."

"Brilliant," chirped a hungry Terry, "What we got to eat?"

"We? We haven't got anything," scoffed Buckley. *I* however, have some bread and cheese coming. *You,* matey-me-boy, have bugger all because *you,* didn't order anything, did *you?*" Buckley over-emphasised the 'I' and 'you' to reinforce his assumed dominance. "Breakfast finishes at 9.30 you wally!"

"Thanks for that *mate*," mumbled Terry, resigned to his fate and rumblings of hunger. He over-emphasised the word '*mate*' to instil some guilt in Buckley but it failed to have any effect.

Ms Sharpe, the perfect B&B host if there ever was one, delivered the late breakfast to their room. Always in hope, a guilty pleasure of Ms Sharpe's was to try and catch young men boarding with her in various states of undress. On this occasion, she hoped to see Buckley and Terry, individually or jointly, in some state of partial nudity, or even full nudity if it was time for God to prove his existence and answer one of her prayers. Ms Sharpe took her pleasures where and when she could find them and if that meant a quick glimpse of some naked boy in his room, or better still on the toilet, then she would gratefully accept whatever came her way. Simple observation became the foundation on which she built her fantasies and dreams that would act as a diversion from those jaded memories of marriage and her monotonous, daily routines. Wild imaginings would inject some excitement into her life where she could be carried away by erotic thoughts of being ravaged, taken from behind and filled to absolute capacity.

"There you are, boys... Oops! Should've knocked first. Sorry!" sniggered Ms Sharpe.

It was a very brief and unconvincing display of shocked surprise as the bread, cheese and pickles were delivered into the room. Terry, without discomposure, took the tray from Ms Sharpe whilst still in his underpants. It wasn't any different to his mum bringing in breakfast, or so he thought. Anyway, Ms Sharpe was about the same age as his mum so why should he feel shy or embarrassed. Ms Sharpe's fifty-five year old eyes strayed to focus upon Terry's puny body which, proportionately, made the bulge in his underpants seem a lot more ample than it really was, an optical illusion if ever there was one. She drew her top lip across her bottom dentures to feel sharp pain and the resultant pleasure on her sensitive flesh, a precursor to what she had set her mind on.

"She fucking fancies you!" taunted Buckley, after Ms Sharpe had left the room. "Tel, you can have her if you want. Give her a large portion!

Terry passed the breakfast tray to Buckley and considered the prospect of shagging a woman who wasn't too dissimilar to his own mother. He felt a twinge, somewhere in the region above his knees but below his scrawny chest, that signalled he would probably chance it later.

"Oh fuck off Buckley," he countered, with genuine bashfulness.

It was later in the afternoon that Terry found himself in the unenviable position of gagging on a lengthy tuft of Ms Sharpe's pubic hair, where a piece of dried debris had become curiously entangled. It was a clear cut case of either extracting the hair directly from the host or vomiting. Whatever the outcome, something needed to be done and fairly sharpish at that. A shrill of painful delight left Ms Sharpe's lips as Terry snatched, by their roots, a number of greying, curly hairs with his teeth, then swallowed hard to remove the offending contents from his mouth. After the event, which surprisingly had left both parties completely satisfied, they found themselves affectionately in each other's arms. Ms Sharpe recounted an incident that had taken place the night before; apparently, there had been some trouble at Le Kitty Kat Klub, a few streets away. There had been some shouting and screaming late at night and then, gun shots had been heard and there were sirens and gendarmerie all over the place. Madame Guillard had told her about it that morning in the Boulangerie. Terry felt a panic rise in his shrivelled scrotal sack and knew he should deliver this ominous news to Buckley as soon as possible. He also knew that he could not drag himself away from the effort he was making in trying to extract some milk from Ms Sharpe's right nipple, but no matter how hard he sucked, nothing would come - but Ms Sharpe quietly did.

Late in the afternoon, lethargy abated by a relaxing siesta, the town came alive so Buckley and Terry made their way down to Le Kitty Kat Klub to see what had occurred the previous night.

"I bet it's your fault," said Buckley in an accusatory tone.

"How can it be my fault?" Terry answered defensively.

"You, throwing up all over the place. The area has probably been shut down, quarantined, no one in or out, everything contaminated. What d'you go and do that for, hurling all over the show?"

"Oh, thanks for the empathy," snarled Terry through gritted teeth.

"Sympathy, you twat. S...Y...M...P...A...T...H...Y!"

Buckley spelt out the word slowly to further display his deep displeasure at having to do all of this, having to worry about absolutely everything and on top of it all, having to listen to the sordid details of Terry's encounter with Ms Sharpe's prolapsed labia minor. Buckley felt agitated by the uncontrollable urge to constantly scratch his crotch. Buckley needed to smoke a joint, and soon.

The brown, panelled front door with ornate, ironwork filigree stood before Buckley and Terry like a chequered winner's flag. They had arrived and it was obvious their race was over. They felt uncertain about how they should feel; they felt uncertain about feeling uncertain and subsequently struggled to make any sense of what was going on. It felt like they had taken part in some sort of chase, a chase in which they were now the confused participants who had just crossed the finish line but nobody could determine if anyone had actually won. They both stared at a printed piece of paper with writing on it that neither of them could understand. Atop the text was a printed picture, in blue, of an old building with something that looked like a large chain wrapped around it. Terry recognised a small shape below the picture as being the same as the club's wallpaper – a Fleur du Lys.

"Christ Almighty!" cried Terry, "It's in bloody French!" Somehow he felt the need to validate his outburst with more exclamations of surprise, despair and discovery. "It's all foreign and official. Fucking hell!"

Buckley spoke, "Could be worse. It could be Spanish!"

Neither Buckley nor Terry could tell if the jumbled letters with odd markings were French, German, Spanish or Gobbledy-Gook – suffice to say, neither could comprehend any of what was written on the notice that was firmly pinned to the front door of the Le KKK.

"Ask that bloke over there," ordered Buckley, pointing to the first person he could see walking close by.

Terry dutifully walked over to the smart gentleman in a pink polo shirt and cream slacks with deck shoes on bare feet; under his arm he caressed a bundle of baguettes and smoked a

Gauloise cigarette.

"Pardoney me!" stated Terry in his best French accent. Voose speakio Englisho? Sift ooh plates."

The soft, southern French accent of a well-bred, well to do monsieur, answered Terry in perfect English by requesting that he speak normally. Doing as he was asked, as he always did, Terry explained the situation and politely asked if the notice pinned to the door of Le Kitty Kat Klub could be translated for them. After slipping them both a disapproving look, the notice was read out in French with an immediate, but indirect, translation.

"It says that the club has been closed down by order of the municipality. Any enquiries to the Director General of the Gendarmerie."

Monsieur stabbed his finger at a signature at the bottom of the notice to conclude his service.

"Is that all?" queried an unfulfilled, expectant Buckley.

"Oui!"

With sinking hearts, Buckley and Terry simultaneously extended their thanks to their aide, with an apology for any inconvenience caused. Both were shot further, disapproving looks as the translator walked away, expensive boat shoes flapping at the heel as they slipped on and off his smooth, well-tended feet. Terry watched intently as one of the baguettes he carried desperately tried to escape from the bag it was in, slowly boring a hole with friction of crust upon paper.

"Fuck it!" muttered Buckley.

"Fuck it all! Shall we go home Buckley?" suggested Terry.

"I guess so Tel. Fucking disaster, start to finish mate."

Tucked into the corner of their little room in Ms Sharpe's B&B, Terry sat listening to a song wafting in on the evening breeze. It was in French but he had heard it somewhere before, a long time ago, maybe on holiday or at his Nan's. He recognised the chorus as it rose and fell according to the fine net curtains that billowed as they hung from wooden poles above long, narrow windows. He managed to pick out some lyrics and began to sign along with it in his head, the recording repeating itself over and over again as an old record player picked out the scratches of vintage vinyl.

'Non, Je ne regrette rien...'

Buckley laid on his side, listening to Edith Piaf once more, the needle having been placed into the first chorus groove yet again.

"I love this song," said Ms Sharpe, as she climbed back into her small, double bed.

Pulling Buckley's naked body towards her, she held the back of his head and gently guided his mouth towards her left breast so he might suckle and sleep.

It was early morning the next day when Buckley called for Terry to hurry up. Bags hastily packed, suitcase wheels wildly tracking the paths of smooth, cobble stone joints, the journey home was under way and it would take them past Le Kitty Kat Klub for one last look at what might have been. From the end of the Avenue they turned to look at the club but feared to venture down the corridor of buildings that mocked their ineptitude and misfortune. A large lorry was parked outside the building and standing at its rear was a portly chap inspecting his hand, a finger of which appeared to be bulging with a white bandage. A sharp noise drew his attention so he turned towards the door of the club to direct three young men in green aprons as they manhandled a roulette wheel into the rear of their van. With scant regard for the peace of the neighbourhood, the shutter was yanked shut with a machine-gun, ratchet clicking, rat-a-tat-tat, followed by a reverberating crash as the shutter's metal bar met the van's metal frame. Then the whole affair drove away disappearing into an adjacent street. Buckley felt despair, more so than Terry but then again, Terry suffered in so many other ways. Looking lost and forlorn in the doorway of the Le KKK was the stately figure of Monsieur Blanc. Buckley held up his right hand by way of acknowledgment then tugged on Terry's arm as they made their way towards him, the rattle of plastic wheels fracturing the still, morning air.

"Bonjour!" said Monsieur Blanc, a slight hint of dejection in his tone but nevertheless remaining courteous and polite.

"Hello," said Buckley. "What's going on?"

"We 'av' been clos-ed down," explained Monsieur Blanc. "Maybe we did not pay enough atten-she-on to de-tail? Maybe we just did not pay enough!? C'est pas grave."

"What about the wheel, the roulette wheel?" Buckley enquired enthusiastically.

"It is gone. I sold it to my busi-ness friend Henri, he has a litt-le place in Oostende."

"Oostende in Belgium?" asked Terry, surprising Buckley with his knowledge of geography.

"Indeed. Henri has a litt-le place in Kegelpad. It is a street in the town if you know it?"

"We don't," answered Buckley. "Not yet anyway!"

Buckley turned to Terry, again pulling at his arm.

"Come on Tel, we're off to Belgium!"

***

"It's a lot like France really," was Terry's critical analysis of Belgium.

Both had made the long journey on the TGV overnight train where they had shared a sleeper cabin with four others. Their lack of sleep resulted in the two of them staggering around the coastal town of Oostende, bleary eyed and a lot worse for wear, they looked for somewhere to stay and tried very hard to forget their recent travel experience. Buckley had managed to get hold of some marijuana, good quality gear it seemed, which was readily available and could easily be procured just by asking any of the men that loitered in shop doorways or on street corners. Sitting on the promenade, watching the ferries queue up to enter the port, Buckley smoked himself into a happy zone and a clear revelation materialised as to what they should do next.

"Tel, my best mate, best buddy in the whole, wide world, ever."

"Yep!"

"Get us an ice-cream while I plan something."

"I've only got French funny money on me," said Terry reluctantly.

"No matter mate, they'll take that here, it's all the same."

At a booth nearby, Terry was relieved of several cash notes, overpaying by many times what the value of two dollops of bacteria laced ice-cream should have cost.

Buckley's only thanks came in the form of an observation. "These cones aren't like ours Tel,' he said. "They're too thick and kind of quilted. Bugger to bite into!"

Terry lapped furiously at the vanilla dome that sat proudly on the rim of his waffle cone, then Buckley flicked at the dollop with a grubby finger to launch Terry's ice-cream into the air, whereupon it landed with a splat on the pavement. Buckley laughed the uncontrollable laugh of a hash-head who would not, or could not, explain exactly why he thought it was all so funny. Terry starred at the splodge of ice-cream at his feet; slowly melting, it looked like a suicide case as vanilla gloop seeped from an icy head wound. Terry starred at it some more, as though he were willing it by the power of his mind to reform and jump back onto the crispy, cone shaped pastry. Buckley continued to laugh maniacally without care or reason, wild, childish, irrational and intoxicating hilarity. Terry nibbled on his headless cone, still starring at the melted mess on the floor. In those few moments Terry began to formulate his revenge.

The small hotel that had agreed to take two men in the same room was cheap, cheerful and conveniently midway between the market square and the seaside cornice, it felt pleasant and safe. The owner, a Monsieur Gaston, had two sisters who shared the ownership and running of the hotel. He also had a resident niece who was no more than twelve or thirteen years old but looked significantly older. To Buckley, she certainly looked significantly older but to Terry, he thought she looked just about old enough.

To make sure they got to the right place where they might find the wheel, as directed by Monsieur Blanc, they took a taxi giving written directions in English and Flemish, which had been prepared for them by Monsieur Gaston: *Lotuslaan, right into Bikkelpad, across road and 1ˢᵗ left into Kegelpad.* It seemed simple enough but after an hour of touring the streets in a vehicle hailed from the roadside, Buckley had doubts about the cab driver's honesty and integrity. There was nothing for it, he would hand over the fare paying responsibilities to Terry, after all, he considered, Tel was more of a people person than he was. Arriving in Kegelpad, Terry bade a fond farewell to more of his cash, paying a little over ten times what it would have cost someone with local knowledge to take the journey. In his ignorance, Terry just believed that Europe was an expensive place and Buckley was just plain ignorant of the facts. What was before them could well have been the exact twin of Le Kitty Kat Klub. Affixed to a three storied building with plain white stucco exterior walls was an unlit neon sign that read, 'Whisky-A–Go-Go.' In a glass cabinet, affixed to the wall next to a panelled, wooden front door, was a notice with a picture of a roulette table. Neither Buckley nor Terry could read the words but the picture was as plain as day - roulette was now being offered nightly and this was the place they would find their wheel. It was time, at last, to start making those elusive dreams come true with big money, big living and big boobs on big, beautiful babes, or so thought Buckley. Opening hours appeared to be '20:00 heures,' as was written, so they turned to take the same taxi back to their hotel only to find that it had already left. A twenty minute walk at a gentle pace returned them to their hotel and this was confirmation that their taxi driver had ripped them off. By way of consolation, they retired to a nearby bar to eat, drink and oust their humiliation.

It was almost 11pm when Buckley and Terry staggered up to the open door of the 'Whisky-A-Go-Go.' Both stood unsteady on their feet as two rounded figures in dark suits with black ties eyed them up. After some awkward stares from both sides, Buckley decided to demonstrate his assertive nature and lowered his head for an insistent, but gentle, barge towards the door. Terry stood quite still, awaiting the outcome. It was only four steps before Buckley felt the steel like barrier of a forearm preventing his way forward. If anyone had been close enough, they would have heard a pitiful, 'Ouch!' but would not have been able to determine from whence it came.

Buckley looked up to see two, pale blue eyes staring back at him. The face that housed the pale blue eyes shook slowly from side to side.

"Drunk!" said the mouth in the face that contained the pale blue eyes. "Go away!" the mouth ordered.

Buckley knew better than to argue. He had seen the

consequence of drunks trying to get into a night club back home. He had once witnessed two bouncers eject a drunk from the 'The Sweet Bar', as it was called back then, and the drunk got a darn good pasting outside in the street. With a dip of the head and a twist to the left, Buckley was now staring at Terry and Terry stood motionless, arms dangling by his side with a perplexed look on his face. "WELL!" shouted Buckley.

"Well what!?" shouted back Terry.

"Well, fucking do something, Tel!"

"Like what, Buckers!"

Buckley turned and drew himself up to his full height, puffed out his chest and held his arms straight out from his sides, face on to Terry now, his open palms displaying twitchy fingers that sent menacing signals.

"I told you not to call me that, you cunt!"

"I'm not a cunt. You're a..." Terry hesitated, unsure whether he should proceed or not. What the hell, he thought, "...CUNT! YOU'RE A CUNT, BUCK...ERS!"

As a prelude to what was about to happen, Buckley looked over his shoulder, to his left and then to his right, searching the doormen's faces for signs of approval for the ensuing violence he was about to initiate. Buckley walked towards Terry with purposeful strides and nodding his head as affirmation of the violent intention, he prepared the knuckles that would plant themselves into Terry's facial features. Terry stood his ground as the two doormen looked on with excited anticipation.

"Come on then!" screamed Terry, rage filling his insufficient body as he pulled back his right arm to display a tightly clenched fist poised at the end of it.

He blatantly showed Buckley what he could expect if he came any closer, in fact it was a little too obvious and overly melodramatic, like an old black and white movie punch-up between two comic characters engaged in fisty-cuffs over a waiting heroine. Buckley spotted the weakness in Terry for Terry was, he considered, basically weak and one punch would surely send him in to the middle of next week. Buckley's eyes carefully gauged Terry's right arm, waiting for the tell-tale twitch that would announce impending action. Suddenly, there was a crack and then a sickening thud as Buckley fell to the floor, a searing pain in his neck as his head twisted forcefully and unnaturally to one side. Terry's left hand, it's journey complete, rested by his right shoulder – a sucker punch and one which Buckley just did not see coming. Had either been sober, both would have seen the other's intentions but for these two drunken Brits abroad, it was an entertaining interlude for the doormen who could not resist the temptation to point and laugh at Buckley's demise. Terry felt quite proud of himself and he revelled in this brief moment of triumph, appreciating the accolade of two thumbs up from amused doormen sporting wide grins. This one chance to be one up on Buckley, this one moment of respite from ridicule, this one moment of victory, it would all be so very short lived. For an instance thereafter, for just a brief moment in time, everything appeared to run in ultra-slow motion and a deathly silence prevailed. Then, just as briefly, the world seemed to be in super-fast motion to quickly catch up to itself; a cacophony of noise assaulted the senses and Terry found himself reaching down to help Buckley as he rose to his feet feeling for the damage to his striking features. There was no blood and no swelling, that was clearly apparent, however there was a long smear of green mucous across Buckley's right cheek.

"Is that snot on your face?" asked Terry.

"Shut up, Tel. Let's get back to the hotel before I kick someone's teeth in," snivelled Buckley.

Buckley wiped his face with the back of his hand, checking for blood as he did so.

"Sorry about that," whined Terry, with more sincerity than the situation required.

"It's alright mate," assured Buckley, "I probably deserved it anyway. Nice left hook. Didn't see that one coming."

"Sorry Buckley," apologised Terry once more.

The two sorry states staggered off to find a taxi and as they took yet another unnecessary and unessential journey through the streets of Oostend, they concocted a plan to jointly give the hotel owner's niece the best time of her life.

Dreams had come thick and fast in that testosterone fuelled atmosphere but come the morning, Buckley and Terry remembered very little of the facts, other than there had been a disagreement between the two of them and they had been refused entry into the 'Whisky-A-Go-Go.'

"It's our own fault," admitted Buckley. "We got too drunk and no one will let a drunk into their club. Not a British drunk anyway. You know Tel, us Brits are renowned for our drinking and hell-raising?"

"Are we?" said a very hung-over Terry.

"Yeah mate. Ibiza, Aya Napa, Magaluf, popping pills, foam parties, shagging, wild shit and stuff."

"You done all that then?"

"Well, not really. But some mates of mine have and they say it's amazing and it's always the Brits that are the craziest ones and everyone envies us Brits and we're like kings wherever we go," explained Buckley.

"That's nice," Terry managed, before burying his head under a pillow that provided very little comfort but provided excellent sound-proofing. Buckley agreed with a silent nod and suggested a revised plan to an oblivious Terry - they would get dressed up smart, stay sober and revisit the club that evening with an apology for their behaviour then, once inside, they would adopt the same protocol as before. They would act appropriately, survey the premises, identify the wheel and get some serious bets down. Without any objection from an unresponsive Terry, Buckley took the silence as confirmation of his good idea and he lay back down in order for some headache tablets to take effect. Two tablets remained on his bedside cabinet next to a small bottle of water as Buckley lay on his bed wondering why the tablets weren't working. Terry, head buried deep under foam and cotton, barely able to breathe, sucked on two Aspirin and recalled a time, not so long ago, when he was certain that he had tasted the sweetness of a mother's breast milk. It was salty, slightly sweaty and barely noticeable by volume, but he was sure that he had tasted Mother Nature's Nectar. What else could it have been? You suck on a tit, you get milk, right? He pondered the idea as he drifted into a disturbed sleep.

It appeared, at first, to be a classic standoff. Just as darkness was ushering the last vestiges of twilight into oblivion, Buckley and Terry faced the same two doormen outside the 'Whisky-A-Go-Go.' This time, sobriety would see them through, or so they thought. Unfortunately, this time, sobriety counted for nothing and the two, well dressed, rotund men of shallow personality and even shallower patience, closed ranks to prevent entry.

"Oh come on guys!" begged Buckley.

"You gotta be kidding!" added Terry.

"Guys, Guys, come on now. Look at us, we're respectable gentlemen. We're British," pleaded Buckley.

"We know!" stated one of the plump persons preventing their passage.

"British always trouble," chipped in the other portly one immediately afterwards.

"You not come in now or never. No trouble with British here," informed the first.

"Goodbye!" bade the second.

Both corpulent carriers of extra weight waved an over-animated farewell and Buckley knew better than to argue. A sudden pang of pain about his face reminded Buckley of the previous night's furore and he looked at Terry who was now walking towards the door with a clenched, right fist.

"Whoa!" cried Buckley. "Easy Terry tiger," he added, grabbing both Terry's shoulders from behind.

It didn't take too much to convince Terry of the grave error he was about to make so, yet another taxi ride was made back to the hotel. Terry thought he recognised the driver from their very first ride and now fired up from the night club stand-off, he thought he would instigate a confrontation.

"You're the one who ripped us off a few days ago, aren't you?"

spat an accusatory Terry.

Buckley sat in silence to await the rebuttal. Either the driver did not understand what was being put to him or he was staying guiltily silent. Terry looked at Buckley and Buckley shrugged his shoulders with bewilderment.

"I'm talking to you, you cunt!" vexed Terry.

Buckley's face distorted as though he had heard something unsavoury, which indeed he had. Still the driver remained silent, his eyes fixed on the narrow streets ahead before briefly driving along a motorway then ending up in another dark, narrow street. At the end of the street, the driver braked so sharply that Terry slipped forward off the plastic sheeting that covered the back seat and knocked his head on the pillar of the car door.

"Fucking hell!" he scolded. "What you fuckin..."

The driver turned and leaned over the back of the front passenger seat, which made Buckley flinch as he had, of late, become a little nervous of unexpected movements. The rear door was flung wide open.

"Go! Go now," spluttered the driver.

Outside, there was a blaze of headlights as a large number of taxis sat idling their engines in a square of abandoned buildings.

"Christ! It's a taxi gang!" was Terry's instant explanation.

"It's just their meeting place by the looks of it – we best go," reassured Buckley, in a sensible, non-confrontational tone.

An outstretched hand that was heavily creased but spotlessly clean was accompanied by a menacing demand.

"Hundred Francs!" growled the taxi driver.

Buckley handed over two notes then grabbed Terry by the arm to lead him away from the sounds of a yelling taxi driver who, rather surprisingly, appeared to be decrying the fact that he had not received a tip. It was all a very efficient, well organised, highly effective and an often employed tactic used by local taxi drivers who faced non-payment, abuse or threats of violence from their fares. Buckley and Terry had no alternative but to make their way home on foot. Five hours later, having walked at least twice the distance required, they crept into bed just as Monsieur Gaston's niece started to practice her trombone recital.

"Arghhhhh!" screamed Buckley.

With both arms, Terry secured his head deep beneath the comforting pillow and it immediately brought back soothing thoughts of Ms Sharpe and her motherly, sagging breasts.

For the following few weeks, with nothing to do and money beginning to run short, Buckley and Terry faced an uncertain future. They sniggered at the 'Manneken Pis' in Brussels, wondered what the 'Atomium' was all about, delighted at mini-Europe - where Buckley felt even taller than usual - they loved the 'Armed Forces and Military Museum,' wandered in and out of more cathedrals and churches than they would care to admit and generally got drunk and smoked far too many illegal substances. Buckley decided it was game over but they should have a last blow out in Amsterdam.

"Please, please. I'm begging you, please," insisted Terry.

"No!" barked Buckley. He was having none of it. "It's costing too much as it is. It's too expensive and we can't afford the time either."

"Please Buckley. I have to. I'll never ask for anything else again, please, please!"

"No!"

"Please, please, please, please... I won't stop saying please, please, please, until you say yes... please, please, please, please, ple..."

"Okay, okay!" surrendered Buckley.

"Ah! Thanks mate. Thank you, thank you, thank you, thank you, thank you thank y..."

"ENOUGH ALREADY!" screamed Buckley, losing his patience as well as his will to live.

With ice-creams in hand, Buckley and Terry waited patiently for the train to Brussels to see, once more, the Manneken Pis.

"Unbelievable, isn't it?" exhorted Terry.

"It's just a statue of a boy pissing, Tel, that's all."

***

It was another two weeks before Amsterdam beckoned on the horizon - a glowing icon of debauchery, fun and fulfilment. Buckley's dream had always been to make it to 'hash-head' heaven and Terry could barely contain his excitement at the thought of all the sexual gratification that was on offer. The journey had been eventful, hitch-hiking most of the way, they had been propositioned by people traffickers, drug dealers, several individuals whose gender could not be immediately determined and Terry had, on one occasion, engaged in a highly questionable act that had been orchestrated by Buckley whilst off his head on a cocktail of unidentified pills and powders. Fortunately, Terry had not really been aware of what was going on either and that was just as well because it had involved more than one protagonist. All that Terry knew was, it wasn't pleasant and it now hurt a lot when he went for a number two. He even told Buckley as much but Buckley seemed to be at a loss for any plausible explanation and was very reluctant to discuss the matter further. Buckley would always wonder if Terry might ever have that moment of epiphany, at some time in the future, when he would suddenly recall that his best friend was one of the people who took part in a very unnatural and defiling act.

Down at the bottom of the town, where the canals stop crisscrossing each other, where you can walk without coming across yet another thinly channelled stretch of water, where there is an expanse of greenery and open space in which to meander, there can be found a modern building which houses a very modern and legal casino. Sex could wait, thought Buckley, but a joint could not, nor a beer as it happened. In a bar that displayed a motorbike mounted on an interior wall, as well as a number of chapter badges from Hell's Angels, Buckley and Terry found themselves flicking through a menu of soft drugs and paraphernalia that was on offer from the bar. Buckley pointed to a picture labelled *'Sensimelia'* and having paid for it, as well as two lager beers, he offered Terry some advice.

"You've got to stand up for yourself mate. Stop letting people walk all over you. You need to be assertive, like me and stand up for yourself. It's the forthright positive insistence in the belief in one's own rights, mate. Stand up for what you believe in. Okay?"

"You're right Buckley," agreed Terry, the truth hitting home like a sneaky, unexpected slap across the face. "That's fucking brilliant," he continued, "How d'you know all that stuff?"

"I don't," replied Buckley, "I'm reading it off a sticker on the wall behind you, you sad muppet!"

Buckley laughed as the waiter delivered a small, clear plastic bag containing something green and organic. Two beers with large frothy heads were quickly followed by a small piece of paper with some handwritten figures.

Terry turned back from reading the sticker on the wall behind him.

"You got any Guilders?" asked Buckley.

"Fuck off!" replied Terry.

Buckley waved some Francs at the waiter who helped himself to what, both assumed, was probably the right amount for the price. At that particular moment in time, Buckley would have paid anything for what the small, translucent packet contained. Ramming the contents into the quickest joint he could assemble using some Rizla papers he found on the table, Buckley sucked long and hard as he lit the touch-paper, then practically collapsed as the immediate effects of the drug assaulted his brain's operating system. He held the table for support just as a leather-clad pseudo biker, standing close by, leant in to breathe garlic and tobacco into Buckley's face.

"Skunk mate!" the fusty, allium mouth interrupted. "You want to go steady with that stuff - it'll knock your socks off!"

The leathered and generally foul smelling, wannabe-motor biker dragged his hand from the table that supported him and helped himself to Buckley's stash, discretely palming the bag and contents into his pocket before briskly walking away. As soon as Buckley felt that his eyes had stopped rolling around in their sockets, he passed the funnel shaped joint to Terry who, during his exhalation, described the occurrence of theft that had just taken place. A moment of anger welled up in Buckley but he quickly accepted the shameful act by assuming that another's need was greater than his own and anyway, it was readily available so he'd just buy some more. Buckley looked into Terry's eyes and Terry looked back at Buckley wondering why he was looking at him. Buckley began to wonder why Terry kept staring at him and as Terry began to wonder why Buckley was giving him that look, the stare off began. Buckley eventually broke the pointless exercise with a drug inspired outburst.

"I love you Tel and if you want to, only saying mate because I really do love you, but don't take it the wrong way or anything, you can have me up the arse if you like?"

"Nah, you're alright mate," comforted Terry with an immediate refusal, but then considered it was perhaps worth bearing in mind for leaner times.

The joint now smoked right down into the cardboard roach, beers dispatched, the active ingredient tetrahydocannabinol doing its job admirably, led by adventurous instinct and spirit, both made their way out into the chilly night air to walk, hunched against a bitter wind, down towards the park and the casino.

Le Palais was a typical, continental casino, just as one might expect to see in a movie or on the television. Lavishly decorated and very stylish, it hosted a number of familiar games as well as some that were very local indeed. Feeling fairly competent and at home in such surroundings, Buckley and Terry parted company to wager on their favourite games, flicking and shuffling chips as they sat at their respective tables, obvious ex-employees of the industry, their intentions more recreational than professional however. Terry threw money down onto a table where a game was being played but it was one he could never hope to fathom. He enjoyed a winning streak as a Jack was drawn by the dealer but still he had no idea of what the game was all about. He knew not how or why but happily enjoyed himself nonetheless. Buckley was attempting to count cards on Blackjack but his system was not working too well. Every now and then he would win but it was just sheer luck that saw him through as skill never came into the equation. The hours rolled by and rarely did the two come across one another, neither knowing nor caring where the other was. During a break they momentarily met at the cocktail bar where they enjoyed a drink and talked as though they were two old friends who had not seen each other for many years. They boasted of their gambling prowess and the luck they were having. It was one of the few times that Terry felt happy and Buckley didn't feel the need to deride his loyal friend. By the end of the night, Buckley had recouped a large proportion of all the money he had spent and Terry had amassed a sizeable sum that he decided to keep a secret from Buckley. Unbeknownst to both, interested eyes followed them around the casino but their dreams of being professional gamblers meant they were not aware of the sexual opportunities that were openly genuine and abundant. The admiring eyes of middle-aged housewives, along with some daughters too, looked upon the tall, handsome winner who appeared to be without a female companion. A local man and his daughter followed Terry with their eyes but they merely wondered why this strange looking foreigner should have all the luck. Buckley and Terry resumed their acquaintance outside the casino and made their way to the red-light district where, having consumed a cone each of 'Frites 'a' Mayo,' they would ogle some prostitutes in the windows before bedtime.

During the meanderings, several girls tried to entice Buckley into their booths. Standing in the window of the tiniest rooms, they displayed their wares wrapped in neon bikinis or little more than a chiffon scarf to concealed their womanly wares. Terry felt an overwhelming urge to partake and as a slim, dark haired girl with almond eyes beckoned with a seductive forefinger, he felt himself inexplicably moving towards her. Buckley's finger pushed a little harder into Terry's back and as they broke contact, Terry turned to hand Buckley a large wad of folded Guilders. Buckley snatched at the banknotes and quickly secreted them into the front of his underpants before the prying eyes of many a North African spotted an opportunity.

During an intense moment of sexual embrace, when the prostitute appeared to be totally overcome with passion but was really acting out a well-rehearsed role, Terry allowed himself to be manipulated and manhandled until he was forced down onto his stomach in readiness for his money's worth. The damage that had already been done was clearly obvious to the transgender manipulator so, having some genuine sympathy for this particular customer's previous, painful experience, he/she decided to offer him a little hand relief with a courteous demand for some extra cash. None the wiser, Terry agreed and having duly handed over a ten Guilder note, watching as it was expertly folded and popped into a small, wooden box in front of a mirror, he delighted at the furious left hand that got to work with its masturbatory magic.

Outside, Buckley waited patiently and casually waved to the girls who beckoned for him to enter their parlours. With a large bulge in his trousers, Buckley guarded Terry's cash and considered how he might invest it on his friend's behalf. It was not too long before a flaying arm wrapped itself around Buckley's waist and a sinewy youth, full of excitement and relief, spoke without drawing breath to give a blow by blow account of his third ever, sexual experience.

"Good on ya!" exclaimed Buckley, happy now that his friend had been satisfied and he was in control of the wealth.

"Give us me money back," demanded Terry.

"Not here you wanker! These South Malaccans can smell cash a mile away and we'd get mugged before you could say... Banana Bar!"

"Do what?" quizzed Terry.

"Look, there's the Banana Bar. I've heard about that place. They do a show with girls who can fire things out of their fannies, like Ping-Pong balls and bananas and stuff. Come on, it'll be a giggle, let's go and have a look."

After two and a half hours of watching girls insert inconceivably large objects into their vaginas, as well as spitting table-tennis balls at each other from that very same orifice and then performing bombing raids of grapes into the mouths of prone volunteers, again from that most versatile of openings, it was more than enough for any man to bear so Buckley and Terry departed to walk the canal side route home and to take in some sights along the way. Buckley suddenly became excited by some video booths where, after inserting a Guilder coin, you could flick through a huge selection of sexual depravity and have it shown on the back of a private booth door while seated on a Formica seat. Buckley looked into a booth and asked Terry for a coin. Terry immediately obliged and stood behind Buckley in readiness. Terry looked at the mirror on the door and surmised that the video image was projected onto the wall first, and then reflected by the mirror.

"I've only got the one coin," confessed Terry. "I'll have to come in with you."

"You're fucking kidding, right? You fucking bender Tel!"

"Nah, come on. I'll watch the video on the wall and you can watch the one in the mirror," explained Terry.

"Seems like a plan, mate," replied Buckley, disconcertingly accepting of the suggestion.

Both surveyed the area before attempting an entry and looked decidedly shifty in the nonchalant repose that they adopted so as not to arouse suspicion. The coast, seemingly all-clear, allowed the two to squeeze into a booth designed for one and Buckley positioned himself on the continuously flowing Formica seat that morphed from wall to seat to floor. Buckley spread his legs wide so Terry could sit down opposite him on the floor, back pressed against the door with his knees drawn up to his chest.

"Here we go then," said an excited Buckley, as he dropped the silver coin into the insatiable slot.

Immediately, a hidden projector burst into illuminated life with what appeared to be a home video of some very young girls playing on a seaside beach. Buckley poked at a black, triangular button by the coin aperture and the video immediately switched to a movie showing several men engaged in what appeared to be a homosexual orgy of some description.

"Arghh! NO!" hollered Terry. "Queers! Next one, next one!"

"Shut up mate," reprimanded Buckley. "You'll get us thrown out."

Buckley jabbed his finger furiously at the well-worn forward button and the videos went into a montage of filth and depravity that was well worth one Guilder in itself, so Terry thought.

"Stop! Stop there... back a bit... forward... there, that's the one."

Terry settled back to watch a dusty looking brown skinned goat herder having sexual intercourse with his charge, a mountain goat by the looks of it, somewhere on the side of a hill in a faraway land.

"Ergh! Fucking hell! It's all wet down here," revealed Terry, as he wiped his palm across the smooth, seamless floor. Buckley's eyes were drawn to the box of cheap, paper tissues mounted onto a flimsy wire holder and he pointed with a directing finger to draw Terry's attention to it.

"IT'S SPUNK! SOMEONE'S JISSED IN HERE!! ARGHHH!!!"

Both jumped to their feet and fought each other to unbolt the door. Unfortunately, the door opened inwards and it needed some clever manoeuvring to safely exit from the tight confines of the single occupancy cubicle. Both pushed and shoved and as they did so, they rattled the dry-liner walls which shook the adjacent stalls. It sounded like a fight was in progress so when they finally managed to squeeze themselves from their immoral confinement, it was no surprise that a small crowd had gathered to see what all the commotion was about. Exiting a compartment specifically designed to accommodate one male masturbating over a mucky movie, there emerged two young men, one of whom had sperm spread across and dripping from the seat of his trousers and the other, who was shaking his fingers furiously trying to dislodge the sticky substance that clung like glue. Buckley pushed past an elderly gentleman who was busy with a mop and bucket in the doorway of another booth and Terry quickly followed after him, both shouting their horror and laughing uncontrollably as they did so.

Agreeing to never mention the incident, having wiped his arse on some grass like a dog with worms, Terry loaned Buckley his handkerchief to wipe his hands on. Buckley folded it and passed it back with thanks and Terry, without thinking, slid it back into his pocket. Sometime later, Terry would sneeze into the handkerchief then comment about the strange but familiar smell that he couldn't quite place. It was time to move on so, in the morning, they would make for home, back to Blighty, back to good old England and back to their mundane lives. Failure, previously not an option, was now the only option. Terry asked for his money back but Buckley promised to keep it safe until the morning.

"You can't trust these foreign sorts," he said, for Terry's continued reassurance.

***

The journey home would take them across the English Channel and back to London. Two, one-way tickets from the Hook of Holland to Harwich on the 'Prinses Beatrix' ferry was destined to be their last journey as professional gamblers. With a little less cash than they had started out with, Terry optimistically deemed it all to be as good as a free holiday whereas Buckley sank into despair and depression when reminded of all he had given up for the charade. Their last days in Amsterdam were spent rifling through sex shops, educating themselves for free about man's derisory intent towards women, children and other men. They bought souvenir postcards in the sex museum and made crude jokes about the animated bicycle with the model of the naked girl sat astride it. A soiled dildo, which had been handled too many times by tourists who had disregarded the sign which said, 'DO NOT TOUCH,' thrust upwards every time the pedals went round and round. On every revolution of the cog, a crank caused the rubber cock to disappear into the vaginal opening of the scantily dressed mannequin and she permanently smiled the smile of sexual bliss, or so the tourists were led to believe.

"Come on mate," ushered Buckley, as he tugged on Terry's arm. "Let's get the bus. We've got a boat to catch."

The ferry was a Ro-Ro, whereby traffic, goods and pedestrians making their way across the dreary waters that separated a thriving England from a destitute Europe, would literally roll-on and roll off the ship. The passenger lounge areas smelled of diesel oil, stale cigarettes, sex-starved lorry drivers and unhealthy food. Buckley and Terry wandered aimlessly through the lounges and at the far end of the throbbing, sluggish boat that hauled merchandise and souls back and forth across the English Channel, they came across a single roulette table that was being operated by a middle aged, suspicious looking man and a young, female dealer. The man was taking care of the money, pulling and pushing notes into and out of, what appeared to be, his personal wallet.

"Look at that Tel, fucking roulette if you please," said an excited Buckley.

They stood opposite the dealer who smiled at them. She was dumpy and it was difficult to discern where her breasts stopped and midriff started. She appeared to be a ball of a human being, perfectly rotund with legs and arms sticking out where it mattered. A proportionally small head sat on rounded shoulders and her pretty face, almost pure white with painted cheeks and bright red lipstick, was a beautiful feature only let down by the mass of her round frame. She wore a waistcoat of bright orange polyester that was badly frayed around the front edges and there were grease stains with an obvious hash-burn or two on the lower flaps. Her dexterity with gaming chips was amateur and anything too taxing in terms of calculating pay-outs was done by her dubious boss. Several spins were played by a lorry driver who sported a dirty, grease speckled baseball cap that had "MACK' emblazoned across the front of it in red and white embroidery. Sticking out from under the fabric that covered his oily head were straggly bits of reedy hair. Under the weight of scalp oil, fine strands had stuck together to form pointed barbs where droplets of lubricant hung precariously, threatening to drip but never actually doing so. Buckley stepped back from the trucker whose smell was decidedly obnoxious yet curiously hypnotic. As he took small, shuffling steps to withdraw from the abhorrent player, Buckley sniffed a little harder, a little more intensely, to try and identify the smell, that familiar smell, that aroma that was emanating from the driver, a smell he thought he recognised. Terry watched Buckley's animated sniffing and joined in too, although he was not quite sure why he was doing so, he just didn't like the idea of being left out.

"Mmmmm!" announced Terry in satisfaction, as though he were receiving the first wafts of a delicious, traditional Sunday roast lunch. "Ms Sharpe," he identified, "That's Ms Sharpe's perfume that is."

"What?" Buckley nervously questioned.

"Ms Sharpe's perfume," answered Terry. "I'd recognise it anywhere. It's called Lotus Love. I saw it in her bedroom. When she went to the bathroom I put a dab of it on my knob, to sweeten it up like. It stung like a fucking hornet I can tell you. Definitely, Lotus Love. I'll never forget that smell, I can still feel the pain right now."

"Oh fucking hell!" spluttered Buckley. "The dirty whore! Just think of all that trucker porridge we must have been stirring. Urghhh!"

The slime ball that drove trucks for a living, delivering items throughout France and Belgium before returning to the U.K., making a little extra money by smuggling loose tobacco and cigarettes and finding sexual satisfaction wherever he could, eventually moved away from the roulette table grumbling about the game being crooked.

"Thank you, Sir," called the orbicular dealer after him.

Buckley's, thoughts, still ricocheting around his head, about the unsavoury delights of one-night stands and middle-aged women hoteliers, moved towards the roulette wheel to look for the last winning number. A small swirl of onyx black immediately drew Buckley's eye onto the rim of the roulette wheel as the large swirl of an overweight dealer found his ear.

"Hello Sir," the spheroid squeaked. "Like to play?"

Like a billowing black flag on a wave of white cotton, Buckley could see the mark as clear as day, even under the appalling light of flickering fluorescent strips - it was the mark of *their* biased roulette wheel.

Without any word of warning, without any confirmation or discussion, Terry watched in horror as Buckley dumped all of Terry's money onto the roulette table. The owner, or possibly just a supervisor, snatched up the wad and counted it briskly before holding up five fingers as a signal to the girl. She pushed over 200 black chips at twenty-five pounds each and Buckley shone in his refusal to accept them.

"Give me grands," he ordered, with the authority of someone who wanted to appear wealthy but clearly wasn't. "I want a grand on a number as well," he demanded.

Without hesitation, the man who could, did. "You got it fella," he confirmed.

"Fucking hell, Buckley!" interrupted Terry. "What you doing?"

Without answering him, Buckley watched as the dealer picked up the ball to spin. A small crowd of hopefuls, thieves and scroungers began to form on the peripheries to marvel at the spectacle that was about to unfold.

"Buckley! What you doing man? That's my money."

The ball was in the initial phase of its spin, hurtling around the ball track, rattling loudly as the ship pitched on a heavy swell.

"It's our wheel Tel. It's the one. This is it. I'm going for it mate. No more missed opportunities, no more fuck-ups. Okay?"

Barely waiting for approval, Buckley laid out the five chips on the splits of 5/8, 10/11, 13/16, 23/24, 27/30 and...

Buckley looked into his empty palm as the ball began its decent onto the metal number dividers that immediately sent the ball clacking and cracking back up onto the track before depositing it unceremoniously, and with some considerable force, into a Tier number.

"Thirty–six, red, even," announced an apologetic dealer, who began to back away from the table in anticipation of Buckley venting his spleen.

Buckley stood motionless, still looking at his empty hand and wondering why, wondering how, as a professional gambler, with all his experience, knowledge of the game, the industry and everything else, with all his training and understanding, his skill and expertise, how on earth – how in the name of Neptune, could he have got it so wrong? He had bought only five chips for a six piece bet and was now paying the price for it. A £5000 price, to be exact.

In his role as owner/supervisor/bouncer and sympathetic shoulder to cry on, the man piped up.

"Oh! Tough luck Johnny. Have another go?" he sang.

Buckley felt he was being ridiculed and not wishing to lose face, he reached into his pocket to throw all the Guilders, Francs and some odd Greek and German notes that he had acquired along the way, onto the gaming table. Nimble fingers tapped furiously at a wristwatch calculator before the man signalled to the girl with a flash of five fingers, twice in quick succession. A sizeable crowd had gathered as ten, almost fluorescent, green chips were placed onto the table in front of Buckley. In his left ear, a whimpering Terry tried to talk him out of the madness, tried to get him to reconsider, tried to put a stop to the play, tried to make him see sense, but it was all in vain.

Buckley's look of authority demanded the girl spin the ball and she looked nervous enough to believe that if Buckley won, then her boss would no doubt retaliate upon that rolling expanse of youthful blubber she called her body. She laid down her hand to rest it on the inside of the wheel, the inside edge of her right hand pressing hard onto the inlaid wooden bowl next to the ball track. The ball, held between a sweaty thumb and middle finger, slipped slightly and as she went to snap her stubby fingers together in order to release the ball at high velocity, nerves got the better of her and the snap became a click that sent the ball into a vertical trajectory high above the table. Like a juggler performing a daring feat with fiery blades, the onlookers looked up at the spectacle. Buckley remained stalwart in his composure to continue and watch an empty wheel spinning, much as he thought a professional gambler might do. Terry was stalwart in his lachrymose composure and he continued to plead with Buckley, whimpering and tearful, as a professional gambler should not do. Everybody watched as the ball, reaching its maximum height, finally gave into gravity's inevitable pull and as it fell back down, Buckley began to wonder whether it was too late to back out.

"NO SPIN!" screamed a voice from somewhere behind the table, probably that of the dealer but it could well have been that of an excited man.

A sharp tap, surprisingly painful, caught Buckley just above his forehead hairline where the ball renewed its contact with earthly objects. It bounced onto the roulette table coming to rest just above the zero/three line, but decidedly on zero. Buckley considered this a sign, an omen, a message from the gods; it was fate sending a positive signal, destiny was reaching out and lady luck was sucking him in.

"Sorry 'bout that," squirmed the doughnut shaped dealer as

she positioned herself to spin once again.

Buckley eyed the man who appeared to be suppressing laughter and where Buckley may have reconsidered his options and thought better of the risk, he now felt the mocking sneer of the supervisor, the sarcasm of the dealer and the contemptuous stench of the throng as they gawped with jealous curiosity. It had come down to a show of strength, a demonstration of will and character. Buckley laid down his chips covering the Tier numbers, all the Tier numbers, as evenly as he could, then slid one solitary chip up onto zero. Spectators of a tennis game could not have matched the synchronicity of the crowd as they switched their gaze, swivelling their heads from wheel to layout and back again. Like a single entity they starred and collectively willed the tall, handsome Englishman with stunning green eyes, to lose. The shortness of the spin was not very sportsman like and the ball avoided the metal deflectors altogether as it fell straight into zero without a fuss. There was a moment of instant elation but then the ball popped out again due to the ferocious speed of the wheel. The man shot the dealer a reprimanding look but it was wasted as she had her eyes firmly fixed onto the wheel, trying to focus on the rattling ball amid the mesmerizing blur of red and black that spun before her eyes. The ball skipped, bobbed, rattled and rolled and Buckley's heart thumped hard in his chest. Terry could not bear to look and turned away to hide his tears, his fears and his anger.

After several, coronary inducing seconds, the ball finally bounced its last bounce, pinged its last ping and dinked its last donk between the metal separators that defined one number from the next. There were some gasps of delight and a cheer from someone close by.

"YES! YES! YES!

But the triumphant cry that rang out loud, clear and victorious, was not that of a friendly soul.

"Fucking yes!" was the hasty, conquering follow-up.

Terry spun round to look at Buckley who was standing very still. The owner, now standing at the head of the table, clenched his fist and shook it in front of his chest with uncontrollable exhilaration.

"Get in you fucking beauty!" he cried, just before the dealer made her announcement.

"Four… black… even," she broadcast, with a quivering voice.

Buckley looked at the man with distrust and tried to think of something accusatory to say, to justify the loss, to command respect.

"You're so unprofessional," was all that he could manage and he walked away, dragging Terry by the arm.

"I was trying to tell you," said Terry, wiping the wetness from his nose and eyes in one flustering, swipe of the hand. "How can the bias work when the ship is rolling about the way it is.

The fucking ship is going up and down and all over the place on the waves. How can the wheel work properly when it's doing that, eh?"

Buckley suddenly realised the wisdom with which his mate, Terry, had spoken. There could be no bias on a roulette wheel that was constantly unbalanced. Basic science and simple physics it was, but Buckley invariably failed to see simplicity even when it stood staring him in the face. Terry stared Buckley in the face.

"What now?" he snivelled.

Buckley stopped in his tracks. The ship juddered fiercely as it positioned itself in readiness for docking and disembarkation.

"You know what Tel?" said Buckley quite philosophically. "If I was to write a book about this, no one would ever believe it."

Chapter Eight

Safety and Security

SECURITY CIRCULAR 1100 – 1.57.9.22: July - December

<u>Confidential</u>

Gentlemen and Ladies,

Please acquaint yourselves with the current issues and disseminate accordingly.

Thank you.

A. Happe

Head of Security

C.C. Clubs

Please be advised of the following and take appropriate action where necessary:

1. STUD POKER/BAHAMA BONUS AND CARD GAMES FROM THE SHOE -

    Intelligence on the 'Eastern Block Gang' is still being collated. At this time, it is believed that there are three persons involved – the player and two producers. Confirmation of activity can be confirmed by a van parked outside or within very close proximity to the casino. The player will have secreted about them a small camera which is usually up the right sleeve of a jacket or in a cigarette packet (or similar) which is placed on the table at the lowest level. The cigarette packet (or similar) will, on closer inspection, reveal a small aperture through which a camera lens will be discovered. It is usual to have two packets: the 'camera' packet on the bottom and a genuine packet on top from which cigarettes can be taken. Similarly, a sleeve mounted camera will require positioning of the arm close to the table baize and it will remain almost motionless once positioned correctly. As the dealer's cards are pulled from the shoe, the camera will record the dealer's hand which is inadvertently revealed from the slight bend that the dealer uses to hold the card to deliver it to the table. The information from the camera is transmitted to a van outside the premises where the producers will read the cards and relay this information back to the player via a radio link (please use the RF detector on a regular basis during floor patrols). An 'invisible' earpiece can also be detected on closer inspection of the player's ear. Once the player has received information about the dealer's hand they will make their additional bet accordingly (Poker). The case for automatic dealing machines is currently being negotiated to negate this risk. Ensure activity is recorded on CCTV and immediately inform myself or A/HSO. Previous information – circular: 0200 – 08.08.19 BEW refers.

2. ROULETTE - The Chinese 'Top Hat' gang are still very active and vigilance is required. More information has been received so please familiarise yourself with the details:

    Within a two or three person team: a female will usually distract the dealer once the dolly has been placed on the winning number – although if the opportunity arises it will be BEFORE the dolly is placed. The distracter will cause a commotion, gesticulate and argue, anything to distract the dealer and the Inspector – usually it is the claim of a bet gone missing. Whilst the dealer is distracted away from the winning number, the 'Top Hatter' will reach out using chips secreted in their palm, manoeuvre their hand about the layout, tidying bets or checking their chips or any other spurious activity and whilst doing so drop the secreted chips held in the palm onto a winning bet. So as not to arouse suspicion, they will have taken from the layout, on a previous occasion, another player's coloured chip to put on top of their own. This then looks as though they could not have dropped their chips onto a winning line because another bona fide player's chips are on top. Once the bet has been placed, the 'Top Hatter' will move away from the table and at the first sign of trouble will disappear from the casino. Upon payout, the third member will claim the winnings which will ensure that if he is caught, it is not the skilled artisan that gets nabbed but just the unskilled body. The player whose coloured chip covers the 'Top Hat' never complains as they suddenly have a winning bet. This gang is becoming increasingly blatant and have been seen on CCTV to 'Top Hat' by brushing aside the dealer's hand as they go to place the dolly on the number then actually 'Top Hat' **that** winning number. It is vital that we endeavour to apprehend the 'Top Hatter' himself as the other two bodies are only temporary, unskilled, paid participants.

3. ROULETTE – Be advised that distracting the dealer and the Inspector is often an early indication of cheating.

It is unacceptable for CCTV operators (you know who you are!) to use the surveillance equipment for viewing and/or recording players or staff for entertainment purposes. The recording of female cleavages and other anatomical parts is unacceptable and leaves our department open to severe criticism. Cheating gangs know this is an excellent way in which to distract our security and there is a very good training video, captured at one of our clubs, showing how a female is used to distract the CCTV operator, the Pit Bosses and the Management, all at the same time. It shows a young woman, believed to be of Russian origin, playing from the end of the roulette table trying to place her chips on some numbers in the first dozen. In order to do so, it requires that she stretch right up the length of the table with one leg raised (just like a snooker player might!). As will be seen by the CCTV footage, she is clearly not wearing any lower undergarments and the constant zooming in and out demonstrates where the attention of the CCTV operator is focused. This was initially pointed out by another player, who is now thought to be a member of the team, and a Pit Boss can clearly be seen on the telephone just before the CCTV tracks the woman. During this distraction, several hundred pounds of other players' cash chips were taken and there was a significant increase in winning pay-outs at that time, which suggests improper play was taking place. Please do not let yourselves be distracted by such overt displays of attention seeking. Act professionally at all times and see these distractions as a signal to cheating taking place.

4. ROULETTE – The 'Push Bet' continues to be employed by our not so adept cheats. Placing chips on a winning bet, particularly the outside bets, after the ball has dropped and after the layout has been cleared still achieves results for these players. Placing their 'early bets for the next spin' and then cheating under the guise of it being a genuine error, has become so commonplace that it appears to be the norm! Crack down on this activity please and inform management of those dealers and Inspectors who are ignoring their responsibilities.

5. GENERAL – The police are NOT to be called under

any circumstances. Police records are used against us during re-licensing and it puts the business in a bad light. Deal and eject, revoke membership and add to banned members list where necessary. Police should NOT be called unless it has been agreed beforehand by myself (24 hour contactable) or the A/HSO.

6. ALL GAMES – Theft of players' chips is an increasing problem. Desperate players continue to blatantly steal cash chips from other players, either from the layout or from the table in front of the player. The most common method is for the thief to position themselves sat next to a player that has a fair amount of cash chips on the table in front of them, usually a messy mound of chips where theft will not be easily noticed. As the player stands up and leans over the table to place their bets, the thief will remain seated and slide an arm under cover of the player's own body and take a number of their cash chips. This will continue until such times as the player has nothing more to steal or the thief gets nervous. The genuine player, leaning forward, obscures the act from the dealer, Inspector and CCTV. Reliance on other players' information is the only evidence we have to date. Please be vigilant for this theft as well as players placing chips of their own and palming higher value

cash chips from the table as they do so.

7. BEGGING - This must not be tolerated. It causes valuable players to lose faith in our operation and it makes everyone feel uncomfortable, resulting in lost business. Particularly unsavoury is the praying and good luck chants where a reward is demanded should the player win. Beggars are known to follow players all night, constantly requesting a loan or payment for good wishes, prayers and sometimes outright blackmail. All complaints in respect of this must be dealt with in a robust and timely manner.

8. ROULETTE – **New! New! New! New!**
Identified recently is a device that is reported to be able to predict the winning number on roulette.
BEWARE – THIS IS GENUINE!
Our competitors have recorded substantial losses, over twenty million pounds to date, having fallen victim to this method. A masterclass is being organised by myself and attendance is mandatory for all Management, Security and CCTV Personnel. Usually a team of six carries out this operation. It is very sophisticated and careful observation is required so all the necessary evidence can be gathered in accordance with legal requirements for presentation in court.
An electronic device has been designed to track the

deceleration speed of the spinning roulette wheel as well as the ball. It is a remote computer which is concealed inside a nearby vehicle and the roulette player will have a concealed device about their person, like a Morse-code tapper. He uses the tapper device to time both the wheel and the ball and the remote computer is then used to calculate the winning number. This is based on an algorithm from data gathered and transmitted by the player. The result is then transmitted to the hidden earpiece of the watcher who voices which zone the ball will probably land in. The players, usually three of them, will cover a part of the layout each and slap down chips on the specified zone as quickly as possible, the calculations take a little bit of time and there are usually only one or two revolutions of the ball left before it drops. This method gives punters a considerable advantage over the house.

Initial consultations with the Gaming Board have determined that this MAY NOT be considered cheating as nothing is being done to tamper or alter the equipment or the outcome. You should be aware of the watcher/player who will tap on a hidden clicker, in their pocket or with their foot if secreted in the heel of a shoe, to record the moment when the ball passes a given point on the rim of the wheel. They will also tap using a similar hidden device (sometimes a second player will do this), when a particular point of the spinning wheel passes a particular point on the rim. Over several clicks, algorithms will determine the speed of the ball, the speed of the wheel, the rate at which both are slowing down and the likely area that the ball will drop into. Be vigilant please – this is an ultra-sophisticated method. We do **NOT** want to get hit with this one. You have been warned! Again RF detectors to be used.

9. DIPPERS - Pickpockets are known to frequent the clubs so please take the time to do random sweeps with CCTV and walkabouts to try and catch these despicable characters. Handbags are vulnerable so please give advice to players about keeping their cash, chips and other valuables safe.

10. PROSTITUTES – 'A casino should not be the habitual haunt for criminals or prostitutes,' (Gaming Act 1968 – as you all know?). Too many complaints have been received, usually from wives and girlfriends, of men who have been propositioned. Be on the lookout for slips of paper that are discreet 'menus' for services. The service is usually written along with a

price so it's a fairly obvious piece of evidence. Look for customers disappearing with girls who then return a few minutes later, with or without the girl. Flushed looks are always a giveaway! It should go without saying that any staff member who engages with a prostitute in the course of seeking services will face summary dismissal.

11. COLLUSION – Temptation often coerces staff into colluding with players to commit acts of theft against the casino. Particular players favouring particular members of staff and winning regularly should raise immediate suspicion. Talk between customers and staff should always be of a polite, courteous and professional nature. Take the time to review the table audio recordings and listen in live to ensure compliance. Placing late bets for players, taking unspecified call bets then announcing them after the ball has dropped, over paying or cash chips being secreted in amongst coloured wheel chips are all well-known favourites. Identify possible colluding parties and record all attendances, movements, wins and losses accordingly. Fraternisation between all employers and any club members, both inside and particularly outside of the casino, is strictly forbidden.

12. DRUGS – The random search of staff lockers will

NOT take place as scheduled. Management has determined that were this to happen, we would probably lose half our staff to instant dismissal! I have taken this issue up with the Board of Directors. In the meantime, random searches of staff with respect to casino chips and drugs should continue with special emphasis on illegal substances being hidden on the premises, but not in work lockers – apparently! Case study: It was reported that, for the third time, someone had broken the toilet seat in the staff toilet. On inspection, the DSO found that the plastic toilet seat had been snapped in three places. Initially, it could not be determined as to how or why this was occurring. Vandalism was suspected. As it was always the same toilet seat, suspicion was further aroused and it took the investigative prowess of a vigilant DSO who, upon looking about the area, saw above him that some of the suspended roof tiles had been disturbed, to make the discovery. Standing on the toilet seat (already broken by now) he pushed up a tile and felt inside. The DSO recovered two wraps of what is believed to be Cannabis resin, one packet of an unidentified white powder and three £25 cash chips! Quite a haul! As CCTV is not allowed in the toilets, for obvious reasons, we cannot determine who the culprit is. Suffice to say, devious methods have been utilised here so please pay attention to your surroundings. Most of you are ex-police or ex-military so I would expect you to use your professional skills in ensuring that this sort of thing is identified and offenders apprehended. The chip detector at the bottom of the stairs that leads from the casino to the staff room is functioning again. Please do NOT ignore the alarm signal but stop and search. It is written into company policy and staff have no right of complaint against this action.

13. ALCOHOL – There should be no alcohol in any areas other than those determined by our liquor licence. No alcohol is allowed in any staff area for any reason – and that includes staff shopping kept in lockers. Any staff member suspected of being under the influence of alcohol must be breathalysed using the provided kits and reported to the Duty Manager if the reading is red. No exceptions.

14. RESPECT AND THE RIGHTS OF OTHERS – Please read policy 23.06.1 on this matter and report to the Duty Manager any instances of threatening behaviour, bullying, intimidation or any other matter that is in breach of policy or the civil rights of an individual.

15. AR 4 WHEEL – As discussed with management, the wheel on AR 4 has been moved to AR 1 in order to try and alleviate losses. The 'cabbie,' as we all now know him, should be monitored to see if he is following this particular wheel.

16. CASH TRANSIT THEFT – It was reported recently that the cash transit van delivering money to our sister casino was robbed. Please be aware of this M.O. and be alert: As cash was being delivered to the casino, the case it was being transported in was taken from the van and as the delivery officer turned to walk from the van into the casino front entrance, the case was snatched from his hand. The delivery officer had not even had time to activate the alarm that would have automatically triggered when his grip was released. The force of the snatch sent the delivery officer sprawling into the kerbside and he was later treated for a dislocated shoulder. CCTV footage shows a man, description as per appendix A, who started running from the top of the street whereupon, timed to perfection, he hit his target at full pelt and this force carried him quickly down the street and around the corner where he disappeared out of sight. Suspicion as to the delivery officer has also been aroused due to the alarm not being set. Similar

attempts may be made so observations should extend well beyond the immediate boundaries of the building when cash is in transit.

17. ORANGE ALERT – We remain on orange alert. Please conduct perimeter walks at specified daily intervals, no less than two hours apart. Proper procedures must be adhered to should any suspicious or unattended packages be identified. This does **NOT** mean kicking it to see if it is a bomb (you know who you are, again!).

18. MONEY LENDING – It is against the law for money lending to take place on casino premises. It has almost become commonplace recently and must be stamped out otherwise it will become a threat to our licence. The Lebanese money lender has been told to desist so please monitor him and the Triads have been told to take their business elsewhere, even though they are bona fide players. It must be assumed however, that all involved will continue to push the boundaries on this one. We must adopt a zero tolerance attitude to this activity. Complaints have already been made to the Gaming Board about over-zealous collectors of debts.

19. BLACKJACK – As per gaming rules and regulations, ALL cards must be dealt face-up. There must NOT

be any case of cards being dealt blind, or 'one in the hole', etc. This is usually requested by our American friends and maybe what they are used to in their home country. It is prohibited by legislation here!

20. CUSTOMER TOILETS – Please liaise with the toilet attendants and should they report any matters of concern, such issues should be dealt with respectfully. The recent case of the foetus left in the lavatory bowl in the ladies toilet on the casino floor only goes to demonstrate that ALL reports made by the toilet attendant should be taken seriously. It was regretful that proper assistance could not be afforded to the female who had clearly miscarried and, I should imagine, she must have been in a severe state of distress at that time. At this moment we have still not identified who she is and this matter does not bode well for us having had to report the matter to the police.

The needles found in the gents' toilets have been identified as used by a diabetic. A notice will be placed in all toilets about the safe disposal of sharps. Empty bags containing the residue of a white powder have begun appearing once again in the upstairs, customer toilets. Whilst we must accept that drug taking is endemic in this environment, it must not be tolerated. If seen, do NOT call the police but refer to myself or the A/HSO in the first instance. If unavailable, eject perpetrator and cancel membership. Add to barred members list immediately.

Plastic carrier bags continue to be fished out from the sewer pipes. Someone, for reasons we cannot determine, is intent on regularly flushing plastic carrier bags down the ladies toilets. It would be good to know WHY?

Nothing can be done about the females who insist on standing on the toilet rim to do their business. The attendant must continue to make do with her mop and bucket on that one, I'm afraid.

21. BLACKJACK – Card counting teams continue to attempt to gain an advantage over the house. Whilst this activity is not illegal, it should be discouraged. Similarly, block tracking of shuffled cards should be discouraged by efficient shuffling in compliance with house procedures. Please monitor staff to ensure that the correct shuffle is being performed. However, should an obvious card-counter be losing, then they should not be discouraged but allowed to continue playing. Winners however, must be brought to the attention of the Duty Manager who will monitor and act accordingly.

22. CONSTANT WINNERS – Players who consistently win will be dealt with by a Senior Manager. It will be deemed that it is not in the interests of the casino to entertain such players in our casino but this must be a Senior Management decision. In case of confrontation, a DSO should remain on standby and at the discretion of the Duty Manager, be close at hand in case of violent reaction.
23. DEBTORS – Casino debtors are the responsibility of the Management and Directors. Under NO circumstances should debtors be approached or any conversation entered into regarding debts, or repayments thereof, by security personnel.
24. CCTV – Under NO circumstances is any CCTV footage or audio to be played to a third party without the express permission of a Senior Manager. Playing or viewing company CCTV footage for pleasure, especially at staff parties, is STRICTLY FORBIDDEN. Any contravention will result in summary dismissal.
25. NEWS – The recent story of the manager held to ransom is true and all managers should now be aware of their duties and responsibilities in respect of this issue. All managers' details should now have been added to the 'Leopard File' system and audio

recordings made of themselves and their family members in case of kidnap. Managers have been advised to vary their routes to and from work. As a result of the recent case, bolt cutters have now been stationed in every cash desk so should a claim be made by anyone claiming they have been handcuffed to a briefcase containing a bomb, it can be dealt with in situ. In the recent case, bolt-cutters were not available and the so called bomb would only be released when the manger delivered a large amount of cash to men waiting outside in a van. The threat to detonate the bomb in the briefcase if the manager failed to deliver was deemed to be genuine at the time. On subsequent examination, the briefcase was found to contain a household brick wrapped in bubble-wrap. Because the theft was successful, it must be assumed that the same M.O. will be used again in the future.

26. PLAYERS – The unacceptable behaviour of certain players must be monitored closely to ensure that no offences are committed but more importantly, players have no cause for complaint against our staff. The recent case of the dealer swearing at Zayer is a good point. Audio clearly hears the dealer swearing, calling the player a 'fat bastard' and as such, we as a casino,

have no defence. Also, players' behaviour should be recorded in case of claims made by dealers for assault. In the case mentioned above, Zayer lifting the roulette table could well have resulted in serious injury to staff with a legal claim for damages. As such, recordings are required for evidence. In all cases, please ensure that, at all times, at least one DSO is available to assist the manager upon request. In the latter case, ensure that our presence is discreet and non-threatening. I must remind you that any form of violence, be it instigated or retaliatory, is unacceptable and certainly NOT a 'perk of the job,' as was overheard recently.

27. Male security personnel are **NOT**, under any circumstances, to use the female toilets for any reason and the practice of photographing excreta will desist immediately. Non-compliance will result in dismissal.

GENERAL – In all instances, clarification should be sought from your line manager should there be any uncertainty as to instructions, procedures, house rules, gaming law or otherwise.

Staff – HSO x 1, A/HSO x1, DSO x 5, CCTV x 4.

Chapter Nine

The Big I Am

YEARS OF GROVELLING had led me to the upper echelons of casino management – well almost. One or two nasty, insecure and less able managers could see my threat and they would set me up to fail at every opportunity. It mattered not because I still had a few supporters who saw my contribution to the greater good as being more important than petty, management point scoring. With just the right amount of brownie points attached to the same sleeve on which I would always wear my heart, I was gloriously awarded the honour and privilege of being allowed to wear a two piece, double-breasted suit and neck tie, rather than the dinner jacket and bow-tie I had worn since training school. A lot had happened inbetween, some of which I was immensely proud of and some, best left forgotten.

Having finally achieved the rank where I was required to do very little, but would always be in the firing line for other people's fuck-ups, I could take it easy and count my management perks, which were indeed plentiful. Tickets to shows, accompanying punters to events such as football, tennis, polo, the theatre, clubs, restaurants, parties and anything else a punter wanted to do with a Casino Manager in tow, were all mine for the taking. There was a generous suit allowance and Kenzo was just about the best that this would stretch to in my case. An option to purchase old stock from the casino wine cellar, which was expensively old and particularly delicious, was more often than not purchased for resale and profit; however, one or two bottles of the finest were unceremoniously quaffed. There were meals in the casino restaurant and glasses of wine to accompany that culinary experience, superb food of unquestionable quality, exquisitely prepared. The best treats came from punter's left-overs, believe it or not. The wine that is, not the food – that would be disgusting! Unused, bottled wine, always controlled by the Sommelier, would be delivered to the manager where maybe the glass and a half that was left remaining would provide an immensely enjoyable dining experience. Some of the vintage wines had a menu price of £1800 or more so each glass, even by conservative estimates, would retail somewhere in the region of £400 a glug. You could taste the silky smoothness of that handsome, full-bodied red; it was like drinking pure gold and you could almost sense the money trickling down the back of your throat as it slid effortlessly into the gut where, sometime later, it would no doubt give you a bit of jip and probably the shits. There was Ascot races - bigging it up with the knobs in a box and wondering what all the fuss was about. The go-kart racing, the river cruise dinners, the company car, the fuel card and most revered of all, the business card with embossed ink that said, just under your full name, 'Casino Manager.'

"I've arrived Mum," I heard myself scream one glorious night while pissed out my head and it certainly had nothing to do with the nameless tart that lay underneath me at the time.

No, it was the realisation that all of my dreams had finally come true and my new dreams were all ready and waiting to be fulfilled. There was also the Mont Blanc pen with which to endorse multi-million pound cheques, not to mention the club diary with matching card holder in embossed, blue leather. Can you imagine a royal prince changing places with a pauper? For the prince it must have been a pretty rum deal but for the pauper, well, can you imagine it, just for one moment, how it must have felt? Well, if you can, multiply that by a couple of hundred and you'd be close to how it felt to be a casino manager. Like an athlete who had sacrificed everything for his sport, to finally be crowned champion of the world, it was the best feeling ever!

The job itself involved stepping back and letting everyone else do all the donkey work. My job was to be the figurehead, to stand in judgement, the one who would sort out all the mess and make all the important decisions: 'Yes, that's okay. No, not that one. No more credit. A cheque for a million? No problem! That's against the law I'm afraid.' Endless decisions that, generally, were of little consequence as the casino pretty much ran itself. Of course, if the shit really hit the fan then I could always pass it up the line. They'd always be someone senior hanging around on the end of a telephone, maybe a Director on call in a titty-bar somewhere giving it a lot larger than I ever could. These people were paid to be contactable twenty-four-seven and I too hoped, one day, to be that available. Anything that might go badly wrong was always referred to someone senior, for should it ever fall apart, then everything would go to hell in a hand-basket.

A lot of the managerial work was poncing about looking sophisticated and important, meeting and greeting punters that frequented the place and acting the hospitable host for the benefit of the rich, the famous, the filthy rich and the downright filthy. I can attest to being one of the very first people to know the sexual preferences of a very famous pop star who was, at the time, barely under suspicion. Years before he 'came out' I saw him with his hand down the back of another man's trousers. Although I could not say for sure and it would never stand up in a court of law, I still hold the honest held belief that he was upto no good but, as I say, I could never prove it.

There were a lot of foreigners about at that time, some of whom were very foreign indeed and the majority of us were racist, to all intents and purposes.

"Hello! Mr Abu," I recall greeting a very dark skinned man of short stature.

Mr Abu had that very high hairline and shiny forehead that is most resplendent in the light of a savannah sun, a royal bonce one might surmise, from somewhere down in the deepest depths of uncharted Africa. As he was procuring funds from the cash desk and I waited in readiness to employ my managerial nod if required, I chatted to Mr Abu as he signed a number of cheques for gambling.

"Where are you from, Mr Abu?" I politely enquired.

"From Africa!" came his immediate reply, in Radio 4 Receiveed Pronunciation.

"That is a big place," I said, assuring him of my geographical knowledge of Africa and all the major countries therein.

As though he was reading my mind, he offered the name of his home country.

"Really!" I exclaimed, genuinely surprised by the tongue twister he delivered and the fact I had never heard of it. "It must have a lot of wealth?" I said, but this was based solely on the fact that Mr Abu was a consistent punter who was capable of regularly losing some £10,000 a day.

Laughing the laugh of a Nigerian, although he wasn't, he went on to explain, but need not have, how it was he could afford to spend the sums that he did on this favourite hobby of his. He also had a very healthy appetite for classy prostitutes, not to mention the finest Sevruga caviar. A man I can really relate to.

"Man after my own heart!" I quipped, trying to ingratiate myself to this wealthy, very black man from Uganda, possibly. Now, coming from Africa, where in the past they have been known to eat people, my saying that he was a 'man after my own heart' may have sounded like I was accusing him of being a cannibal or something. But I was not – that would be silly, I think. I mentally prepared my defence should this matter crop up in a disciplinary hearing.

"In my country," he forgivingly explained, "I am the finance minister and a businessman. My country has little by way of industry, exports or tourism. However, we are the recipients of a large aid budget from the United States as well as your good country."

"I'm from Peru!" I teased.

Mr Abu carefully considered my one liner before continuing.

"Additionally, we receive a lot of food aid which I sell in my shops – my many shops. There are clothes too, and machinery."

Bold as brass, tell it like it is, he seemed quite proud to admit that he was squandering the proceeds of foreign aid from other countries – humanitarian aid by the sounds of it. I considered the moral issue but then decided it was not for me to take the moral high ground on this one, so I offered my assurance that his secret was safe with me.

"That's nice!" I said.

I thought this would give the impression that I had not at all understood anything he had said and so could not, therefore, repeat anything disparaging or accusatory. Like a couple of old chums, me and the man from Kenya, maybe, walked over to lucky roulette three where he gave his military command, "Spin the ball!"

Apparently, he was head of his country's military as well! With another managerial task completed to the satisfaction of all, I took to the manager's table on which was placed the manager's phone and waited for the next exciting aspect of this wonderful career to present itself for my managerial attention.

The raising of one index finger, as the waitress slunk by, was the recognised and accepted signal for a cup of tea and the showing of the front of a cigarette packet, as though it were an FBI badge, could mean nothing more than a new package of fags was immediately required. It was like a game that only the 'in-crowd' could play; secret signs, gestures, subtle facial expressions and furtive signals, all secret codes that could only be gained from many years in the business observing other managers, so as to learn the correct way to converse without words. Gesturing was a sign that one had done one's time, served an apprenticeship, risen through the ranks, put in the hours to be finally deemed worthy of a superior position; to sit above all others at the end of the casino floor next to the cash desk, sipping tea, smoking company fags and waiting for the manager's phone to ring.

In all those years, during all that waiting and sipping of tea, the phone only ever did ring once, and then it was a wrong number. Nevertheless, I answered it on that one occasion and I could feel all the jealous eyes watching me as I spoke into the managerial phone – me, the manager, *the* Casino Manager, mumbling the words, 'Sorry, wrong number!' to a stores man on the other end. On all other occasions, the phone would ring at the other end of the Pit and I would be beckoned by the frantic waves of various Pit Bosses who would tell me, in hushed tones, that it was for me.

"Why can't they ring the manager's phone?" I'd ask, but I never did receive a logical reply. Maybe it was a jolly-jape they were having at the new boy's expense? But I wasn't always the new boy! I still wonder, to this very day, why my phone never rang.

Now, this management title did not come without a great deal of sacrifice. It was incumbent upon me to ensure that I was seen as management material long before I had any hope of being promoted and this meant having to do things, sometimes bad things, which may be considered a little underhand or vindictive, such as spilling the beans on the drug stash above the gents' toilet for one thing. I also had to discretely inform on the competition and the nature of what I had to say, well it meant that my competitor, suddenly, was no longer a viable contender. Nothing to do with his newly acquired circumcision I might add, more to do with the story behind it all; who was involved and the illegal substances that were being used and anyway, I saw him with my own eyes sniffing on a tube down at the club one night, and it definitely wasn't a nasal inhaler! Dog eat dog in this gaming world and quite frankly, at the end of the day, I won and he lost. I was the one in the comfy chair overseeing the casino floor, sipping Earl Grey, smoking free fags and waiting for the phone to ring. End of!

"Billy's in!"

I thanked the Pit Boss for the information, having got out of the 'not so comfy' chair after all, not so comfy after two hours of sitting on it at any rate, to go to the other end of the gaming floor to see what all the hysterical waving was about.

"Why can't they ring the manager's phone?" I asked, but it was met with silence and a shrug of the shoulders.

Why? I thought, as I went to the top of the stairs to do the meet and greet stuff, such as my position demanded. I stood looking down on my domain, master of all I surveyed and my loyal subjects looked back up at me, in adoration, no doubt considering me to be their rightful master, their manager, their manager-king, heir to a directorship. I rather suspected that they thought I was a megalomaniacal wanker at times, but they never said as much. I was management and they were not. End of!

Where is the fucker? I thought, wiping my sweaty palm on the clean, pressed handkerchief that was neatly folded into my trouser pocket. Nervously, I reached into the cigarette packet in the lower inside pocket of my beautifully tailored, off the rack, Kenzo suit jacket – amazed that they had thought to install a fag pocket discreetly inside the lining. As a conjurer might pull a white dove from the secret compartment of his theatrical coat, I produced a single cigarette and flipped it up to my mouth, where it promptly fell to the floor. Fortunately, I managed to kick it on the volley and sent it flying through the air where it bounced off a wall to finally land behind a display cabinet. Looking around for appreciation, in order to give the impression that I had meant to do it all along, it seemed that no one had noticed so after performing a brief jig, just in case someone had indeed been observing, I went back to dabbing my hand discretely on the comforting, cotton square in my trouser pocket.

How fucking slow can you be? I thought. How long does it take one fat git to get up some stairs? Two options presented themselves: I could go back to my seat of authority and wait for the phone to ring or go down to the reception to find out what the bloody hell was going on. Professional reputation always foremost in my mind, I took the trip down to reception and made purposeful movements to demonstrate this commanding and authoritative decision. Of course, it demonstrated nothing of the sort but in my mind, it worked a gem.

There is nothing like the feeling of walking in leather soled shoes upon sumptuous carpet laid on the most expensive of underlays, all of which covered a finely sprung, wooden, ballroom dance floor. The casino floor was probably one of the best in the world and it was tantamount to orgasmic pleasure; walking on fluffy clouds of angel dust heading towards the door that led down the side stairs to the reception where, gracefully, one would emerge into the reception area to appear like magic from behind a concealed door that looked like a wall mirror. But before then, the sumptuousness suddenly stopped and the harsh reality of industrial flooring and slip-grippers, in black and silver, fixed to the edge of stair-treads, greeted this pedestrian like a slap of bamboo upon the soles of bare feet! Staff stairs did not warrant expensive covering, so I resolved never to walk on staff flooring again.

Popping out from the 'secret' door that was indiscernible from the reception mirrored panelling, caused two work-shirking receptionists to snap into action and they quickly busied themselves to look as though they were doing something important when, in fact, clearly they were not.

"Where 'd man at?" I said, in my mock, West Indian accent.

"The gentleman is just outside" replied the elder of the two, work-shy judges of good character and financial capability. "There was a gentleman in here earlier," he continued in a posh tone to make my Jamaican chat seem cheap and tactless. "He looked pretty rough, French or Belgian I think. Seemed very odd but he had a Patek-Phillipe," the receptionist informed me.

"That'll do for me!" was my critical, managerial confirmation.

"We gave him membership so he'll be in this time tomorrow, I would think."

"Right, let me know," I said, now thinking they were ganging up on me.

The receptionists had used their superior skills which allowed them to determine a shit-bag from a money-bag and there was nothing I, or any other manager for that matter, could ever add to such appraisals. Barely, if ever, was a receptionist's judgement of wealth and character ever wrong. All day, every day, they spent their time eyeing up people's habits and behaviours and this was what they were very, very good at. They were also very good at looking busy when there wasn't a lot to do.

"Here he comes now," informed one, lethargic receptionist.

Walking from his car, which was an enormous, red Cadillac with cream leather interior and no roof, came the self-proclaimed King of Tarmac – one Billy 'Boy' Lee.

"Billy!" I called, as he pushed his fat frame into the reception area. "Where you been buddy?"

Now, such familiarity is the sole reserve of a manager. We were encouraged to talk to 'our' punters like mates, old chums, best buddies or however we saw fit in order to build and maintain strong, working relationships with them; ones that would keep them happy but more importantly, keep them loyal. Complimentaries, gifts, food, cigars, tickets and even prostitutes could be made available, depending on a punter's worth.

There was the obligatory shaking of hands where my smooth, pale, professionally manicured portions were enveloped by the course, bitumen stained bunch of bulbous bananas that served as fingers for the great oaf of an imaginary royal. He was a typical gypsy sort but he liked to refer to himself as a traveller. I, on the other hand, suggested that living in a caravan on a council site did not constitute being a traveller by any stretch of the imagination and this I pointed out to colleagues, explaining that I had probably travelled much more just by commuting to and from work.

Billy reached down to pick up the bulky carrier bag that he had put down in order to take my managerial mitt, which he shook in a traditional, 'travelling sorts' fashion. Instinctively, I looked down and could clearly see, packed to the brim of the carrier bag, a vast number of twenty-pound notes. Underneath the notes were an even greater number of notes, all twenty pounds in denomination, precisely banded with elastic rubber and stacked, or maybe thrown in, haphazardly. As if it wasn't clearly apparent, I questioned the contents of the carrier bags – plural, because he had another in his other, sausage-fingered, claw-like grip.

"What you got there then Billy, money?"

From the corner of my eye I could see the head of an idle receptionist turn slowly to look at me for stating the bloody obvious, but I chose to ignore him. I was the manager and he was just a receptionist. End of!

Billy looked me in the eye and gleamed, "It's money!" he

informed me, merely because I had asked.

There's a certain beauty, a fresh naivety in such a response and it brought a warm, tingly sensation into the mix; it made one proud to be a part of an intelligent, management team. Looking down on Billy, in height as well as social standing, I gave him a quizzical look – a look that said, 'Don't lie to me you thieving, gypsy bastard.'

"There's more out the back," called a slothful employee from behind our beautifully carved and ornate reception counter.

"Really?" I said, genuinely surprised, before walking around the counter to crane my neck into the coat hanging space where I saw four more bags full of money.

I carefully considered my response and then, after a short while, I heard myself say, "Fuck me Billy! Where'd you get that lot from?"

"I won it up north," he offered, by way of explanation.

"Bingo?" I suggested.

"Nah! Cards. I got a tractor and two horses an' all," he declared.

"Blimey!" I said.

Blimey seemed woefully inadequate, under the circumstances, but I was already worrying whether an over officious security officer might have picked me up on the audio swearing with, not *at* or *to*, I hasten to add, a valued customer. The odds were in my favour I reckoned, mainly because it was fairly quiet so one would expect the security officer to be sleeping, copying illegal DVDs or looking at porn; the chances of me being overheard, let alone recorded, were pretty much negligible.

"How much you got there then?" I asked Billy, not really expecting a definitive figure.

"No idea," replied Billy. "Maybe a hundred quid!"

He laughed the hacking, phlegm riddled, guttural rasp of a future lung cancer patient and I stood there adopting my best managerial stance as I tried to avoid the winged, wet bits that flew out from his mouth. A small droplet of green, marbled mucus stuck to his bottom lip and within it was a distinct swirl of deathly, obsidian blackness. A black swirl such as that portends to a most unfortunate episode, I thought.

With the help of a receptionist who was first cajoled, then finally ordered, into doing some real work for once in his life, the carrier bags were transported, two apiece, to the cashier's desk and the cashier, upon spotting the work that would be required to sort and count it all, put down his half-eaten banana and sighed heavily.

"Count that lot Reggie," I lampooned, with wetted finger flicking the air as though it were racking up cash notes.

The counting machine was slammed heavily onto the cash desk just as I offered Billy, with an inviting gesture of hand and sweeping movement of arm, to a seat at the manager's table.

"Yes Billy, the small table there, the one with the phone in the middle. Tea?" I offered, suspecting the answer would be something quite base.

"Ta very much," said Billy. "Lapsang-Souchong, if you please." The cheeky, upstaging bastard I thought, before smiling to concur.

I raised a forefinger to summon the delightful waitress, Jane, and requested two teas.

"Lapsang-Souchong," I snorted, as if I was used to this fine and refreshing black tea with its rich, smoky flavour.

Jane nodded in agreement but I somehow suspected we would get the builders tea, as usual. We sat for a while in silence before I broke the monotony.

"So, tell me all about it Billy. It's good to see you by the way. What card games you been playing then?"

Billy sat and slurped on his tea, which appeared surprisingly quickly, dunking the accompanying shortbread biscuit in twice before putting it all in his mouth to mush.

"I was at the horse fair," he began, "And I got to be there 'cos I'm still the king and all that. I used to be the bare-knuckle fighting king an' all, but I give dat up 'cos me sons now does it."

Personally, I did not doubt for one moment any aspect of his life, or the current story, that he ever told me about. If he had told me he was the new boyfriend of Princess Diana I probably would have believed him.

He went on, "I was playing brag with the boys and as you know, it's the one with the most money that always wins. Well, I had a shed load o' money 'cos I been selling me horses at the fair, so I puts it all down on me prial of aces and I wins. I got a Massey-Ferguson and a couple of Piebalds, as well as all that cash."

Reggie leaned over the counter like he needed to address a child on the other side.

"A hundred and twenty dead," was the result of frantic counting by an agitated cashier and a machine that was temperamental when it came to used banknotes.

"Thanks," I replied, twisting my neck to look back up at Reggie's odd expression of surprise, his slender body leaning right over the top of the counter.

In both respects, we were unnecessarily animated in our exchange.

"One hundred and twenty thousand," I confirmed to Billy, who drank the dregs of his tea without acknowledging whether this was the total he had expected or not.

I suspected old Billy 'Boy' was far too shrewd not to know, precisely, how much money was stuffed into those six carrier bags.

Billy chatted some more about horses and fairs, fighting and drinking, the police and how to avoid capture plus the finer subtleties of having officials on your payroll and I tried to suck up to this wealthy, n'er-do-well by taking a keen interest in all his, highly questionable, activities. There was talk of a place in Spain, a backroom boxing club in the East End, cars whose parts were shipped abroad and a lucrative business smuggling contraband from Europe whilst posing as a truck driver. Not for one moment did I doubt any of it and not for one, infinitesimal moment, did I ever think I would become embroiled in any of his illegal activities but I would, and this put my walking capabilities, if not my life, in serious jeopardy. Eventually, I introduced Billy to a waiting Blackjack table and with one hundred and twenty grand on credit, he settled himself down armed with three packets of complimentary cigarettes and a saucer of boiled sweets. Every so often Billy would raise his head and run his fingers through his greasy, long mane - lank, greying hair swept back between fat fingers which left an oily residue to be wiped from the palm onto the table baize. A little bit of Billy left behind on the table top. How sweet! It mattered not, apart from the disgustingness of it all, as another cloth could easily be put onto the table but the thought of all that hair oil and cream, that grime, that slick scalp and those horsey hands, it sent one or two female dealers running to the washroom and refusing to deal to him. As the manager, I considered that to be a fair excuse so I sat down to await the details of Billy's Blackjack capabilities and his final win/loss figure.

Watching his heavy fingers tap at the table when requesting another card, sovereign rings and bracelets jingling and jangling at the end of powerful arms, it led one to believe that this was the sort of gentle giant that could quickly lose his 'gentle' status if pushed. Most of the stories Billy told were absolutely true and rarely did they ever need embellishing; they were so outlandish they could not be anything other than credible accounts of Billy's colourful, fantastical world of criminal activity. Rumour had it that he had mixed with the big, bad boys back in the day; the days when crooks were gentlemen and London was a much safer place for it. Rumour had it that he was present at all the funerals of the Krays and were anyone ever to question it, he would pull from his pocket a folded mass of newspaper cuttings by way of verisimilitude. In a way, I admired him and saw the good in a man that had fought, literally, to make some headway in what might have been a very miserable life otherwise; the struggles he endured to gain respect and his hard work which afforded him the means with which to treat his family and friends decent were truly admirable. Others saw him as an out and out rogue, an inglorious thief who deserved whatever he got – especially the bad things.

I turned to replace the teacup and saucer that I had been

nursing, even though it was empty, back onto the manager's table and Reggie caught my eye with a curious, feminine wave.

"Did you see the notes?" whispered Reggie out loud.

"I did," I replied, expecting there to be a punchline.

"They're all Scottish," he advised.

It was my turn to lean right over the counter to look on the other side of the cashdesk where, uniformly laid out, were bundles and bundles of Scottish, twenty pound notes.

"All of them?" I probed.

"All of them," confirmed Reggie, using his hand in a whirling gesture that was meant to denote 'all of them.'

"It'll have to be reported," I said.

Reporting large or suspicious movements of cash was the normal function of casino business and, being the manager, the onus was upon me to undertake this menial task. I had my doubts about this methodology of giving information to the authorities and my reasoning was that if anything were to come of it, such as breaking a drug cartel or solving a crime, I would be in the criminals' sights for aiding their demise. As the reporting officer I would, essentially, be grassing on Billy 'Boy' to the National Criminal Intelligence Service. However, the significance of what I was actually doing, at the time, didn't really materialise in my managerial head because, in the confused noodles of my mind, life continued to be one, endless merry-go round of beautiful waitresses, free fags, exotic teas, along with a solitary phone that never rang. In this instance, I would be grassing on a criminal whose violent history was well known and just in case there were any doubts about his reputation, his forceful nature was often remarked upon by way of polite but intimidating conversation - this was a man who used his fists first and only ever asked questions if he really, really had to, and even then it was most improbable. This was a man whose life was based on respect and honour and little else mattered, especially the well-being of some pompous, casino manager. At the end of the day, at the end of this particular gaming day, Billy lost all his money and thought nothing of it. He reckoned he still had the tractor and horses and even with the cash gone, he was still quids in.

Forsaking the fine wine list, Billy opted for a bottle of 'Blue Nun,' which was his favourite, so he said, but it had to be bought in special because there really was no call for it in the casino restaurant. In fact, there really was no call for it anywhere in civilised society and most people were amazed that anyone could have a preference for it. For one hundred and twenty grand of Billy's loss, it was well worth the while sourcing that poor excuse for a wine and cooking up the best Vindaloo that Vijay the chef could knock up from scratch. Finally, Cadillac door wide open, it received the stuffed 'traveller' and off he sped into those places that decent folk dare not venture.

During a quiet moment, NCIS reporting officer head well and truly screwed on, I managed to fill in the blanks on the official reporting form. All the details, as requested, were noted and it was duly signed in the appropriate box along with my title, 'Casino Manager' then, top copy in an envelope to the Head of Security to be forwarded to NCIS, middle copy to same for records and bottom copy on file. Another job well done! Smugly, I informed the Head Cashier of my excellent work, only to receive astonished looks for my trouble.

"Are you mad?" questioned the Head Cashier.

"Why?" I asked, in panic.

"You put your name on an NCIS report? You don't have to do that you know? You can leave it blank and the Head of Security will put their name on it instead."

I should have known why, of course. I thought I knew everything. I am the manager after all. But I didn't know why I should not have put my name on the NCIS report, so the Head Cashier enlightened me.

"What if they prosecute Billy for money laundering? Under the rules of disclosure, the defendant, 'Bonkers Billy,' will get to see who has shopped him to NCIS and there, in fountain pen ink, will be your name. Guess who he'll blame for stitching him up and sending him to prison?"

I considered the life threatening fuck up I'd made but could not be seen to lose control over my managerial bowels for this faux pas.

"Do you think I'm scared?" I said, fronting it out. "I know all that and I really don't give a toss about Billy. He's all talk and no trousers."

Deep down inside, I was shitting it.

Subsequent visits by Billy 'Boy' were of a similar nature and we began to think that he'd actually robbed a bank up north. He casually lost in the region of £350,000 and all of it was in Scottish banknotes. It was generally believed, by most, that the notes were in fact from a heist, stolen from that place where they take old bank notes to cremate them. Thinking back and come to mention it, the notes had been rather tired and suspiciously grubby looking.

Unbeknownst to me, the wheels of justice had already been started. Nevertheless, further NCIS reports were dutifully completed but only after heeding good advice and omitting to put my own name on any of the forms. There were times when Billy made visits with no money at all and we would joke with him that he had either lost at cards or that no one would play with him because he was so lucky. He never quite got the ribbing, or maybe he did, it could all have been a rouse to get us to believe that he was just a bumbling idiot when, in fact, he was probably a criminal mastermind. I subscribed to the former and promptly began to forget about the superficial and hypothetical threats.

On one occasion, having been called down to reception to greet Billy as usual, I naturally assumed he had, yet again, come armed with carrier bags full of cash. However, upon arriving in reception, having taken the customer stairs with the carpet that felt soft and comfortable underfoot, I saw Billy emerging from behind the reception where the coats and umbrellas of customers were kept. The only receptionist on duty at the time, sad Dave, looked directly at me with fear in eyes that narrowed under perplexed eyebrows. He stood in complete wonderment for a while then motioned with a pointed finger for me to look in the back room. As I did so, Billy barged by me on his way in, arms loaded with long, colourful boxes that struggled to contain their contents. "What's all this Billy?" I asked with rising tone, as a parent might to a naughty child.

"I've brung these in for yer staff," was Billy's explanation. "I got 'em all for you, look..." he said opening the lid of the box in his arms. "Look at this fucker!"

It's an inadequate reflection of my astonishment to say that I could not believe my eyes but, I could not, seriously, believe my eyes. Inside the thin cardboard box was an array of various sized, shaped and coloured fireworks. One was as big as a man's thigh. Others were less alarming as they lay next to cylinders with names such as "Pharaoh's Fountain' and 'Black

Widow'. There was even one called 'The Devil's Porn' (suspected Chinese typo from 'Devil's Horn') which had a dark blue touch-paper that appeared to be weeping some kind of viscous fluid.

It seems Billy brought out the best of my colloquialisms and I exorcised, from deep within, an almighty, 'FUCK ME!' just to please him.

"Where did you get this lot from? Why's it here?" I asked.

Billy explained that, yes, he had won a consignment of fireworks, recently imported from the Far East, in a game of cards up north. He had also won two whippets which were, he said, 'Very good at rabbiting,' but only if I was interested in that sort of thing.

"You're shitting me, right Billy?"

"About the whippets?"

"No, about the fireworks!"

"Give 'em to the staff. Tell 'em, there from Uncle Billy."

"I'll do no such thing. Look at them. I bet they don't comply with British Standards," I said. "Where's the fucking kite mark, Billy?"

"No need for that old bollocks," reassured Billy. "They're as good as gold."

"You can't keep them here Billy," I protested. "They're explosives and look, there's shit oozing out of them."

"I'm not putting them back in the van," stated Billy, before casually leaving. The door to his van was slammed shut and a furious revving of a worn out engine preceded a hasty, slipped clutch getaway.

Times such as this are when a manger comes into his own. The receptionist looked bemused, entering punters were totally bewildered, the CCTV operator, smiling with sick intent at his porn collection, was oblivious to it all and the manager, me, the calm in the storm, the font of all knowledge, the cool, calm rock in such rough, tumultuous seas, finally spoke.

"Dave, get me a Director on the phone – any will do."

Fortunately, after a short while of guarding explosives, a van arrived with two young boys dressed in three-quarter length shorts and quilted gilets. Billy's lads hastily loaded their van with the unstable, fully primed and ready to explode goods and drove away with a short screech of tyres on tarmac. A most welcome grab and quick getaway if ever there was one.

Sighs of relief all round.

With confirmation given to the Director that I now had the situation fully under control and that everything was okay, I gave the all clear and retired to the manager's chair to drink tea and wait for the phone to ring. I took a long drag of a newly lit cigarette and considered the implications of Billy's actions. I fully believed that he had no real understanding of the possible consequences of his kindness and generosity, the trouble it might cause me or the danger it put everyone else in. It would have been a very messy business indeed were we to have witnessed worst case scenario, and then questions would have been raised as to my management style and effectiveness. And that just would not do! I'd report the fucker for the misdemeanour, just to be on the safe side. I took another lung full of carcinogenic fumes and signalled to Jane to clean the ashtray. Jane was always very attentive and why wouldn't she be? I was a manager after all and what a prize I would be for someone such as her – a waitress! Whatever next! Surprisingly however, from that moment on, from that very second right there and then, as the damp tissue she held so elegantly wiped the rim of the ashtray before replacing it for me to foul again, in that one instant when her hand brushed mine and her eyes looked at me just as I focused on her cleavage, when thoughts ran amok with ideas of things other than tea, free fags or even a nice sandwich, Jane would be forever infatuated with me and I with her but sadly, it would never end up in cohabiting bliss. That's not to say there weren't times when hearts spoke and souls listened – it's just that it was never destined to be, that's all.

I flicked through my casino issue address book wondering who I could call in order to look busy and important. One could always pretend to call someone and make out one was having a conversation on the phone. I'm sure I had witnessed other managers doing exactly that, making themselves look professionally hectic and significant. I decided against the idea. Knowing my luck, I would only get caught out and my credibility would be washed away along with my outstanding ability to remain popular. I would wait for the phone to ring, all by itself...

If the truth be known, it got a little boring sat there night after day after night. Finding most punters difficult to talk to, most punters whose first language was not English, I took to the ancient art of staying silent and observing people as they went about their business. There were, obviously, some scintillating conversations to be had but they were few and far between. Because of this infrequency, such exchanges became very memorable which, in my book, is better than having a shed load of meaningless interactions that cannot be recalled. Quality, not quantity, was the watchword for me.

I am favourably reminded of a middle aged, 'B' movie actress, an ageing and respected socialite who propositioned me on a number of occasions. Having been around the block a few times, looking like she had been dragged from the back of a car, she had an endearing quality about her that could not be ignored and it was this that attracted me to her. Also, I was mesmerized by her arse which was always delicately covered in a short, pleated skirt, the hem of which would swish from side to side as she walked her mature, womanly walk. It reminded me of the bottom hem of a pleated, hospital curtain that had been drawn very quickly in order to prevent prying eyes from seeing some horror within. She was well known as a temptress, a siren and this maternal matriarch had once, a very long time ago, had a clandestine relationship with a very famous head of state somewhere in the Middle East. Had she been of the correct religious persuasion, he may well have married her but being Jewish, it was a no hoper from the off. It was also known, from tittle-tattle, that she had been involved with one or two very famous and well respected Hollywood actors. I desperately felt the need to be sexually satisfied by her but upon receiving her personalised Christmas card, which had on the front cover a photograph of herself between two luscious daughters, I thought better of my desires. Eventually, I came to realise that she was, and would always be, completely out of my league and I could never have come upto her exacting standards in any shape or form; or be a match for all those affairs, her fame, her fortune and all the handsome, fit, young men that still sought her company. I considered myself fortunate for her passing attention and my smutty thoughts.

The more one knows, the more temptation is put in one's way, or so it would appear. Being a simple dealer meant dealing the game, getting paid and going home to drink copious amounts of alcohol and getting stoned. Being a manager, on the other hand, is a completely different bowl of cherries. Apart from all the propositions, both sexual and monetary, other temptations present themselves when one least expects it.

It was Reggie again, that schoolboy face appearing round the pillar as I was trying to hide, who asked me to enter the cash desk for a look at the books. Why not? I thought, not much happening out here. Inside the claustrophobic recesses of a particularly snug cashdesk, Reggie explained the deposits book to me. The book, a real ledger of a book, bound in blue and green leather with oversize pages full of fountain pen scratchings and scribblings, was where the records had been entered as to monies that had been placed on casino deposit. These sums, along with a myriad of other financial odds and sods, made up the cashdesk balance sheet. If one cared to review the accounts, daily weekly, monthly or yearly, there would be a notation that read '*Money held on account.*' Flicking through the ledger pages was like going back in time, like an afternoon at the National Archives researching a family history. Names and amounts going back to the 1970s, as Reggie explained, was money that was still in the possession of the casino but was actually owned by individual customers – it was simply money that had been left on deposit and never claimed.

"Like how?" I enquired, my inquisitive, managerial brain stepping up a gear.

Reggie began excitedly, "Imagine a punter comes in, puts money on deposit to play with, then goes home and drops dead. He never comes back to collect the money. Or maybe a punter who has a dispute who gets paid but is adamant that it should be more so he walks out refusing to accept it. The money goes on deposit so it can be given to him on his next visit but he never comes back. He's too pissed off with the casino for that and he decides never to play with us again. Or imagine you put money on deposit and you take what you think you have then forget about the rest. You never ask for it because you have no reason to think you have it and it never gets offered because no one gives a shit or remembers anyway."

I offered my standard response to such matters. "Blimey!"

"So, I did some digging around," whispered Reggie, like he had the definitive answer to the Stone Henge mystery. "I had a look at the attendance lists and found the majority of these punters haven't been in for years and years. Probably dead by now, but their money is still alive and sitting right here in this book. Let's say," Reggie began his hypothetical scenario, "Let's say, just for the sake of argument, just for a moment, that someone, not me of course, were to take the actual cash and write off these accounts with a zero balance. Look, no one ever, ever checks these books. It's an old volume too and I only came across it because I was bored and started snooping around the back. The money on deposit always fluctuates wildly because it is linked to the day's action so no one would suddenly see the figure drop and wonder why that was. An entry could be made in the book with a bit of scribble which says 'repaid' and an illegible signature added. The punter will never come in and ask for it as they are most likely dead and if they were going to claim it, they would have done so by now. No one here will question it as I doubt anyone knows or even cares."

"Mmmm! I like your thinking Reggie," I said, with one finger pressed against my chin, the position in which you usually see Sherlock Holmes in the pictures of him. "So what you're saying is, we should defraud the casino by siphoning off this unclaimed money, eh?"

I made it out to be a joke, just in case he was trying to ensnare me in some sort of integrity trap, and Reggie made all the apologies just in case I was about to bring down my managerial clout upon his dishonest head.

"No! I'm just saying that someone *could* do it," explained Reggie.

"Just saying, were you?" I said suspiciously.

"I thought it was a risk that I should point out so ..."

"A risk eh? You identified a loophole eh?" I interrupted.

It was a brilliant plan and Reggie had calculated, even by leaving the most recent deposits alone, about fifty grand could be siphoned off and no one would be any the wiser. I knew that Reggie knew, and Reggie knew that I knew, he knew. We both suspected the other of entrapment so we decided to laugh off what was probably one of the best plans of fraud ever concocted by two casino employees with only half a brain between them. Reggie solemnly put away the ledger and I returned to my corner to stare at the silent phone.

As a dealer, during idle times when players had seemingly abandoned the idea of gambling as an amusing pastime, when the casino remained empty for uncomfortably long periods of time and we wondered if we would get paid at the end of the month, we would play word games with the table Inspector. We'd go through the alphabet naming dogs, countries, cars or whatever else came to mind. One particular game that gave me an insight into the honesty and integrity of all casino staff went something like this, in a two-way banter, it mattered not as to gender:

"You know that fat bastard, ugly cunt of a punter, Zayer?"
"Yes"
"For how much would you let him fuck you?"
"Not for a million quid!"
"Really, not a million pounds?"

"No! He's fucking gross."

"What about five million then?"

"No way."

"Alright, fifty million?"

"No…"

"Think about it seriously, fifty million quid for one shag. It might only take two minutes and you'd have fifty million pounds to spend; F…I…F…T…Y, M…I…L…L…I…O…N… quid!"

"Yeah, I suppose I would then."

"Just for arguments sake, he gives you the cash but it's short, he's only got forty-nine million, nine hundred and ninety-nine thousand, nine hundred and ninety-nine pounds. He must have dropped a pound somewhere. Is that still okay?"

"Yep, it's only a quid."

"Okay, so he's handed it over to you but dropped another pound down the drain. You'd still do it for two quid short of fifty million, right?"

"Yep, of course."

Goodness me! He's counted it wrong and he's five quid short…"

So on and so forth it would go. The two issues being: firstly, once an initial price had been determined and agreed (fifty million pounds in this case), we found that, eventually, everyone's price is negotiable. At the time, if it was a quick version of the game, we'd chip in with the remark, 'Now that we've established *what* you are, let's negotiate price?' and secondly, it suggested that, for a price, depending on what that was and everybody had their own figure, we were all willing to act dishonestly and/or immorally for monetary gain. In all my years of engaging in this mindless distraction never once did I, or anybody I ever spoke to or heard about, ever meet a person who did not eventually agree a price. For some it was in the billions and others a lot less but, every single one of them had a price for which they could be bought. My price however, was not the trifling amount suggested by Reggie, so I sipped tea and watched Jane's slender, inner thighs as she bent over to deliver drinks and a snack to the side-table of an ungrateful punter. Anyway, I was a manager and such immature thoughts of ripping off my employer had to remain firmly suppressed and what's more, I only had to consider Mr Abu, who was clearly dishonest, immoral and selfish - such greed and gluttony, not to mention all the other earthly sins, will be jolly difficult to deny or explain when stood before the omnipotent one on judgement day. I had to concentrate on my career, on something else, something like Jane to stop the bad thoughts of deceit and fraud entering my managerial head.

Days, weeks and even months drifted in and out of each time spectrum; a boring day could last an eternity and a good day was over in a flash. How many lifetimes were spent wishing away lethargic hours that could never be recorded.

Jane and I drifted in and out of each other's lives, with brief interludes where we missed each other terribly only to find ourselves unhappy in each other's company. Jane was like no other – the only girl I ever knew who, when I wasn't with her I desperately wished I was and when I was with her, I desperately wished I wasn't. In the end, one of us would lose our minds and although it was only a temporary period of complete insanity, it was a frightening experience as a passive lamb was slain by the might of madness.

Leaning on the pantry wall, watching Jane prepare sandwiches with delicate fingers and a dribble of spit for those punters who did not tip well, I had a moment of intense boredom when I thought the highlight of my career had passed me by and I hadn't even noticed it. It seemed boredom came in blocks of weeks and sometimes months. A whole new breed of punter seemed to have morphed from the sad saps that we were used to and Far Eastern players were now the new kids on the block, rather than the Middle Eastern studs that had once dominated the gambling scene; our customer base changed according to the global fortunes and shifted so the *nouveau riche* were no longer the revered boys in town. The clever money, and a lot of it too, was pouring in from astute businessmen who seemed to own everything east of Bombay and these perceptive entrepreneurs openly scoffed at the excesses of yesterday's, flamboyant playboys. The sums involved were mind boggling and just when it seemed that profits could never reach such dizzying heights again, they quickly did and often surpassed previous ones in the process. Business was booming and Christmas bonuses instilled in us a sense of satisfaction and self-worth that lasted all summer long.

One old lag who reared his weathered, ruddy face after a long period of absence was Billy 'Boy' Lee who, it was generally believed, had either died or gone to prison. It was almost the latter as it happened.

Billy called for me to sit with him in the cocktail bar where, along with an entourage of cauliflower ears listening in, he explained his absence to me. That very day, on the very day we were sat there talking, he had just been acquitted of the charge of smuggling contraband. The celebration for this was to take place after our little chat and I, on behalf of the casino, would authorise the complimentary nosh up as well as all the booze. He told me as such, to my face:

"You're paying for everything," he said, which left no leeway for negotiation.

A certain cashier, with a certain piece of advice, had been most prophetic.

Billy leaned forward in his chair and his greasy head got

uncomfortably close to mine as it began to swing back and forth due to the resultant momentum of his upper body. I considered head-lice to be preferable to the contempt of his family and friends, all of whom looked like caricatures gathered round Mr Bumble from Oliver Twist, so I decided to stay put and listen intently. Then, inexplicably, I suddenly felt an overpowering urge to ask for 'some more, please Sir!' It was a bit like watching yourself on television and knowing it is only a drama, all fictitious and made up, something to ridicule for not being anything like real life. Unfortunately for me, it was all very real and the life in question was my own.

"Please Sir! Can I have some more?" I heard myself say out loud.

"Do what?" asked a bemused Billy 'Boy.'

My management mind fired up a trillion neuro-receptors at once, electro-chemicals whizzing around at lightning speed, all trying to justify the twaddle that I had just spoken.

"I said... Pizza! There's some on the floor," I chanced.

Billy looked around his feet and his entourage followed suit.

"Where?" Billy asked, eyes darting about the carpet, which was soft, luxurious and devoid of any pizza.

"Ah! ... It's gone now," I said, as though it was the most common thing in the world for a slice of pizza to suddenly appear on the floor and then disappear just as quickly.

Billy fell for it, and so did his pals and they collectively nodded to confirm my version of events. Some even added a short, 'Oh!' to further convey their acceptance of my explanation.

Billy got back to the issue of explaining his recent court appearance and subsequent appearance before me.

"It's not your fault," he said.

I looked into his eyes and noticed they were weeping like a sea-lion's, all glassy and wet with sincerity and relief. And that, in a nutshell, was all I wanted to hear. Billy had let me off the hook with those few, god-fatherly words.

"What happened 'Billy?" I asked, tilting my head to look all concerned and sympathetic, now that the threat had waned.

"I know your name was on the report, I saw it myself," Billy informed me.

He was still in fatherly mode but had definitely ditched the god aspect of it. Too fucking right it was, I thought. And what a big, fucking mistake that was.

"Go on Billy," I counselled, trying to tease from him the gory details.

"Well, I was bringing some gear in from the Hook of Holland and I was being watched all the time. They confiscated me lorry, the bastards. It's just as well I lost all me cash playing the roulette table on the ferry otherwise they would 'av' had that an' all."

"Blimey!" I said, utilising my very durable and often employed response.

"In court today, your name comes up, right, as reporting me for all that money I brung in your casino..."

"Ah, yes," I quickly interrupted. "You know I wouldn't have done that if I knew where the information went Billy. I only fill in forms... this one, that one - I don't even know what happens to all the forms I fill in or where they go. If I'd known they were going to be used against you, I wouldn't have... look, if you had asked me, I would have been in court for you Billy, I would have been there for you and said that you got the money from playing cards up north and told them whatever you wanted me to tell them Billy."

"I know you would have," reassured Billy, in a calm manner that led me to believe he either genuinely cared for my welfare or the kiss of death was looming. "Anyway," he continued. "If I thought you had anything to do with it you'd be dead by now."

Billy 'Boy' Lee smiled at me and his eyes seared into the depths of my soul as a small pocket of air escaped from my sphincter. Like everything he said, I had no reason to doubt his word and I fully believed that what he had just said, even if I had reservations about anything else he had ever claimed to have done, I knew I was walking and talking solely by his grace and his grace alone.

"So, how d'ya get off?" I boyishly added, in the hope of

changing tack from me being the focus of attention to someone else more deserving of violent intent.

Giggling like a village idiot, Billy looked around at his faithful congregation who giggled in harmony with their wild expressions of solidarity, devotion and mental inadequacy. Billy calmed himself and then spoke.

"The main prosecution witness, right, some Dutch bloke from 'olland; he was supposed to be in court but he couldn't make it."

"Oh! Why's that then?" I foolishly enquired.

"Because he ain't got no legs no more!" spluttered Billy.

"Blimey!" I blurted out, a wholly insufficient form of exasperation but one I felt would suffice for the time being.

A small bubble of white spit formed in the corner of Billy's mouth and as I looked at it, it began to morph until there, before my very eyes, I saw a good-looking, lean and fair-haired Netherlander who nursed two bleeding stumps that had once been fine athletic legs with feet attached to their ends. Blinking sharply to dispel the startling image, I relayed my shock and concern to the man who I fully believed could make all my nightmares come true.

"You're kidding me, right Billy?"

"Of course I am boy," he reassured me.

But his words were empty and his tone was sinister. This was the only time when I felt that Billy was not being totally honest with me. He picked up a glass of water from the table next to him, a glass that was not even his, and poured a small amount of the liquid contents onto the formed, gnarled knuckles of his right hand, letting it trickle across his rough, combat hardened skin. Some old tattoos, long bled into unrecognisable letters on the backs of his fingers, were highlighted by the moisture and he slipped those watery knuckles firmly across my chin in a slow motion right hook that neither hurt nor damaged, but was mesmerizingly symbolic. It was immensely demonstrative of his power and instilled within me a healthy respect for this harbinger of gratuitous violence, this King of Black Tops, this undefeated champion of bare-knuckle fighters and brilliant brag player.

That evening, friends, family and anyone else he deemed worthy drank all the Blue Nun we could lay our hands on and then they polished off some cheap Pinot Grigio followed by a case of Liebfraumilch, before tucking into sandwiches of ox tongue, chicken and sliced roast beef. It was a very small price to pay to keep Billy & Co. happy and essentially it put the value of my life way down there in the bargain basement. That was the last time I ever saw Billy and, for that matter, it was the last time I ever wanted to see him. I always worried that I might slip up and say or do something wrong in his presence, only to find myself sat next to a legless Dutch guy in hospital sharing stories about having crossed Billy "Boy' Lee, the traveller who took our bipedal limbs with a chainsaw. When Billy eventually left, he offered me some advice from his view of the world and wealth of experience; he told me not to be such a twat. His final parting words to me, whispered in my ear with true conviction and terrifying venom were, 'Now, fuck off!'

And I believed every word of it.

Curiously, that wasn't to be the last that I ever heard from Billy. Several years later, whilst at another casino, having risen like cream to the top of Senior Management, I received a small box wrapped in faded Christmas paper. The festive season was long gone and the next was too far ahead for the gift to be anything to do with religious affairs; it wasn't my birthday and I hadn't been particularly exceptional in my performance, so the package was a complete surprise. Inside the poorly wrapped parcel was an expensive watch which had come from one of the hotel gift shops nearby; it still had a small, paper price tag attached to the strap and it was wrapped around a miniature cushion which had served to better display it in a shop window, perhaps. The watch had been broken, deliberately by the looks of it. There was a small piece of napkin, torn from a drinks coaster, the sort that is found in most hotel bars, and on it was written in juvenile, capital letters, 'IN TIME, MY TIME, YOUR TIME, TIME TO...' and it was signed, 'Boy.' Rarely, if ever, did I call Billy by his nickname, as this was reserved for family members and very close friends. I could not understand the significance of the watch, the deliberate damage to it or the meaning of the words. It obviously meant something but I could not fathom what it was. It would be many, many years before I found out the answer to this coded conundrum.

Newly retired, sat inside my favourite Pie & Mash cafe, staving off the chill of a winter's afternoon with two Pie, Mash, Stewed Eels and Liquor, sitting alone, I eyed the diner opposite me as he tucked into a bowl of piping hot eels. As he did so, and cleverly multi-tasking I might add, I saw him tear the corner from one of the napkins that sat in a cheap, plastic holder at the end of the table. The lunchtime rush had subsided and there was only one other person in the place besides me and him. From the pocket of his great coat he took a ballpoint pen and wrote down in uneducated, capital letters, the words, 'IN TIME: MY TIME, YOUR TIME, TIME TO...' and he signed it with an illegible scribble.
"Excuse me," I said, waggling a finger across the table in case he was hard of hearing. "Sorry to interrupt and I don't wish to appear nosey or anything bu..."
"No probs," he interrupted, in a warm, East London accent.
"Can I just ask what you're doing with that piece of paper? Why have you written that on it?"

"Oh this!" said the surprised cockney, now waving the portion of napkin to and fro.

"Yes that, what does it mean?"

"It don't mean nuffin, me old mate. It's what some of us do round 'ere for a giggle. We send it to people."

"Why?' I asked, now on the precipice of having an answer to the question that had haunted me for so long.

"No reason me old china. Gangsters used to do it before the war but now it's only funny 'cos it shits people up, gets them all panicky and stuff. They fink bleeding gangsters are after them. It's just winding mates up really."

So that was it. After all that time, the years of wondering, I eventually found out that Billy probably regarded me as a mate, a close friend, at least close enough to play a prank on. The watch, I could only assume, had been broken during a robbery of some sort and it obviously couldn't go back for repair or be returned for replacement. Anyway, Billy 'Boy' probably won it in a card game up north.

Chapter Ten

An Unsavoury Affair

TOYN CARPEE STOOD amongst the intricate pattern of an Axminster, twist wool carpet surveying his domain. A short specimen of a man, it was merely his managerial position that supported an obvious height deficiency. His perverse sense of justice was brought about by 'little man syndrome' and it manifested itself as megalomania in the most malicious of ways. His hair was scraped back across the top of his head and being fine and sparse, it lifted in the middle to produce a distracting bouffant of wispiness. It was always a challenge to keep one's eyes from drifting up and over the smooth, rounded forehead to observe, in casual amazement, the orangey strands that appeared to defy gravity. Yes, it was orange! A terrible hue of admission that spoke volumes as to one's thriftiness. The result was a bastard attempt that merely served as an admission of one's true worth as a member of the human race. The colour itself had an iridescence about it that was decidedly carroty under certain lighting conditions but then, it was decidedly shitty under others. Beady eyes like headlamps shone from below a botoxed forehead where fake, tanned flesh slowly descended like a roller blind towards a dehydrated and crusted upper lip; the corners of his mouth were awash with a milky moisture that caused stringing as the aperture opened and closed to speak. Carpee's stature was stiff and defiant as he drew himself up in some hopeless, vain attempt to look taller. As he did so, his trousers rode up with the effort and this caused their hems to dangle about his ankles, flapping in the wind as he walked briskly with piston arms pumping the void ahead. The three inch heels of his black, Cuban boots with zippered sides did little to help in the height deception and no one was fooled by such vanity. Suit and tie of expensive cloth and a white cotton shirt could not detract from the obvious fact that he looked like a sack of shit tied in the middle. This nasty little piece of work, having evolved from early years of being on the receiving end of youthful ridicule and torment, now revealed itself in the form of a recently appointed Assistant General Manager. He felt everyone was taller than he, which was indeed true. This included most juveniles for it was a most unfortunate hand that had dealt him this fate because had he been just a tad shorter, he would have qualified as an official dwarf and subsequently received all due respect, kindness and consideration for such physical inadequacy. Had he been a tad taller, then he would have been in the shorter range amongst normal men but he was neither; his height sat dead centre of the 'laugh out loud and let's mock the short-arse' gauge. It was very, very difficult to keep a straight face when confronted by him, especially as he tried to exert his new found authority. It was a bit like taking orders from a three year old who tried very hard to look and sound like a grown up. Yep! That was him, right there; a fucking three year old trying to be a man.

"What's he doing?" questioned Carpee, having sidled up to the Pit Boss who was trying to concentrate on a game of roulette.

A Pit Boss' duties are many and varied and even when it looks like they are standing around doing nothing, things are buzzing away in their frantic brains – calculations, table-odds, break-lists, buy-ins, cash-outs, running scores, who to shag, blag and tag, weekly rotas, reports, sick leave cover, wins, losses and the price of cocaine in the Candy Bar. Having some vertically challenged despot with nothing better to do than ask impertinent questions in order to justify his presence, interrupt a train of thought so fine and precise that all of humanity's existence might rest upon its deliverance, was not only tiresome and confusing it was, in the case of this particular Pit Boss, psychologically damaging. Also, fighting the desire and showing all due restraint to prevent the top of Carpee's head being slapped with an open palm was a lot tougher than the Pit Boss might have imagined.

"What's he doing?" crowed Carpee.

Unfortunately, the Pit Boss, whose head was actually full of useless trivia at the time, did not know what that specific person, the one in question, as pointed out by the goblin, was in fact doing. In that split moment, in those milliseconds that will often determine our fate, the Pit Boss made the unwise decision to employ some avoiding tactics to pretend that somebody more important required his immediate attention – which was not the case at all.

With a palm held up above the troll to signal a halt, the imprudent words were spoken to the top of his head,

"Hang on a minute,"

And off did the Pit Boss foolishly trot.

Effectively, this left the leprechaun to stand in the middle of the gaming floor looking like a klutz (or a right cunt in old money), having been shunned by a subordinate; the rest of the staff looked on at the funny little fellow left stranded in the centre of luxury floor covering. He looked like a garden gnome who had just been discovered down at the end of an allotment, transfixed by the gaze of his discoverers, he remained motionless. It was this moment, this one defining moment, that secured the demise of, most probably, one of the finest Pit Bosses that any casino had ever had the good fortune to employ. For many years thereafter, the pygmy would hound this particular Pit Boss, traduce him at every opportunity, vilify him, criticise him and denounce his very existence until finally, no amount of negotiating could prevent the two Pit Bulls from tearing each other apart, in a preamble before legal counsel, during an employment tribunal.

It was a busy night. Balls rattled upon the tracks of roulette wheels and cards were pulled at lightning speed from Perspex shoes whose 'brakes' creaked as the next card was slipped out by a compelling, middle finger. On busier games there were cries of 'No more bets, thank you, that's all now' and the vocal count of Blackjack hands sounded as punters tapped their fingers on the table baize to signal for another card as they sought to reach a score of twenty-one without going over: 'five, seven, sixteen, twenty-two' and in a flash the losing hand would be swept away. 'Four-fourteen, six or sixteen, twenty-one; split twos or four, seventeen, sixteen,' then on until each player had either bust their hand and lost their stake to the house or they sat waiting for the dealer's hand to be revealed and where, maybe just this time, fortune might stroll their way. Standing alone in the middle of the gaming floor, having been rejected by a lowly

Pit Boss, stood the impotent imp who, at some point in time, would have to walk away from the embarrassment.

An argument could be heard emanating from the roulette table at the cash-desk end of the casino. Roulette One, it appeared, was beginning to erupt into a distracting commotion over a losing bet and an irate punter was making the most of the fracas. This was the perfect excuse for the hobgoblin to exit stage left so he made his way to see what was going on and excused himself from scrutiny. The bet in question was a table chip that lay very close to, but not quite touching, a winning line.

"Somebody's moved it!" argued an enraged punter.

"But you're the only person playing," countered the Inspector, who had risen from his high chair at the end of the table.

"The dealer's moved it then!"

"The dealer hasn't touched the table, Sir. You have only four chips on the layout."

"The dealer straightened my bets!"

"No, Sir. She did nothing of the sort."

"Pay him out for the split," ordered the Halfling manager, who had taken twice the number of steps an ordinary sized person might have taken to reach the table.

"Pay him!" ordered the Inspector.

The dealer adjusted the table chip to a winning split and the punter received seventeen chips for his noisy, attention seeking effort. In itself, seventeen chips doesn't sound very much however, the table minimum was £3000 on that occasion so each pretty, red plastic chip was worth £3000 each. That's a payout of £51,000 for what was, essentially, a cheating bet. And the winning stake was returned too!

"Why?" sassed the dealer, a look of astonishment on her face.

"I'll speak to you when you come off," reassured the Inspector before the game proceeded as normal.

The little 'un wandered off, happy that he was no longer the subject of ridicule, although in fact he constantly was, then as the changeover of dealers took place the outgoing dealer on Roulette One stood next to the Inspector for an explanation.

"Okay," began the Inspector in a low voice that could not be heard by any of the punters nearby. "It's like this - sometimes we pay out even though we know they are cheating."

"What!?" exclaimed the dealer.

"Shush! Bear with me. We pay out on losing bets when the punter contests it because we don't want to upset them. Look, we pay the same odds as every other casino in this town and we offer the same service, so the only thing we can do to keep our customers is to keep them happy, so they'll always come back for more. It's all about customer retention, you see? Fact is, we know they will lose those winnings back plus a lot more besides. It's just economics really and nothing to do with your dealing. So don't worry."

"Oh, okay," accepted the dealer. "If you say so."

***

A futile war was being played out somewhere in the world. An explosion followed by wailing sirens and then the cacophony of endless, morbid chanting. There was brief respite as the situation was explained, 'In Middle Eastern culture it is the done thing to beat one's chest exhorting the virtues of martyrdom whilst at the same time mourning loss'. The crackle of semi-automatic rifle fire, an explosion and then all hell broke loose. 'Man's inhumanity to man...' an unidentifiable voice momentarily interrupting the discord. Then silence.

The face was familiar, very familiar actually and although aged with the harsh wrinkles of a tough existence, there was a youthful beauty that shone through. The years seemingly peeled away and as they did so, the sweetest face glowed from beneath the prone and arched body to reveal a contorted montage of every boyhood sweetheart but somehow, somehow there remained the notion that all was not well. Knowing the vision to be a lie, knowing the features to be masking some hideous form of a deceased step-mother, ejaculation seemed all but impossible but determination held firm and the thrusting continued – desire and hatred smudging the edges of sanity.

"Fuck!" gasped a sweaty Carpee sitting bolt upright. "The fucking heating's on?"

Carpee felt sick as his head swam in the guilty pleasure of his dream and the closed bedroom that had no ventilation produced a suffocating, sickening, stifling heat. The radiator pipe beneath the floor tapped its unidentifiable Morse code in quick succession, increasing in speed until it suddenly stopped with a long, insidious creak. A nauseating headache that had formed in Carpee's awkwardly shaped skull, the combination of an over-heated room as well as having slept for too long, clouded his consciousness and those dreams, those worrying dreams of violence and paternal loving, all of a sudden, strangely made sense.

"Cup of tea on the table for you... news is on," was the shrill wake-up call of a thin, dishevelled and sinewy figure engaged in domestic duties downstairs.

"I'm already awake," shouted Carpee, as he slipped on some boxer-shorts to soak up the excess sweat from his gusset. "Fucking heating's on! It's still October for fucks sake," mumbled the midget as he stomped down the open-plan stairs into the mezzanine dining room.

"Fucking heating's on and it's only October!" despaired Carpee again to his waiting partner, who held out a blue and white mug of tepid tea.

"There's a big war happening on the tele," was the explanation for Carpee's nightmare. "Poor little kids caught up in all that fighting, that's the sad thing. Maybe we should adopt one?"

"Are you fucking mad!?" choked Carpee. "How could we ever afford it? All our money goes on the heating bills. This tea's cold."

"Oh, stop your cackle and drink up, sweetie."

"Fucking heating… October for Christ's sake!"

"Someone's got out of the bed on the wrong…" and the words drifted away, as did the utterer who was now in the kitchen extension at the back of the house, clanking pots and pans on cooking rings and Formica tops.

The house was circa 1878; an old railway cottage that sat proudly amid a row of seven which had once served a family of modest railway workers quite well but now, there were no such memories and all traces of former tenants were long gone. At some time, ten years previously, a small extension had been added to the back of the house to change the two up, two down into a comfortable two bedroom terraced house with an indoor bathroom. Fronting what was once a village road, the property sat high up on a bank standing defiantly over modern day traffic which utilised this popular rat-run into town; in silent disapproval, crumbling bricks and mortar faced the advancement of modernity and social indifference. Nevertheless, behind the closed doors of this insignificant residence was a love nest, cosy and warm, albeit piping hot at this particular point in time.

"Why is the fucking heating on?" questioned Carpee, his headache showing no signs of abating.

"I'm fucking cold, that's why."

"You're always cold. Why don't you put some meat on your bones? You're too skinny, that's your problem!"

"And you're too sh..."

There was a limit to the severity of the banter that this couple could employ as any reference, any inference, any allusion to height or being short could, and most probably would, result in a sharp slap to the small of the back. Nursing a pounding head, Carpee failed to comprehend the start of such derision.

"Give me some headache pills and make yourself useful," he groaned.

Two, smooth white pills were dropped into a smaller than average palm and with an exploratory ruffle of fading, orange hair, the offer was made to recharge the root colour where shades of grey were beginning to announce their arrival.

"D'ya want your hair doing, sweetie?"

"Go on then, give it a quick colour before dinner," agreed Carpee.

Kneeling and leaning over the bath would have been a lot easier had Carpee's chest been hinged in the middle. Unfortunately, his size meant that he remained almost upright as he knelt against the bath's edge and only his neck could help direct the water onto the avocado coloured slip-mat below. As the dye was being squeezed out of the tube and massaged in with a pair of rubber protected hands, rivulets of watery orange began to form down the side of Carpee's neck and it ran onto his chest to randomly trickle between the gaps of flesh and cloth below. Caressing fingers traced the streams of coloured liquid over pasty, freckled skin to where no waistband could stop the carnal intention. Deep down in Carpee's groin, rubber squeaked as it caressed his misshapen manhood and slung below, like a Chinook helicopter carrying a lopsided load in its cargo net, two, very odd shaped testicles, sagged.

"Give that a good colouring too, shall I?" said the amateur hairdresser.

Clinical rubber worked energetically against taught flesh to produce the inevitable weak spurt and forced sigh of gratitude.

"There now, that did the trick, didn't it sweetie?"

Carpee looked up as the purveyor of pleasure bent down, right down, to give him a long, salacious kiss that suggested more might follow but reciprocation was preferred.

"Get on with my hair!" snapped an agitated Carpee, satisfaction having departed in an instant. "You're wasting the hot water."

"You and your money! Aren't you forgetting something?"

"If you think I'm returning the favour, you must be joking. Like I always say, get in first because when it comes to payback, there never is any!"

"Selfish to the last, you old sod!"

Head tightly wrapped in a fraying, cotton towel that had previously been stained with orange dye and turned black with mildew, Carpee sat to watch the slim figure of his partner tidy up after him.

"I was thinking… we should… maybe get married one day, when it's legal like," stuttered Carpee, with no real intention of doing anything of the sort.

"You like to shock me, don't you?" came the reply, knowing all too well that such offers were never, ever serious.

"One day, my sweetness, one day we will be wed," promised Carpee, sarcastically.

"You know I want to be married, so why make fun of me? Once you made a promise to me…"

"Talking of promises," interrupted Carpee. "I'll make a promise to you right now."

"Go on then."

"There's a Pit Boss at work. You might know him. I swear I'll fuck him up forever and a day."

"Fighting talk that is sweetie!" said Terry, as he made his way into the kitchen.

"Honestly Terence, I'll get the runt if it's the last thing I do," avowed Carpee.

"If it's Buckley then you have my blessing!" shouted Terry. "He deserves everything he gets for what he did to me."

Carpee changed his tack as well as the tone of his voice, "You never did tell me the story of what happened when you and Buckley went on that wild goose chase through Europe? Go on Terence, spill the beans, tell your Uncle Toyn all about it. Go on, go on, go on, pleeeeease."

"Stop goading me. I can't face that memory right now," despaired Terry. "I'll tell you another time and, it wasn't a wild goose chase, so there! Tell me who it is that will be on the receiving end of your wrath Toyn."

"The other night, I was getting to grips with the floor and, being the new manager onboard is never easy, as you know Terence, so I thought I'd check out a few punters and see what's what. There's this Pit Boss, smarmy looking git, been through the ranks pretty fast by all accounts and he's the blue-eyed boy who's Malloy's favourite at the moment..."

"Malloy?"

"He's the Director. Well Terence, I edge over to the Pit Boss, his name's Vere-White I think, and I ask him what a particular punter's doing. I was nice about it, polite and professional as I always am, but he looks at me like I'm a bogey on his dinner plate and he turns away, says nothing and buggers off. Can you believe it? He snubs me right in the middle of the fucking gaming floor."

Quietly, Terry smirked in satisfaction as he licked the fingers that had inadvertently slipped into the gravy that would soon smother a potato and aduki bean combination; the perfect, red dragon pie.

"I'll tell ya Terence, I was fucking livid," shouted Carpee from the armchair. "He just stood there, gave me the hand, right in my face, and then fucked off. I thought, you absolute cunt. I'll get you for that. He might be the golden bollocks right now but you wait and see, his career is going down the Sewanee if I have anything to do with it. Now, I'm not a vindictive man, as you know Terence, but I will not have a twat of a Pit Boss make me look like a fool!"

"But you are a..." Terry stopped short of saying what he wanted to. He really wanted a little revenge, a little redemption for all the abuse, the belittling, the patronising and everything else derogatory that Carpee had dished out, "...Senior Manager," completed Terry. And in case there was any doubt he added, "You deserve respect you do, especially on the gaming floor."

"Exactly Terence! It's all about respect and he showed me none at all."

"Right," agreed Terry, returning from the kitchen.

"For that, he will get his comeuppance, you wait and see,"

hissed Carpee to finalise his intent.

Terry leant forward and massaged the damp towel around the pimple shaped head of undulating hair that appeared to thin as it dried.

"None too shabby," said a self-congratulating Terry. "A little on the 'Papaya-Whip' side as opposed to 'Bittersweet Shimmer' like it says on the packet, but none too shabby though I say it myself."

"What are you on about Terence?" questioned Carpee, although he did not wait for an answer. "That'll do," he said, snatching the towel from Terry's hands before brushing him aside with weak authority.

"I'm not one of your Pit Bosses now you know?' countered Terry.

"You would know it if you were," retorted Carpee through gritted teeth. "If you ever decide you want to be the giver rather than the taker in this relationship, then you just let me know and I'll help you pack your bags. I'll even give you a lift to the train station. Now, turn that fucking heating down, for crying out loud!"

***

It had never been Buckley's intention to be living with a girl, not so soon after returning from Europe at least. As oft' times before, alcohol and recreational drugs had totally altered his perspective of life, one thing had led to another, a promise was made, an ideal lived up to and the best was all that he could have hoped for.

"I'm pregnant!"

Two words, both magical and despairing, encapsulating hope and dread and fear and fortitude, were delivered as three syllables in a single breath. Veronique's announcement was as much of a shock to her as it was to Buckley, who drew so hard on his joint it instantly lost half its length; the red tip glowing brightly as the tightly wrapped contents crackled and spat their repose.

"No fucking way!"

"I am!" confirmed Veronique.

Buckley considered this cataclysmic, life-changing event and sighed heavily.

"A baby?" he wheezed.

"Der....Yeah!" replied Veronique.

"Fuck me!" said Buckley, before falling backwards into the waiting arms of a soft cushioned armchair. A hot, grey speck of ash broke free from the glowing tip of his joint and it fell indiscriminately to land upon the armchair seat just a second before Buckley's arse made contact with it. Searing hot ash quickly burnt a perfect round hole in the soft, white cotton boxer shorts whilst simultaneously burning an identical hole in the faux velvet cushion cover to leave a black dot in a sea of red cloth. An intense burning sensation made itself known to Buckley's right buttock; lower half, to the left.

"Shit!" screeched Buckley as he lifted his butt cheek. "Something just bit me. This chair's got fleas."

He scratched at a small, red mark that would eventually leave a scar on the rear of an almost perfect thigh.

"So, what do you think then?" asked Veronique, expectantly.

"Let me think…" Buckley teased, to give the impression that he wasn't sure about it all and needed time to think. In reality, Buckley wasn't sure about it one bit and he needed time to think.

"Brilliant!" came his answer, believing this to be what was expected of him. "Absolutely, fucking brilliant!" he reiterated.

But deep down inside, Buckley was already beginning to despair at this unwanted interruption in his life and he would bemoan the fact for a very long time to come.

"Of course, if you're thinking of getting rid of it, then that's okay with me as well. Probably for the best I suppose. I mean, you're ready to apply for pupillage as a lawyer, aren't you?" probed Buckley hesitantly.

There was a nervous uncertainty in Buckley's voice as he outlined his true wish, which was not so discreetly hidden in his open desire to support Veronique in any decision that she made, especially if it was an abortion.

"You fucking idiot!" cried Veronique.

"No babe, I just meant... whatever you decide to do is okay. I mean, let's have a kid and all that. I already have one anyway, so another one won't make any difference."

"Just listen to yourself Nigel."

Buckley knew he was in trouble and he began to flounder like a flat fish on a dry deck. No one ever, ever called him by his first name, not even his own mother. The last person who had uttered his first name had been Terry who, somewhat non compos-mentis, had pleaded with Nigel to stop hurting him up the bottom. Buckley shuddered the thought away and sucked between tight lips to extract the remnants of burning smoke from a barely smokeable number. A blister would soon appear on Buckley's bottom lip that would be a subtle reminder of this defining moment in his life.

"What about your career?" asked Buckley, in the hope of redeeming himself. "You don't want to have a kid messing up your job and everything you've ever worked for, do you?"

"What about my career? You numbskull!" retaliated Veronique. "I can take maternity leave and go back to work. They can't discriminate on those grounds anymore. It's against the law you know?" She continued by spelling out the word L.A.W. to emphasise that she knew what she was talking about.

"Nice one," sniggered Buckley.

"What are you laughing about now, you moron?"

"You said it's against the law and you're a lawyer. Get it?"

"I'll tell you what's against the law" chided Veronique as she walked up to Buckley and bent down to put her face directly in front of his. "You can stop the illegal substance bullshit right now and sort your miserable life out. And if you don't, then you can get out of my flat and that's only if I don't have you arrested in the meantime. OKAY!?" Veronique maintained her awkward position so she could hold her stare until Buckley would, finally, have to shy away. "O...KAY!?" she repeated, standing motionless, awaiting an answer.

Had Buckley had a tail, it would have been firmly curled up and tucked under his backside with only the very tip wagging back and forth in submission. He spoke in a whimper,

"Alright, okay."

As if to reinforce his commitment, he stubbed out a small speck of white and black that had been burning into the flesh of his thumb and middle finger.

"There you are, I've started already. Happy now?"

"And you can tip your stash down the toilet too!" demanded Veronique.

Buckley jumped to his feet, taking with him an ornate wooden box inlaid with fine marquetry which was no bigger than an average paperback book.

"I'm not throwing the box away," he said defiantly.

Buckley marched out of the room and into the toilet, then tipped the contents of the box into the waiting mouth of an Armitage Shanks toilet bowl and pushed on the chrome lever to watch most of the green and brown dust bubble up to remain on the surface of the water. He held the box with the lid closed upon his fingers then held it aloft like it was a holy relic and he was about to reveal an ancient truth. In reality, he cut the figure of a defeated man on a soapbox who liked to preach about tolerance and injustice.

"Happy?" muttered a suddenly reticent Buckley, who had many a secret to hide along with other stashes of marijuana and cannabis.

"You make your own choice about our baby Nigel. I want you to take your time but you have to make a decision. We either do this together, as a couple, like normal people, or I do it alone. I'll give you the opportunity to walk away, if that's what you want, but if you do…" there was a long pause for maximum effect "…if you do, there's no coming back. Ever! And I won't ever come looking for you either. I won't ever make a claim for any money, maintenance or anything else but that means you will have nothing, and I mean nothing at all, to do with us. You will have to promise us that. You won't see us, talk to us, visit us, send us cards, presents or have any contact with us whatsoever. That's the deal Nigel. Take it...or don't take it. Your choice? Best you start thinking, eh?"

It was bad enough being patronised but this was going to be a very difficult thing for Buckley to do as he had just lost his best, most loyal support – that being his marijuana. For a moment, just for the briefest of moments, Buckley filled his head with drug addled memories and he wondered what might have been, what might have been had he and Tel found fame and fortune somewhere in Europe; what might have been had he told Tel how he really felt or what might have been had he had the courage to admit that two men, in these modern times, could have found happiness together?

"Right you are," said Buckley, as he screwed his face up to show that he was giving it some serious thought. "I'll give it some serious thought then," he said, to reaffirm the seriousness of it all.

"You truly are, a wanker," screeched Veronique, as tears began forming in the corners of her eyes. "Why are you thinking about it?"

"Because you told me too, didn't you?"

"Yes, but I didn't want you to think about it."

Buckley was getting more confused than he would normally be under the influence of a strong smoke.

"But I thought that's what you wanted? You told me to have a long think about it. You'll have to help me out here, I'm losing the plot."

"Why are you thinking about it?" wept Veronique.

"BECAUSE YOU BLOODY WELL TOLD ME TO!" shouted Buckley.

"Don't you shout at me," cried Veronique, sobbing uncontrollably before turning to hide her face into the waiting comfort of a sofa cushion. She announced her frustrations before leaving the room. "I want you to want this child, not think about wanting it. Don't you get it?"

Buckley didn't get it at all and no sooner had Veronique left the room, he jumped up and pulled with him a large matchbox that had been pushed down deep into the armchair's inside. Sliding open the inner chamber with his thumb, it revealed a clear plastic bag packed with a number of dried buds that smelt strongly of cat's piss.

"I don't get it," muttered Buckley to himself, as he prepared to ponder it all on a large joint of the finest green. "I really don't get it."

***

Cherry and Reggie were a regular item around the clubs. Reggie looked terribly out of place, often surrounded by hardened gang members of Asian origin but his dreams had come true and he proved his worth by slipping a solitaire diamond ring onto Cherry's delicate finger. It had set him back three months' salary but it's what he felt he should do. More importantly, it was what Cherry demanded he should do. 'It was all about respect,' she had said. Not hers, of course, his. He would not, and could not, command respect in the Chinese community if he didn't put a 'rock' onto his girl's finger. Cherry too would lose respect if she were to sport a mediocre diamond in the company of her peers. Having taken the time to spell it out to Reggie, Cherry was happy with what appeared to be an expensive diamond ring but just to make sure, she had had it valued at a local jeweller's shop whilst Reggie's back was turned. Quite literally, Reggie had turned away in the High Street, went into a shop to look at a pair of trainers and when he came out, he caught sight of Cherry leaving the jewellery shop across the road. Cherry made no bones about it; up front and as bold as brass she told Reggie she had just had the ring valued and it was okay.

"Oh, that's alright then," said Reggie, somewhat confused.

Had everything not been alright, Reggie would gladly have paid twice more for the privilege of being Cherry's man. He loved her and she loved him loving her. Both expressed their total satisfaction with this arrangement but it wouldn't last any longer than Chow Mein on a chopstick. Reggie had, sadly, too often taken second place to drugs, both being dealt and consumed, as well as being side-lined when it came to conversations involving those for whom English was not the preferred language. On one occasion, a defining moment in their relationship, when Reggie felt he had no more to give and less resilience with which to fight the indifference that he was being exposed to, Cherry had turned up at his house quite unexpectedly. Unable to state how she had got there or by what means, whether anybody had been with her, where she had been, why she had come or even what day it was, Reggie felt powerless to save their relationship. Cherry looked like shit but no less perfect in his eyes. Pockets filled with illegal substances and cash concealed about her person, she was like a rag doll stuffed with the type of filling that could get you five to ten years in prison.

"Oh, Jesus!" exclaimed Reggie. "Are you okay, babe?"

"I frucking ruv you," sang Cherry.

"You've a funny way of showing it," lamented Reggie.

All questions went unanswered and Reggie knew that come the morning, Cherry would have little, if any, recollection of the events that had occurred twenty hours previously. Reggie carried the slight, Oriental figure into the bedroom, holding her in his arms she felt like a child and he desperately felt the need to protect her. Undressing her he noticed congealed vomit on the thigh of her leggings and considered that they would need soaking straight away. Now naked, he looked at her perfect form, golden-hued skin, jet black hair with wispy sideburns and her closed eyes which were beautiful, narrow incisions in a flawless complexion. Cherry lay awkwardly and as Reggie yanked at the quilt underneath her body, she flipped over to expose buttocks of little substance that were smoother than silk. It was not enough for Reggie to feel her protector, it was not enough that he had taken care of Cherry both now and all those times before, it was not enough that he had done the right thing in helping her during those moments of physical and mental crisis, it was all too much to bear that she treated him with disrespect and ingratitude. Reggie spread Cherry's buttocks apart with his left hand to reveal a dirtied, tight anus. With the middle finger of his right hand, wetted by his own spit, he repeatedly thrust it hard into the small, wrinkled opening until a trickle of blood appeared over his cuticle. Satisfied with the punishment so delivered, Reggie checked her over for any signs of having had sex. This extended to a close examination of her underwear which revealed nothing more than the usual, stubborn under-stains of a girl whose basic hygiene was somewhat rudimentary.

Before leaving her to sleep, Reggie tucked her in, opened a small window to let in some fresh air, kissed her lips gently, licked both her nipples, then left the room. He finally decided, at that moment, it would be too risky to get involved in her plan to launder money for the Triads.

***

"He's in, he's in!"

Word spread like wildfire; from the first sighting on CCTV by security to the gaming floor phone call, everyone was talking about the biggest punter in the Western Hemisphere being in and ready to play. Billionaires were few and far between and most casinos employed Public Relation Officers specifically to target such wealthy players; these fat, slow moving, slimy individuals who could make or break a casino, 'snails,' as they were called, attracted the interest of casinos worldwide. Where Las Vegas could fly them in on private jets and endlessly entertain them, London could only provide a Bentley taxi, tickets to a West End show and some fine wine and grub. These snails, just like their gastropod counterparts in the realms of French cuisine, were highly prized, much sought after and unashamedly revered beyond all good taste.

Slowly ascending the stairs, at a snail's pace, like a god walking amongst his prone worshippers, the obscenely wealthy carcass of Mr Yerrk Preack came into view. Yerrk was the worst type of billionaire, assuming there was a good one, of course. He was self-made, started with nothing but the fluff in his pocket; a young immigrant into New Zealand from the Eastern Block, he had had a vegetable stall when he was only eleven years old but now he owned most of the media outlets in Australia. He had a daughter who, unfortunately for her, looked exactly like him and she would go on to inherit all his wealth and administer the business in the only way she knew how – the way she had been taught by the master himself, the nasty, dictatorial, tyrannical, megalomaniac that was Yerrk. Yerrk wielded power like a schoolboy wagging a stick at a dog - for no other reason than to torment it. He sought out the weak and vulnerable, to deride and demean them and all solely for his own, demented pleasure. Yerrk owned his own horse event team who competed regularly on the world circuit, their success mainly due to the financial backing they received and the persuasive clout that such a wealthy man could command. Out of season, a number of riders would accompany Yerrk on his worldwide travels, some with their wives and girlfriends and some of them alone. Yerrk appreciated the company of single men who helped him feel less inhibited during the sort of expensive orgies that only the seriously wealthy could afford. Wives and girlfriends usually came to the casino in the evenings and this entourage, in its entirety, followed Yerrk like rats after the Pied Piper, only this time it was the melody of money that these rodents found so irresistible. Yerrk knew all too well that every one of them, every single one of them, had a hidden agenda for tagging along for he was not the sort of man to have genuine friends - they were business acquisitions and nothing more. He owned them, provided their living, their fame and their fortunes. Yerrk loved having them around, if nothing else than just to mistreat. During gaming, in the Salle Privée, during a shuffle or when Yerrk needed to vent his frustrations after losing a hand of Blackjack, he would signal to the group, who stood and sat behind him, that he had some 'spare' gaming chips to give away. Yerrk played chips with a value of £25,000 each, so no one ignored these little games that could result in the acquisition of a small fortune very quickly. The chips were a lot bigger and heavier than usual and this gave them considerable substance, it ensured that they never got mixed up with any other cash chips. They were unworn, clean and had very, very sharp edges. They had been specially commissioned for Yerrk's plump, sweaty hands and only he was ever allowed to play with them. Playing all seven boxes on Blackjack, with splits and doubles, could, if the cards were right, create a game with a value of £700,000. It was always a spectacle to watch and more amazing to deal.

Dixie took cover as Yerrk held up the first chip in order to show his team what they could expect. It reminded Dixie of a time when he was a young boy and played in goal during a football match at school. A penalty had been awarded to the other side and as he faced a hefty, centre-forward, who looked as though he could blast the ball into outer space, he had been torn between trying to shield his goolies, his face, his entire body and the need to be rightly positioned in order to save the game. He recalled the awkward fidget that had inexplicably assaulted him as he failed to fully commit either way. He remembered the uncertainty about how he should best cover himself with skinny arms to try and protect his pre-pubescent, private parts. Similarly, six grown men and their respective wives and girlfriends began to fidget uncomfortably as they sought to protect themselves by sucking in groin areas, bending over and cowering behind inadequate armour. With so many of them squirming, it looked like they were in a silent disco, listening individually to some music but dancing together in the surrounding silence; it was hilarious to watch but the dancers cared not how they looked. A dozen adults writhed in anticipation of the hard discs with sharp edges that would be very painful and damaging to delicate flesh, should contact be made. Yerrk held the first chip, about the size of commemorative coin, in the curled forefinger of his right hand and he let it loose in a sudden burst of action, as though he were skimming stones across a pond.

"Catch this!" he dared.

First chip and first blood. Someone's wife had been too slow for Yerrk's perfect aim and she paid the price for her sluggish response by succumbing to 'chip bite'. A tiny gash opened on the left side of her forehead, just above the eye, and a dribble of blood began to appear. Ordinarily, any husband of any worth would have taken exception to this affront of his manliness, this vicious assault on his good lady, but not in this case. The injured party scrabbled alone on the floor in her feeble attempt to retrieve the £25,000 that caused her injury and indignation. Her husband waited, with hatred in his eyes, as another disc sought out its mark but the ingenuity of one chap brought the wrath of Yerrk down upon them all. Cleverly he was using an ornamental book to deflect the trajectory and resultant force of the disc away from the body where the damaging energy could be absorbed and the chip safely retrieved. Unfortunately, this was not the game that Yerrk had in mind and he let it be known that his pleasure was only in their pain.

"Get your slags to stand still while I throw!" he barked at the men. "You lot stand fucking still too!"

Like skittles awaiting the blow of a ferocious strike, they tried their best to stand motionless but nervous flinching could not be totally suppressed. Yerrk let off a salvo of chips, twenty-three in all, with hateful savagery. Pinging off the walls, the furniture and those souls waiting in hope, over half a million pounds lay scattered amongst the greedy horde. Even before all the chips had found new homes in pockets and clutch-bags, Yerrk had already sat down to cut the cards for a new shoe. Dixie looked on in amazement as the injured tended their wounds before surreptitiously counting their riches. Verbal abuse was often employed when physical abuse was clearly not satisfying enough.

"You're a bunch of leeches and your women are fucking ugly!" bawled Yerrk over his left shoulder.

The catch on the Salle Privée door clicked and Dixie instinctively reached out to prevent entry. Expecting some nosey cheapskate to be on the other side, Dixie was surprised to see a tall, well-built American gentleman, dressed in what could only be described as office-cowboy attire, being pushed and ushered in by one of the senior receptionists. A whispered exchange took place and the American gestured as to whether the seat next to Yerrk might be free.

"Free for a price," provoked Yerrk, knowing full well that there were few who could afford his minimum bet in the Salle Privée. The American casually tossed a marbled pink coloured £500,000 plaque across the table, which landed directly in front of the dealer's tray.

"Name's Randolph, Randolph T. Palowski the Third," said the American, introducing himself to Yerrk. "I'm from Texas. Austin Texas. In the United States of America."

"Yerrk," said Yerrk, without looking up from the table or his placed bets.

From that point on, the American did not stop talking and

bragging about who he was, what he owned, where he had been and what he was worth. Jen flashed the cards in quick succession to their respective boxes and waited on fingers that signalled delight or contempt. Bust hands were shooed away with flapping hands while chips from winning hands were stacked together with a hard 'clack' to show the superiority of a win.

"One time," began the American, "I played in the biggest poker tournament in Las Vegas. Boy oh boy! I can tell ya, there was a million bucks or more in that pot and I went all in and geez, I crapped out... Goddamit!" The frustration was more for the current hand of Blackjack than for the Las Vegas story. "Jeeeesus H! I shoulda split those mothers," huffed the American to excuse his loss, if not his incompetent play.

On and on he went, recounting his early days and how he had built up an empire in the lumber business all from nothing and this was quickly followed by a chain of builders' merchants, then a bit of diversification into trailer parks and office refurbs. He was, so he informed all present, the biggest lumber supplier in the Southern States and he had the respect of every builder South of Minnesota. He laughed in mock surprise at his own success but was quick to relate just how much he was enjoying the fruits of his hard work and dedication. There was a ranch down in Texas where he bred American Quarter Horses, he had an apartment overlooking Central Park in New York, a

Penthouse in London and a small chateau in France, a twelve berth Sunseeker motor-cruiser moored in Oman, a small collection of cars that included a Ferrari F40, a Rolls Royce Phantom, a Mustang once driven by Steve McQueen and a Lamborghini Diablo that could barely accommodate his towering frame. He had a place up in Vermont that he used for winter breaks and a villa in Florida for summer vacations. The list went on and on and on: trinkets, jewellery, antiques, exotic pets and even a mistress that awaited his arrival in Monaco every year. He had a collection of Rolex watches and an interesting watch that only cost a mere $100,000.

"Omega it says at the top," he said, looking at the watch on his wrist before holding it up for Yerrk to verify and admire.

Yerrk had had enough and slapped his chips down onto the table. There was the unmistakable crack of plastic upon plastic as they hit the green baize. The room fell silent as the entourage knew an outburst was imminent. The magnitude of the eruption could not be anticipated as Yerrk was predictably unpredictable, but everyone knew something, something very bad was about to happen. Jen put the game on hold and looked to Dixie for guidance. Dixie gave a slight nod and screwed his eyes up momentarily to signal that a pause in the game would probably be appropriate right about now. Jen's eyes motioned down at the float lid that hung under the table and she gave a quizzical look at Dixie as she sought his direction on whether the float should be secured. If something physical was about to happen then high value chips could not be allowed to spill onto the gaming floor - Salle Privée or no Salle Privée. Dixie shook his head from side to side in small movements so as not to be noticed but more importantly, so he wouldn't be misunderstood or misinterpreted by Yerrk. Jen read the signal and remained motionless as Yerrk leant on the table and twisted sideways to look, with a slightly cocked head, at the American who was still talking.

"I'll tell ya bud, when the market crashed I made a killing..."

"Do you know who I am?" interrupted Yerrk in a forceful tone.

"Why, yes I do. You're the media guy from New Zealand," replied the American.

"Yes. I am. And do you know what I'm worth?" asked Yerrk.

"I reckon about the same as I am," said the American, not wishing to demean himself.

"I reckon that's so mate," agreed Yerrk and he closed his right hand to make a fist.

Everyone feared the worst and braced themselves for the maelström.

"I've listened to your incessant bragging and bull-shit talk for the last hour," said Yerrk, and he began to balance a cash chip on his hand where the forefinger was curled around the tip of his thumb nail. He held out the fist in front of the American and then paused before speaking.

"Everything you own, against everything I own. I'll toss you for it?" he said.

The American sat quietly, for once, to process the information and a short puff of air emanated from his nostrils as he realised the magnitude of the wager. Yerrk had a reputation for making outrageous bets, as well as paying up and collecting on them. "You're kidding, right?" squirmed the American, who knew all too well that he wasn't.

"All of yours against all of mine," offered Yerrk. "Take the bet or piss off!"

The American was now in a very dark place. The bet, to a gambling man, was an invitation that demanded serious consideration and it beckoned like a siren to a sailor about to meet his watery demise. For the winner the spoils were immense but for the loser, it would be utter ruin and degradation. The American toyed with the idea for a deceptively long time, going over and over in his head what the chances of victory or defeat would be. Every ounce of the American's gambling spirit wanted to take the bet, see Yerrk ruined and humiliated, show dominance in this premier league of the rich and powerful; to have more and be more, this was the ultimate wager.

"Well, mate?" asked Yerrk, whose patience was wearing thin.

"What d'ya say?"

"Too darn rich for my liking," surrendered the American and with that, he stood up, scooped up his chips and promptly left the Salle Privée.

No doubt, in a bar somewhere in the Southern States, where rednecks hang out to watch working Mums flash their tits and cavort seductively to put food on plates for their fatherless children, Randolph T. Palowski the Third would retell this story. In his version however, he would be the one making the challenge, offering the bet which would finally see off some loud, parvenu foreigner who found the stakes just too darn scary. A loud laugh audibly ridiculed the American as he left the Salle, the flagrant taunt reverberating around his confederate head as he sought to join his wife in the restaurant where he would seethe over an enormous, bloody rare steak.

Dixie looked at Jen and mouthed the words, "I love you," before winking a cheeky wink of real affection.

Jen read his lips but mistakenly received the word 'colourful,' the mouth and lip movements of both being practically indistinguishable from one another. Indeed, it was a colourful episode, thought Jen. After a further two shoes of cards, Jen was released for a well-deserved break and she crept up to Dixie, who was standing by the door watching the new dealer go through her shuffle procedures.

"That was so cool," whispered an excited Jen. "Do you think he meant it?"

"I guarantee he meant it," said Dixie.

He then went on to retell the rumoured history of some previous bets that had taken place between Yerrk and other punters.

"Later, I'll tell you about the time when Yerrk bet another man to swap their wives. And he bloody meant it too!"

"Really?" said Jen, with scepticism.

"Absolutely," assured Dixie. "I swear it."

"Would you wager on me?" asked Jen, coyly.

"You might be my wife Jen, but that doesn't mean to say I wouldn't trade you in for something better!"

A short, sharp kick made contact with Dixie's left shin.

"You bastard!" replied Jen affectionately. "Have you called your Mum to see if the twins are okay?"

"Yep, they're fine," said Dixie. "Now get on a break or there'll be nothing left of it. Love you babe."

"Love you too," uttered Jen.

"Love you three," countered Dixie.

"Love you... for... ever," cooed Jen, and the short repartee was over.

Jen left the Salle to take what was left of a thirty minute break and Dixie stood alone, seductively eyeing up the new dealer, watching the game and wondering how his life had ended up like it had.

***

I remember standing at a roulette table in a Chinese casino doing my very best to pick up the chips that had been, for the umpteenth time, scattered about the chipping area after yet another spin. Long before the days of chipping machines and automatic wheels, auto-shufflers and virtual gaming, one's hands were the tools of one's trade. There was even a good business in insuring those tools and a top dealer with good dexterity of mind as well as fingers was worth their weight in French plaques. Before muscle memory had any chance to establish itself, before calculations were pre-sets of the subconscious and long, long before confidence had been secured, I was asked how long I had been dealing.

"This is my sixth week," I said, wondering whether I should include the odd days as well.

"It shows," said the voice of experience.

Looking on and trying to learn from this 'one-eyed king' in my blind world, I did my very best to be seen as competent and cooperative, to be the essential ally for the dealer who worked his magic about the roulette layout. Arms and hands swishing in and out, around and about, all over the layout, it seemed that the only thing lacking from this one man show was the word,

'Abracadabra!' But, at the time, I knew no better and I was there to watch and learn.

"How long have you been dealing?" I asked politely.

"Ten years," came the proud reply.

Shocked by the length of service and the commitment required to maintain oneself at such a low, professional standard for so long, I forgot to give my name, but I suspect it would not have been remembered anyway. I must have sounded like the new boy that I was, in awe of this 'Master' who had willingly given up such a large proportion of his working life to this one game of chance. I could never, ever, imagine myself as ever being in such a situation. EVER!!

***

There was always so much paper work to be done and never enough time to do it. Always, always, there would be some incident or accident that required intervention by management and being the only manager on duty; it was my role to get things sorted out with the least amount of fuss as possible. Quite frankly, Pit Bosses could not be trusted to do anything properly and Junior Managers just didn't have the wherewithal like I did when I was climbing the career ladder. For a start, they taught too many games in all those training schools that had sprung up in order to satisfy the constant demand for trained staff - merely profiting from the scarcity they had scant regard for quality. The requirement from most casinos was that all new dealers should be trained in at least five games. Five games! In my day we learned one and one only. We trained and dealt roulette. Just roulette and only roulette. We dealt roulette for a minimum, for an absolute minimum, of eighteen months before ever being considered ready to learn another game. Blackjack was the usual follow up game so anyone dealing blackjack was easily recognisable as being at least one and a half years in service. We were masters of our game, knew it inside out, upside down and back to front. We knew the wheel, where every number was in relation to every other number and call bets such as the 'Red Serpent' and the 'Bond Bet.' We learned multiple bets, complete maximum bets, overlapping maximum bets and neighbour bets that were neighbour bets of those neighbour bets and all this required lightning fast calculations for total stake and the correct change to be given. It would only be seconds before pay-outs would have to be calculated and this might involve several different odds in several different denominations. We could work out cash values in twenty-five pence, fifty pence, one pound, five pounds, twenty-five pounds, one hundred pounds, one thousand pounds and, if necessary, hundreds of thousands of pounds. We could calculate multiple odds to arrive at pay-outs in pieces or cash or any part thereof.

We could deduct for next or regular bets, give cash chips and coloured wheel chips in multiple denominations, calculate change, if any, and all in a matter of seconds. Accuracy was paramount as any over-payment was always a devil to recover. We were masters in our time and we were well looked after. The best employers took care of their staff extremely well and they did it with excellent pay rates, bonuses, corporate days out and fun activities (within the boundaries of normal, work life). Everything was paid for and we wanted for nothing. Then the proverbial arse fell out of the business and us 'masters,' once so revered and favoured, were no more than monkeys sent out to perform their menial task. Technology gradually took over our beautiful domain and we melted into the shadows of automated gaming. Occasionally, there was the odd moment when it seemed a revival in fortunes might be in the offing, but such moments were few and far between for there never was any real prospect of returning to those glory days of my training. But staff below me never knew any of these things; their training had been quick and easy, lightning fast with the emphasis on extent, not excellence.

"All quiet," reported my Pit Boss, as he leant on the lectern where I was trying too input the previous night's gaming figures, the bastard excel spread sheet not wanting to accept any of my formulas.

"You've bocked it now," I told him. "That'll put the right mockers on it, you saying that."

"You're not superstitious are you?" he enquired.

"Not anymore," I replied, "Although I do sometimes wonder how powerful our minds might be. I could tell you some strange stories about the power of positive thinking. I've seen things you people would not believe."

"I have as well," the Pit Boss concurred.

"How long you been in the business then?" I casually asked.

"It's my sixth year," stated the Pit Boss, his voice draining away to a faint, almost embarrassed whisper. "How long for you?"

"Thirty years?" I coughed.

Then, like some warped, space-time wormhole, I could see myself standing next to that self-styled 'King of Roulette,' and as I marvelled at the mastery with which he worked his craft and listened intently to his fantastical stories about casino life, it suddenly it occurred to me...

I am all of those people.

About the Author

Born in London during the late 1950s, he was once described by a law court judge as having, 'led a very colourful life.' Considering himself to be a great traveller and thinker, he has embarked upon an epic journey of discovery and has visited more than 152 countries thus far; currently residing in the Middle East, he writes articles for national magazines and local newspapers. Married with at least five children and three goldfish, the latter of which will probably be dead by the time you read this, he is forever hopeful of being able to enlighten and entertain.

Thanks for reading! Please add a short review on Amazon and let me know what you think!

Other books by the same author:

Pippa – When love leads, an unexpected tale follows.
living IN A DREAM – A Practically True Story.
On Holiday, Forever! - A travel log.
An Afternoon Adventure - Illustrated verse.
Have You Ever Thought? - An illustrated poem.
Is It Really Too Much To Ask Banksy…? - amusing emails

Please check my website for more information at:
www.rowntreetravis.com